A Comprehensible World :

On Modern Science and Its Origins

Also by Jeremy Bernstein

The Analytical Engine: Computers—Past, Present and Future

Ascent: Of the Invention of Mountain Climbing and Its Practice

A COMPREHENSIBLE WORLD:

On Modern Science and Its Origins

JEREMY BERNSTEIN

Random House · New York

FIRST PRINTING

© *Copyright, 1961, 1962, 1963, 1964, 1965, 1966, 1967,*
by Jeremy Bernstein

All rights reserved under International and Pan-American
Copyright Conventions. Published in New York by
Random House, Inc., and simultaneously in Toronto,
Canada, by Random House of Canada Limited.

Library of Congress Catalog Card Number: 67–12740

Manufactured in the United States of America
by American Book–Stratford Press, Inc.
Designed by Victoria Dudley

All of the articles in this book appeared originally
in *The New Yorker.*

The Robert Frost quotation is from "Fire and Ice" from
Complete Poems of Robert Frost. Copyright 1923 by Holt,
Rinehart, and Winston, Inc. Copyright 1951 by Robert Frost.
Reprinted by permission of Holt, Rinehart, and Winston.

TO PHILIPP FRANK

in memory

*"One may say the eternal mystery of the world
is its comprehensibility."*

ALBERT EINSTEIN
Physics and Reality (1936)

Contents

Introduction

IN THE FALL of 1960, I returned to the United States after spending over a year in France on a National Science Foundation Fellowship in physics. Before leaving the country, I had accepted a job at Brookhaven National Laboratory, in Upton, Long Island, and the people at the laboratory had been kind enough to keep it open for me while I was away, so unlike many returning expatriates, I didn't have the problem of looking for work when I got home. Brookhaven was, and is, a superb scientific installation, but it is set off in the countryside, and as a bachelor, I found that there was not much to do when I was not working. For lack of anything else, I began to spend the evenings writing. I had never written anything for publication except scientific papers, but as a hobby, I had always kept a notebook in which I jotted down random observations for my own amusement.

As with any novice writer, the first question that arose was what to write about. My nostalgia for Europe, and especially for France, was the thing that dominated my feelings, so I decided to write about some aspect of my time there. I had spent the summer of that year on the island of Corsica, teaching physics in a newly organized summer school for French students. Corsica is the most beautiful island I have ever seen, and the contrasts between the Corsicans, the Continental French, our physicists, and the general, almost dreamlike atmosphere of the setting was so rich in humor that Corsica became the inevitable subject. Each evening, after almost everyone else had gone home, I would come back to my office at the laboratory and try to recreate the atmosphere of the island. After a few weeks I had produced a sizable manuscript, which I gave to a few friends to read. I think it was the physicist Edward Purcell, then spending a sabbatical leave from Harvard at Brookhaven, who suggested that I send it to *The New Yorker*. Without much hope, I put it into a manila envelope with a brief note and shipped it off to the magazine.

Months passed, and just when I had more or less forgotten about it, William Shawn, the editor of *The New Yorker,* phoned to say that he had decided to publish it (it is the first article in this collection) and invited me to come to New York to talk to him. We met a couple of days later. I have no idea what Mr. Shawn's impression of me was—I think that I was the first physicist he had ever talked with at any length—but what impressed me about *him* was his seriousness about the magazine and about writing. We had talked about physics and physicists for well over an hour when he offered me a challenge—to try to write about physics as experience. He pointed out that while an enormous amount had been written about physics and physicists—about the two cultures, the bomb, and all the rest— no one (at least no physicist of the modern generation)

had ever tried to express the experience of actually working at physics. It is not hard to see why this is true. Physics,
like any science, is incredibly demanding. When one is
engaged in a physics problem, it is hard to think of much
else, and it is all but impossible to disengage oneself
sufficiently to write about it. The great physicists of the
older generation—Einstein, Bohr, and others—in their
later years tried to reconstruct the atmosphere that surrounded the discoveries of their youth. But these recollections, as wonderful as they are to read, inevitably lack the
sense of immediacy, bewilderment, and elation that they
would have had if they had been written when the work
was being done.

In talking with the physicists of my generation, I discovered that in addition to the fact that they were deeply
immersed in their work, they also felt that it was somehow
infra dig to try to write about it for a general audience.
(Several told me that they were saving their writing for
their declining years, after they had retired. I refrained
from asking them whether they felt that their grasp of
contemporary physics in their declining years would be
any better than the grasp displayed in the somewhat anti-
quated and remote writings of their predecessors.) This
feeling that writing about the atmosphere of one's work
somehow demeans it seems to me to be peculiar to scientists. To be sure, no one would be interested in hearing
from scientists the same sort of interminable descriptions
of the sources of inspiration that often accompany the
unfolding of a new art form, but surely some middle
ground is possible.

Apart from the sheer pleasure and satisfaction that one
derives from writing about something that one knows and
loves, there is also, it seems to me, a special responsibility
thrust on scientists to try to explain their work. This
responsibility can be put in two ways. In the first place, the
twentieth century is the most revolutionary century for

science in the history of man. While one could hardly argue that modern artists and composers are expressing themselves more strongly than Leonardo or Beethoven, there is absolutely no doubt that contemporary science completely dwarfs the science of the past. More has been learned about the nature of the universe in the last fifty years than in the entire prior history of the human race. A layman who is not let in on the accomplishments of modern science is simply shut off from some of the most significant and enduring aspects of our century. If the scientists are not prepared to write about what they are doing and discovering, who will?

In the second place, the achievements of modern science are more and more dependent on public support, especially in a democracy like ours. For example, a group from Columbia University working at Brookhaven a few years ago found that instead of there being one species of neutrino, as had been thought for years, there were actually two. For physicists this was an important and exciting discovery, and I once estimated that counting the costs of the accelerators, it costs every taxpayer in the United States at least twenty-five cents. The question that occurred to me was: How many taxpayers would have willingly spent a quarter to learn about neutrinos—or even a nickel. Yet if taxpayers are unwilling to spend larger and larger sums on pure science, it will stagnate. In the long run one cannot trick people into supporting scientific projects by fostering the notion that they inevitably lead to rapid and highly visible technological advances. Someone who had backed, say, Einstein's discovery of the equivalence of mass and energy in 1905, would have had to wait until the 1940's to see its first technological application, with the invention of the self-sustaining nuclear reactors. And someone who in 1915 had backed Einstein's greatest discovery—the general theory of relativity, which has replaced Newton's theory of gravity—would have nothing practical to show for his investment today, and probably never will have.

While discoveries in pure science often turn out to carry remarkable technological implications, I believe that the only really sound ground for the public support of pure science is the return it offers in intellectual satisfaction— "seek the source and not the shapes," as the Vedic phrase has it—and such satisfaction is impossible without understanding. In fact, scientists are now discovering, to their extreme discomfiture, that government support of pure science is beginning to be withheld in favor of vast expenditures on space projects, which have little or no pure-science content but which are readily understood by the public. If this trend is not reversed—and it can only be reversed by public understanding—pure science will certainly wither and possibly die.

Needless to say, these somewhat grandiose thoughts did not occur to me in the spring of 1961, when Mr. Shawn made his suggestion. On the train back to Brookhaven, I began to try to think what the experience of practicing physics meant, and to try to recall what my own experience had been. My entry into physics came comparatively late in life—that is, in my early twenties. Most physicists I know were extremely precocious. A colleague of mine who is one of the most brilliant contemporary mathematical physicists once told me that when he was still so young that he was being put down for naps, he had hit upon the notion of the convergent infinite series one afternoon while lying in his crib. He began adding up quantities like one plus a half plus a quarter, and so on, and realized that the infinite sum approached two. This is a somewhat extreme example of mathematical precocity, but it is quite common to find physicists among my colleagues who knew the entire undergraduate mathematics and physics curriculum—and a good deal of the graduate curriculum to boot— by the time they entered college.

In my own case, although I was proficient in high-school mathematics, I disliked it, and I disliked the physics course even more. When I entered Harvard, in 1947, I had more or less decided to be a journalist and to take the fewest science courses possible. At that time the standard way to escape science was to enroll in one of the general-education courses, which gave one the minimum smattering of science that Harvard considered a necessary part of the intellectual baggage of the educated modern man. I duly signed up for one of them, and, as in high school, I did well but disliked it. In fact, everything proceeded according to my expectations until around Christmas, when the theory of relativity was introduced briefly into the course. Up to that point most of the work had seemed just as tedious as my high-school course, which had been greatly concerned with the distinction between weight and mass and the like—hardly the stuff of which intellectual daydreams are made. The theory of relativity, of which I understood next to nothing at the time, clearly represented a new and disturbing set of concepts. In the first place, it was genuinely hard to understand. I got several books about it from the library, and the more I read, the less I understood. In the second place, the conclusions that it led to were both patently absurd and patently true. For example, the idea that a clock placed on the earth's equator ran at a slower rate than a clock placed at the North Pole, simply because the clock on the equator was in motion relative to the pole (one of the conclusions drawn in Einstein's original paper), was so weird that I soon became determined to learn enough about the theory to understand how it could possibly be true. Fortunately, at about this time I discovered that a somewhat more advanced general-education course on the ideas of modern physics was available, and that it was taught by Professor Philipp Frank, an expert on relativity and a lifelong friend and associate of Einstein's. As soon as I could, I enrolled in Professor Frank's course.

Philipp Frank, to whom this collection is dedicated, was the first real physicist I ever came in contact with, and he is the best teacher I have ever known. He was born in Vienna in 1884, making him five years younger than Einstein. As a young man he studied physics in Vienna with the great Austrian physicist Ludwig Boltzmann, which links him to the most profound traditions of classical physics—the pre-Einstein physics. When still a student, he became deeply interested in the philosophy of science, and he first attracted Einstein's attention in 1907, the year he took his Ph.D., with a short paper on the apparently tautological character of the usual concept of causality in science. (Professor Frank wondered how the law of causality could ever be refuted, since any seeming violation of it could always be argued away by assuming that anything that presented itself as a new effect following from the same cause was really the result of an undetected change in the conditions of the experiment. How could one tell that two experiments were really identical, apart from the fact that they led to the same effect?) Many years later Professor Frank wrote, with the humor that was characteristic of him, "While I was still a very young man I published a philosophical paper on *The Law of Causality* in which I made sweeping and amazing assertions. This paper attracted Einstein's attention and he wrote to me that he liked it but found its claims exaggerated. From that time to this we have always been in scientific and personal contact."

In 1912, at age twenty-eight, he succeeded Einstein as professor of theoretical physics at the German University of Prague. There he met his wife, Hania, who was a physics student and a close associate of the artistic and intellectual movements of the city, including a literary group that counted Kafka among its members. In his student days Professor Frank had helped to found the Vienna Circle, a philosophical movement that eventually developed into logical positivism. In fact, in the 1960's when I was studying for a while in Vienna, I met an old waiter in a coffeehouse who told me that he remembered some of the impassioned discussions that the Vienna Circle had held in his restaurant before the First World War.

From the beginning, the Vienna Circle had for its ambition no less than an attempt to unify all of knowledge, especially the sciences and the humanities. Professor Frank later reminisced, "Our field of interest also included a great variety of political, historical, and religious problems which we discussed as scientifically as possible. Discussions about the Old and New Testaments, the Jewish Talmud, St. Augustine, and the medieval Schoolmen were frequent in our group. Otto Neurath the economist even enrolled for one year in the Divinity School of the university in order to get an adequate picture of Catholic philosophy, and won an award for the best paper on moral theology." And he added, "But we returned again and again to our central problem: How can we avoid the traditional ambiguity and obscurity of philosophy? How can we bring about the closest possible rapprochement between philosophy and science? By science, we did not mean natural science only, but we included always social studies and the humanities."

When I went to the first of Frank's lectures, I was unaware of any of this, and I had no idea of what he would be like. He was a small man, bald except for some unruly spurts of white hair around the sides of his head. He had a perceptible limp, brought about, he later told me, by an encounter with a Viennese streetcar. His smile was absolutely luminous, and his lectures, which were delivered in an extraordinary accent composed, it seemed, out of the remnants of the more than half a dozen languages that his wanderings through the academic communities of the world had impelled him to learn, were punctuated by jokes and anecdotes. The anecdotes inevitably began with the phrase "I remember very well, really . . ." This was followed by a long pause, a series of wonderful inner smiles, and then an indelible story, brought vividly to life by the fact that Professor Frank had almost total recall. (On one occasion he stunned an Iranian graduate student by producing a perfectly written literary phrase in Arabic, and when I asked him how he had ever happened to learn the language, he told me that he had studied it for a few weeks in night school in Vienna near the turn of the century because he wanted to read the great Near Eastern philosophers in the original and because, as a young man, he had been fascinated by one prospect of a Vienna-Baghdad railroad connection.

Professor Frank's genius as a teacher of scientific ideas was built on his complete mastery and intuitive under-standing of physics—at least, physics up until the end of the Second World War. It is important to realize that a physi-cal theory—even a very profound one like relativity or the quantum theory—often has a very simple, almost pictorial idea at its center. The great physicists have all been masters of what has come to be known as *"Gedanken experiments"*—experiments existing only in the mind, un-performed and probably unperformable, which, when contemplated, put physical ideas into new and striking juxtapositions. For example, Newton became aware of the universal character of the law of gravitation by imagining an apple tree so big that its branches held the moon like an apple. Just as an apple in a small tree falls to the earth, so, to Newton, must the moon be falling in the gravitational field of the earth. Einstein, at the age of sixteen, wondered whether he would continue to see himself in a mirror if he, and the mirror, were able to move with the speed of light. Would the light ever reach the mirror? He soon came to realize that no matter how he answered this question in terms of the conventional physics of his day he was led deeply into paradox, and in contemplating these paradoxes, he arrived at the special theory of relativity. Heisenberg, in the late 1920's, imagined a microscope through which he could try to measure the position of an electron in an atom, and then realized that the light quanta reflected from the electron into the microscope would inevitably change the momentum of the electron—a realization that is at the heart of the Heisenberg uncertainty principle. And so on. In Professor Frank's course we were taught the ideas of modern physics by means of these pivotal images, and I came away with an entirely new sense of how scientists—at least the great ones—have been able to visualize and create natural laws.

By the time the course was over, I had decided that, come what might, I wanted to continue studying with Professor Frank. Since he was not teaching any other lecture courses, I enrolled in a reading course he was conducting in the philosophy of science, from Aristotle through the philosophers of the Middle Ages (such as Buridan and Ockham) to the modern writers, like Wittgenstein, Whitehead, and Bridgeman. (Bridgeman was still active at Harvard at this time, and on occasions when we reached an impasse in our reading we would descend into his basement laboratory and ask him to help us out.) Some of our discussions were held in the cafeterias in Cambridge, which for Professor Frank represented the nearest available approximations of his beloved erstwhile Eastern European coffeehouses; the rest took place in the incredible chaos of his office. It was packed with books, unopened letters, manuscripts, and scraps of paper. When he retired from Harvard a few years later, I helped him clear it out, and we opened a few of the letters, some of them nearly thirty years old; after studying them, he remarked that their content "was not so important as one might imagine."

He found a dust-covered etching of Einstein, signed by him, which Professor Frank gave me, and it remains one of my favorite souvenirs of my studies with him.

Long after I left Harvard, I kept in constant touch with Professor Frank. Since he rarely answered letters, most of my contacts with him were on my periodic visits to Cambridge, where he and his wife lived simply in a charmingly decorated apartment filled with the mementos of his long life, including a collection of wonderful photographs of the great scientists of his generation. The last time I visited him he was preparing to leave the apartment for a nursing home where he could live in comfort with his wife, who was not well. He told me that he was "somehow surprised to have lived until over eighty," and that he could no longer recall very well the events of the recent past, although the memories of his youth were still vivid. On July 21, 1966, he died in Cambridge at the age of eighty-two.

Very soon after I began studying the philosophy of science, I came to realize that such a study could never really replace the study of science itself. I still had no idea of how I would eventually earn my living, but it was clear to me that even if it were to be in philosophy, I would never be able to contribute anything if I did not really understand the details of science. The details of physics are in the mathematics. While the basic images may be simple, their mathematical expression is not. In fact, modern theoretical physics has become progressively more and more mathematical. (This point was vividly brought home to me recently by an article about the origins of the quantum theory. After Heisenberg, in 1925, had afforded the first glimpses of the quantum mechanics, the theory that replaces, for the atom, the mechanics of Newton, Max Born, one of the most learned mathematical physicists of his generation, wrote that following "eight days of intensive reflection and probing," he suddenly realized that Heisenberg's mechanics involved a form of algebraic manipulation known as "matrix multiplication," which at the time was regarded as a recondite mathematical discipline. It is now taught as a matter of course to sophomores in college, and often to high-school students.) I soon came to understand that the key to learning physics was learning the necessary mathematics, and I began to take all the mathematics courses—even in the summers—that I could cram in. In fact, I became so involved in mathematics that I took my undergraduate degree in it, and only came back to physics after my master's degree, which I took in mathematics in 1953.

In view of my rather peculiar background—courses largely in the philosophy of science and in mathematics—the Harvard physics department agreed to take me in only on condition that I work for a summer as an assistant in the cyclotron laboratory in order to get some feeling of what real physics was like, and then take an oral examination on experimental nuclear physics. Working in the cyclotron laboratory left me with a deep respect for the skill and patience of experimental physics, and the absolute certainty that I would never make an experimental physicist. It takes the patience of Job to tinker day after day with a reluctant piece of equipment, and I was hopelessly incompetent at it. My mind wandered constantly—usually at the most crucial moments in the experiment—and I failed the oral exam and had to make it up by taking a lab course during the spring.

Fortunately, just when I wanted to begin a thesis, I met a young theoretical physicist at Harvard—Abraham Klein, now a professor at the University of Pennsylvania—who had a physics problem he was looking for someone to work on with him. Despite my odd background, he agreed to take me on as a student. I was too inexperienced to be a great deal of help, but in 1955, with Klein's prodding and aid, I managed to produce a passable thesis. The next year, I returned to the cyclotron laboratory, but this time on the theoretical side, and during the two years that I spent there I tried to fill in the gaps in my background and began to do research on my own.

The time I spent in the physics department at Harvard was at the height of the McCarthy terror. "Terror" is the only word that does justice to that period—especially for physicists. Because of their role in weapons work, and because of their generally outspoken liberalism, physicists were especially open to the kind of attack and smear that McCarthy specialized in. If McCarthy had been allowed to carry on much longer, physics in the United States might well have been ruined, just as physics in Nazi Germany *was* ruined by Hitler. As it is, almost all physicists who remember that time, including me, have come away with a profound sense of what a tyrant can do to a community.

While still a graduate student I took a reading course with the physicist Wendell Furry. Professor Furry was constantly being called to Washington, and it was only a little later, when McCarthy came to Boston and put him on public trial, that I realized why he had gone. Furry, unknown to all his students—he never once mentioned politics in his classes—had been a Communist for a brief period in the thirties. In his rampage in Boston, McCarthy used this misstep to create the portrait of a monster conspirator, and worked up the audience to the point where some people literally spat on Professor Furry when he appeared. It is impossible to erase that memory, and it is impossible not to pay tribute to Harvard for having had the courage, despite great pressures, to retain Furry during the worst days of the McCarthy era. About the same time, Oppenheimer lost his security clearance in an action that very few physicists will ever forgive, and it is again a tribute to Harvard that in the spring of 1957, despite protests from some of its alumni, Oppenheimer was invited to give a series of public lectures at the university.

In the summer of 1957, I went to Los Alamos as a visiting scientist, and the next fall, began a two-year fellowship at the Institute for Advanced Study, in Princeton. The two places provided a striking contrast in what the practice of physics had become since the war. Los Alamos was still a completely closed city then—a kind of scientific fortress—and the laboratory was devoted primarily to weapons work. (It is now open, and I am told its character has changed considerably.) Nuclear testing was still going on in the deserts of Nevada, and at the end of the summer I went to see a test. Many people have written about the beauty and overwhelming sense of power of an atomic-bomb explosion, and nothing that I have read appears to me to exaggerate the realities. The bomb is the sophisticated twentieth-century expression of the darkest and most profane aspects of our humanity. As for the Institute, at its best it was an almost complete counterpoint. It is hard to imagine a more idyllic setting for scholarly contemplation. I arrived there in the early fall, after having driven nonstop from Los Alamos. Like all the new arrivals, I was ushered in at once to meet Professor Oppenheimer, who was then the director. After a quick greeting he asked, "What's new and firm in physics?"—a question that I would have found difficult to answer coherently under the best of circumstances. He then recited a list of the visiting members for that year and concluded by saying, "Lee is here, and he and Yang are going to teach us about the weak interactions."

In all postwar physics there has been nothing to equal the surprise and excitement that surrounded the discovery, stimulated by T. D. Lee and C. N. Yang in the early winter of 1956, that the conservation of parity was violated in the decays of radioactive particles. Parity—the symmetry between left and right (it is more fully described later in the book) —was something that physicists had come to take for granted, like the conservation of energy. In fact, the weak interactions—the forces responsible for causing radioactive particles to decay—had become an almost academic subject. Most physicists studying elementary particles centered their interest on the mesons and the horde of new particles that were just beginning to turn up in the big accelerators; weak interactions were a subject that one spent a few weeks lecturing on in a nuclear-physics course and then forgot. With the discovery of parity, non-conservation, the weak interactions suddenly became the most exciting field in physics. Experiments followed experiments, and theories followed theories. It was all but impossible to keep up with the chaos of the new results. That autumn at the Institute, it was the main subject of conversation and study, and we had the enormous good fortune to be able to listen to Lee and Yang, who gave frequent public seminars and private lectures on it. Late that fall, they won the Nobel Prize, which added to the atmosphere of excitement. A few months later, I had the opportunity to collaborate briefly with them on a scientific paper. That experience and the sense of admiration that I, along with every other physicist, had for their extraordinary scientific gifts, and the appreciation I acquired for their devotion to the deepest and loveliest aspects of traditional Chinese life, formed the basis for the Profile I wrote of them in 1962. Since then, both Lee and Yang have left Princeton. Lee has returned to Columbia, and Yang has joined the new and growing physics department at Stoneybrook, near Brookhaven. The weak interactions have become even more mysterious and have remained at the center of physics.

In the summer of 1958, I made a sort of scientific pilgrimage to the West Coast, first visiting the physics department at the University of Washington, in Seattle, then going on to the University of California at Berkeley, and the Rand Corporation, in Santa Monica. Finally, at the end of the summer, I joined Professor Freeman Dyson, of the Institute, who was working on space flight for the General Atomic Corporation, in La Jolla. A short time before, Dyson had become interested in the possibilities of using the energy of nuclear bombs to propel large space vehicles. Like many futuristic ideas, this one, which had its origins with some of the Los Alamos scientists, such as Stanley Ulam, just after the war, appears at first sight to be almost completely mad. This was certainly my own impression until Dyson pointed out that from a certain point of view the automobile engine appears almost equally crazy. The engine operates from the power generated by a regular series of chemical explosions, and the temperature at the time of the explosions is higher than the melting temperature of the metals of the engine; the reason that the engine does not melt is that the temperature of the explosion is maintained for only an instant. It would be possible, Dyson argued, to design a bomb-propelled spaceship that could survive the transitory heat of a bomb explosion in the same way. Dyson also pointed out that nuclear explosions were the only economic propulsion method so far conceived that could deliver enough power for really elaborate planetary exploration. At one point, he expressed his hope that a spaceship weighing a thousand tons could be sent to Mars by nuclear explosions at a cost roughly comparable, per ounce, of delivering an air-mail letter to Europe.

In any event, General Atomic, under the direction of Ted Taylor, a former Los Alamos physicist, had assembled an extremely impressive group of scientists and engineers in La Jolla to see if the thing could be made to work. The project went on for several years, and while the results of the study were highly promising, it was finally terminated for economic reasons. It was an idea a little ahead of its time, but I am convinced that in the near future, after the first moon landings and after the present technologies have been pushed to their limits, it will be revived. The idea of using nuclear-bomb technology for exploring the cosmos—certainly one of the best aspirations of the human race

—would be a fitting solution of how to dispose of the mounting stockpile of atomic weapons.

After my second year at the Institute, I went to France on a National Science Foundation Fellowship. Apart from the delights of Paris and the experience of learning French, this trip led to my first visit to CERN (Conseil Européen pour la Recherche Nucléaire), in Geneva. In many ways CERN is even more remarkable than the Institute. It is entirely devoted to research in the physics of elementary particles—the branch of pure physics that has the least chance of producing new technology. Despite this, it has received the enthusiastic endorsement of all the governments of Western Europe, who support it financially. Physicists from every part of Europe, including the Eastern satellite countries and the Middle Eastern countries, come to CERN. It is one of the few international organizations in which people from many nations have come together to do something concrete in almost perfect harmony. National traits and national differences are accepted and welcomed. The vitality of CERN is in its amalgam of languages, styles of life, and assorted temperaments, all housed in one place and all jumbled together. Discussions are multilingual, with people switching back and forth from one language to another. It is an atmosphere that most people who have worked there have been charmed by, and many, like me, go back again and again. In the third article in this collection I have tried to give the history of CERN and to capture some of its flavor.

After I had written the Profile of Lee and Yang, Mr. Shawn suggested that I try my hand at reviewing scientific books, and after some time I have evolved a kind of philosophy of scientific-book reviewing. Good scientific books written for a general audience are few and far between. At their best, popular-science books can teach not only the layman but also scientists in other disciplines. In fact, as Professor Frank once observed, a really good popular-science book in, say, physics, can teach even the physicist. The reason is that all the ideas must be expressed verbally, with an absolute minimum of technical camouflage. It is often the points that seem almost too obvious to need discussion that are the most difficult to set forth. A scientist who writes a popular book must think these points through with great clarity and extreme detail. He can assume nothing on the part of the reader, or almost nothing, and a scientist reading the results may come to realize that the "obvious" is not so obvious after all. It seemed to me that the best service that a reviewer of science books could perform would be to call attention to those books that appeared to have special merit, rather than to attempt to score debating points against the authors of bad books. The books that are discussed in this collection are all books that seemed to me to illuminate an aspect of science or of the relation of science to society. In reviewing them, I have tried to set their subject matter into some kind of general context so that the reader will not have the feeling that he is reading about an isolated, probably unfamiliar subject in a vacuum.

The last section in this collection may appear, at first sight, to be somewhat anomalous. It consists of three articles that deal with science and science fiction. I am not very fond of science fiction. Unless it is done by a master, it is usually dull literature. In the present explosive scientific atmosphere, most of the futuristic ideas contained in science fiction are either outmoded by the time they are published or are based on some arbitrary tinkering with well-established scientific principles. Of the modern science-fiction writers, it seems to me that Arthur Clarke stands out as a notable exception. He is learned in science and somehow captures the nostalgia that is associated with the contemplation of worlds we can never know and with dreams of the future and the past.

The first article in this section is an attempt to describe

Clarke's art. The second article is a Profile of Stanley Kubrick. It would hardly belong here at all, except that Kubrick and Clarke are attempting to put science and science fiction onto film. This is something that has often been tried before, but I was impressed by the ambition of their project and by the care and imagination that went into it, and I thought that a description of it might be of interest to the general reader. The last article in the book has to do with extraterrestrial life. This subject, like so many others, has until recently belonged to science fiction. The thing that interested me was to what extent, using the best scientific knowledge now available, one could appraise its plausibility, how one would detect it, and what it might mean for our future.

That this writing was ever done at all is due, in the first instance, to the encouragement and guidance of William Shawn. His suggestion that science be viewed, studied, and written about as a realm of immediate experience has been at the center of all the writing I have done for *The New Yorker*. That I ever learned enough science to try to write about it is due to Philipp Frank. His approach to science, his humor, and his sense of the great traditions of our discipline have served as the model of what I have been trying to do.

J.B.

Part I

AN EXPERIENCE
OF PHYSICS

1

Annie of Corsica

BEFORE the summer of 1960, I had a very vague impression of Corsica. I knew that Napoleon was born on the island and that it is still part of France; I had read several French stories that dealt with Corsican bandits of great nobility whose sole activity was robbing the unworthy rich and saving pious girls in black from various hazards; and I had heard innumerable Corsican dialect stories in Paris, all told in a rich Italianate accent and all having to do with Corsican laziness or peasant shrewdness or simple-mindedness. Therefore, one can imagine the general disbelief when I told people that I was going to spend the summer on Corsica teaching theoretical physics. How and to whom?

Since the war, there has grown up among physicists something that a friend of mine calls "the leisure of the theory class"—the summer school. One now finds these schools in such places as the French Alps, Trieste, and Lake Como. Many of them attract faculties of considerable eminence—scientists who are happy to do a little teaching at a spa for an otherwise free vacation—and the students come from all over the world and are at a very advanced level; many have their Ph.D.s and are actively doing research. Some of the schools are now firmly established, and have even taken to publishing their summer lectures in book form; nowadays it is not uncommon in physics literature to see a reference to somebody's lecture notes datelined, say, Les Houches or Varenna.

The school I taught at was in 1960 still in the formative stage. It was situated on a beach in Corsica, and its only building was a half-finished stone summer cottage. The house had been started by two Continental families who wanted to come to Corsica in the summer and live together in the nude. For some reason, they abandoned this admirable program, and what remained was a shell of a house set on a small cliff about thirty feet from the Mediterranean. The families must have been very rich. There were elaborate light fixtures (but no electricity), a fine bathroom (but no running water), picture windows (but no glass in them), and a great, two-level stone living room. Professor Maurice Lévy, of the University of Paris, who was looking for a summer-school site, recognized the possibilities of the house and successfully completed negotiations to buy it. For school purposes, we turned the living room into a lecture hall and mounted two small blackboards on the upper level to make a kind of lecture platform. One of the bedrooms became a library and another one an office. The students lived in tents near the beach, and the faculty in a modest hotel on another beach nearby. There was a freshwater spring, and the town of Cargèse was close enough to keep us well supplied with groceries.

The faculty consisted of three Americans (including me), an Englishman, an Italian, and several Frenchmen, including Professor Lévy, who ran the show. The French-men were mostly from the University of Paris or from the great international research center CERN, in Geneva. Our students were all French. There were about forty of them, and they came from either Paris or Bordeaux. I was at first surprised to find such a large group from Bordeaux, which is not noted as a center of research in physics. The explanation is that everyone wants to teach in Paris, thus creating a tremendous pressure for university jobs there. As a result, up-and-coming young scientists who cannot find a full-time post in Paris often hold two part-time jobs—one in Paris and the other in the provinces. They live in Paris and commute once a week to, say, Bordeaux. Our Bordelais had been brought to Corsica by a young Parisian physicist who worked with them part time in the winter and was happy to have the chance of seeing them more regularly in the summer.

Cargèse, which is near the western shore of the island, some thirty miles north of Ajaccio, where Napoleon was born, was founded about two hundred years ago by some Greeks escaping the Turkish occupation of their country. The *Guide Michelin* has this to say about Cargèse: "852 habitants. Alt. 82 metres. Ajaccio, 52 km.; Calvi, 112 km." It awards a red rocking chair to the Hotel Thalassa, where the faculty lived. A red rocking chair means "quiet and secluded situation" in *Michelin* language and must refer to the fact that the hotel is on a beach at the end of a dirt road that has made a vertical descent of the eighty-two metres from the main part of town. It is a charming hotel, although not very quiet in the summer, when the beach overflows with visitors, mainly students.

The Greek influence has remained in Cargèse. Many of the families have intermarried, and the Greek family names have endured. Some of the people look Greek— cream-white skin and jet-black hair—whereas most Corsi-cans have very swarthy complexions. The native language of the island, Corsican, is an Italian dialect, and you can hear the Italian in place names like Asco, Bastia, Bonifacio, Porto-Vecchio, Vizzavona, and Zonza. The Cargèsians are less reserved than most Corsicans, who give the impression of being a tough, introverted mountain race; indeed, the island *is* very mountainous, some peaks rising to more than eight thousand feet and remaining snow-covered all year.

It is easy to become fond of Cargèse. Life ambles along at a genial pace. There are some cafés that are given over to outdoor dancing at night. There are a couple of restaurants. There is a bus stop and a gasoline pump. There is a postcard-and-record store. When the bus pulls in, two or three times a day, the weary passengers, looking somewhat the worse for the rough ride over the mountain roads, divide themselves between the Café Les Sports and the Café au Bon Repos. To greet them, a loudspeaker from the record store is turned on and we are all treated to Tino Rossi singing "Ma Corse" for the hundred-and-fifty-thousandth time. A few records are sold. Some postcards are mailed home. The passengers are herded back into the bus, which lurches off, and Tino Rossi is put back to sleep. This ritual constitutes the main commercial activity of Cargèse.

Much of the actual physical labor of the island is done by the women. If the men happen to be around, they encourage their wives or girl friends with a few kindly words in Corsican. Some of the men describe themselves as professional fishermen, but no one takes this too seriously, and a breeze that an Atlantic fisherman would barely notice drives them off the Mediterranean and into the bar of the Hotel Thalassa. Here among a swirling crowd of other Corsicans, Continental families, students, and physicists, they ride out the storm—joking, singing, and drinking innumerable Pernods. Sometimes the division of labor between men and women on the island borders on the incredible. For example, there was an elderly Corsican couple who seemed to be around the Thalassa a great deal. In fact, the wife helped out with all the heavy housework. The old boy, straight as a smokestack, would ride up to the hotel every day on his mule and, naturally enough, go directly to the bar, while his wife, arriving on foot, would arm herself with a broom and a mop and disappear into the hotel. I learned after a while that she *owned* the hotel but simply couldn't stand to see good money paid out for cleaning it. This remarkable lady even took over the cooking after her son-in-law fired the cook, a Parisienne. That happened just after breakfast one morning. The reason the son-in-law gave was that the cook had had the impertinence to use *"tu"* instead of *"vous"* in the course of an argument they were having, and the only way he could salvage his honor was to fire her. I must say that the cuisine, which until that day had been excellent, dropped into a bottomless pit of yoghurt, cold fish, and salads with black olives. For some reason, the manufacture of yoghurt is a tradition in Cargèse, and we had it twice a day. I shared a table in the dining room with a French physicist from Paris whose opinion of yoghurt was unprintable. He had a saturnine face, which was bounded below by a long, pointed beard. He was a brilliant pantomimist, and developed a number of routines that he displayed when the yoghurt was brought in; one of them was to drape his head obligingly over the edge of the table, as if he expected the guillotine to fall.

Corsicans feel that they live in a part of France itself—indeed, Corsica is a department of Metropolitan France and not a province—but they are also very nationalistic and intensely proud of the island. The fact that they speak French and Corsican interchangeably and alternately summarizes their attitude. The Continental French, on the other hand, frequently look on the Corsicans as a mixture of bandits and buffoons. They joke about the Corsican blood feuds, which must have existed once, and the enormous indifference and laziness of the men, which is hard to deny. (It is claimed that the size of the olive harvest on the island is determined completely by the wind velocity in the olive groves.) The Corsican accent is so different from the sophisticated Parisian French that Parisians visiting the island, it is said, are sometimes taken for Englishmen. The native accent has become the bread and butter of French stage comedians.

In view of the vast difference in background and interests between the Cargèsians and the physicists, one might imagine that our relationship was somewhat peculiar and strained. This was certainly so at first, but we were soon relegated to the category of harmless lunatics who did mathematics in the summer on a lovely beach better suited to swimming and lying in the sun. We were known as *"les savants,"* said not with respect, especially, but also not with the veiled contempt that sometimes coats the word "professor." We bothered no one, and, in fact, were a modest gold mine for the people of Cargèse, who are very hard-pressed, especially in winter, when there are no tourist buses. Our students did their homework during the day in the cafés, drinking black coffee and Orezza, a natural carbonated mineral water that is bottled on the island. At night, they drank the sweet Corsican wines and danced outdoors. Some even bought Tino Rossi singing "Ma Corse." I bought a vast supply of colored postcards, which always managed to understate the beauty of the island. At the Bon Repos, I became a favorite of the owner. The fact that I was an American made me, a priori, a great expert on the world at large. The Corsicans do not see many Americans; most of the summer visitors are Continental French, and a large number of these are relatively young students. I would arrive at the Repos every morning about eleven, just after my lecture. I was usually in a state of frustration. Since physics lectures are hard enough to understand in one's native language, we Americans did our best to lecture in French, and I found lecturing in French on physics very hard; when I concentrated on the physics, my French would become incoherent, and vice versa. At the Repos, I would order an Orezza to calm my nerves and then begin to read the *Nice-Matin*. While I studied the paper, the proprietor of the Repos could generally be found sleeping lightly in a nearby chair in the shade. If he happened to wake up, he would come over to my chair with *his* copy of the *Nice-Matin* so that we could compare notes. He would invariably begin the conversation by remarking, *"Ça bouge"* ("It moves"). This turned out to be a reference to the world situation, and I was now expected to give a little talk on world problems, during which he would gradually nod off again.

By this time, the students would have begun drifting in—our students and some of the enormous group of young Continental students to whom Corsica is a summer paradise. The eternal triangle on the island was a boy, a girl, and a motor scooter. The couples would buzz around the island until they found an attractive beach on which to set up light housekeeping in tents; hundreds of unclaimed beaches rim the island and are free for the taking. Sometimes the students would set up camp in one of the forests in the interior, but usually they organized beach colonies near a little town like Cargèse. In Cargèse, they spent the hot part of the day commuting between the beach and the cafés, and in both places they talked incessantly. Among French students, the ability to talk brilliantly is the greatest social asset one can have. The biggest catch in Cargèse that summer was a philosophy student who had "HEGEL" painted on his shoes in white—"HE" on his left shoe and "GEL" on his right—and who would vanish into the mountains every few days, usually in the company of one of the most attractive girl students. The second-greatest social asset one can have is the ability to play the guitar. Ah, imagine the man who both talks brilliantly and plays the guitar, perhaps simultaneously! It was nothing to find three guitars going at once at the Repos, sometimes accompanied by group singing but usually all but drowned out by the endless chatter. It is into this setting that I would like to introduce Annie.

The first time I saw Annie was when she came crashing up to the Repos on an ancient black motorcycle. This was no motor scooter but a vintage Harley-Davidson, always on the verge of total collapse. She insisted on driving it barefooted, and could be seen daily careering through the narrow main street of Cargèse, causing man and animal to flee to shelter. She was very beautiful, with jet-black hair, deep-blue eyes, and an infectious laugh. On a good day, she was known to say about twelve words. Although she never asserted herself, one could see right off that Annie was the focus of the student group in Cargèse. When she was around, the conversation and the guitar-playing became even more intense, and when she went bombing off on the motorcycle there was a lull. On her daily visit to the café, Annie stayed only a little while; soon a band of young Corsicans, also on motorcycles, would come by to fetch her. They would salute each other in Corsican, and Annie would remark "*Mes cousins*" and be off.

Pretty soon, I found that I was beginning to wait for Annie's daily visit, like everyone else. I had no occasion to talk to her, since she kept herself very aloof, and as no one offered any explanations, it was quite a while before I could find out much about her. The clue came with the arrival at the Thalassa of a new family from Paris. I was told by our waitress that a wonderful family was coming to the hotel and that now we would be kept amused night and day. Since I was trying hard to finish preparing my lectures, I didn't show much enthusiasm over this revelation. Early in the morning after the arrival of the new Parisians, I was aroused by some prowling outside my window. A man's voice groaned, *"Mais, dis donc, ton oiseau, je m'en fous royalement!"* ("I couldn't give less of a good God damn about your bird!" is a rough English rendering.) I opened the blinds to examine the author of this remarkable statement. He was a small, wiry man in his middle forties, already brown from the sun, and he was addressing a very pretty girl of about twenty who had climbed onto the low roof over the front door of the hotel. The girl was cradling a baby bird in one hand and evidently trying to put it back into its nest. *"Tu vas te casser la figure, et finalement je m'en fous!"* ("You're going to break your neck, and I couldn't care less!") the man said, looking rather desperate. The girl calmly deposited the bird in the nest and slid down a pipe next to the door. She stuck out her tongue and remarked sadly, *"T'es idiot, Papa."* A shutter banged upstairs and a woman's voice called "Robert!" at which father and daughter vanished inside the hotel.

With my day full of classes and students, I didn't catch sight of them again until dinner. My bearded colleague and I were just finishing our soup when they came in. The mother and daughter, with Robert following behind, made a striking pair. They were very brown, and were talking and laughing like two school chums. And, to top it off, there was Annie—in a dress, no less, although still barefoot. Furthermore, she seemed to be speaking whole sentences, one after another, most of them addressed to the bird girl of the morning. Behind Annie came two adults, who were evidently her mother and father; in fact, Annie's mother was a perfect likeness of Annie—the same deep-blue eyes and black hair. Papa was a curious figure, handsome and at his ease but also very distant; he acted as if he were viewing the scene from a telescope on the moon. At the sight of the girls, my bearded friend started a bit and sucked his breath sharply through his teeth. *"Délicieuses,"* he said. During dinner, we made a number of attempts to board their table, but our comments on the yoghurt, the wine, and the general flora and fauna fell on stone. After dinner, they went out to the terrace for coffee and cognac, and we followed. They talked awhile, and suddenly Robert spotted a Ping-pong table at the side of the terrace. *"Le Ping-pong! Le Ping-pong!"* he cried, as if he had just discovered uranium. He leaped to the table and tried to talk someone in his entourage into playing. There were no takers, and he began to look a little unhappy. *"Qui va jouer avec moi au Ping-pong?"* he finally said to the hotel at large, and before anyone else had a chance to say anything I challenged him.

He introduced himself, and when he found out where I was from he labelled the match "America vs. France." At once, we had the entire hotel lined up to watch. I have always regarded Ping-pong as a miserable game, but under the influence of the girls and the cognac I did better than I had any right to, and gave him quite a spirited battle before I went down. However, the real battle was won, for as a reward I was invited to sit with them and have a cognac. I was introduced to the girls and their parents, and we talked on about general things. But suddenly, when it was learned that I was an American physicist, the tone of the conversation became very hostile. I tried to get it down to a more friendly level by arguing that France and America were allies and that for our common survival we had to join forces. This approach only seemed to make things worse, and after a few more minutes of debate Annie's father got up and, without a word, stalked off into the night. Soon everyone else left, and I found myself alone, wondering how things could have gone so badly just when they had seemed to be getting started.

The next day, I saw Robert on the beach. I was going to avoid him, but when he saw me he came straight over. He told me he was sorry that the discussion had been so bitter, but he said that they felt strongly about the United States and especially about the evil of nuclear weapons—the creation of physicists. Before the Hungarian uprising, he said, both families had been very active members of the Communist Party. The two girls had studied Russian, and had even represented France at one of the youth festivals in Moscow. But after the uprising Robert and his family, like many other French Communists, had become completely disgusted and quit the Party. Annie's family, however, had stayed in; in fact, her father was a Party functionary. He was very poorly paid, and they lived on Corsica partly because of the beauty of the island and partly because life there was so much cheaper. Though the girls were still the best of friends, relations between the senior members of the families were somewhat tense. In general, they never spoke about politics, since the old wounds had never healed. Our Ping-pong game had apparently set off an explosion, and I was an innocent victim.

In any case, I now had a chance to get to know Annie. We never again spoke of politics, and I am not sure that she cared about them. It turned out that although she had grown up on Corsica, she had spent her winters studying in Paris. From the Latin Quarter, she knew most of the students who came to Cargèse for the summers. She was not terribly enthusiastic about life in Paris. Most Corsican students who go to Paris to study stay there, or somewhere on the Continent, and sooner or later they are lost to the island; this is almost inevitable, since Corsica can offer them neither sufficient intellectual stimulation nor economic opportunities. Going to Paris is for most of them a little like going to Wonderland, but for Annie it was quite different; in fact, she expected to settle in Ajaccio, with its thirty thousand people. Her most deeply felt objection to Paris was that it was too far from nature. The Luxembourg Gardens can't compete with the Corsican coastline, and, indeed, Annie lived in one of the most beautiful parts of Corsica. Her house (I saw it later) was set on top of a high cliff overlooking the Gulf of Porto, and the view was breathtaking. The Gulf of Porto is a rich-blue inlet cradled by jagged red walls; red mountains seem to soar out of the sea, and at sunset the whole arena glows with a fire that consumes any clouds that happen by. I watched the sunset from those cliffs many times during the summer, and Annie must have watched them many hundreds of times more. If you tried to tell her what she would miss in life by settling in a small Mediterranean town—about the music, the theatre, and all—she would put a finger to her lips and nod toward the sun, which was gingerly placing itself in the sea. There's no competing with a sunset.

2

A Question of Parity :
T. D. Lee and
C. N. Yang

EVER SINCE the explosion of the first atomic bomb
the face of physics has been deadly serious. The
days when physics was almost exclusively a scholarly
activity, carried on in universities and research insti-
tutes, are past, and very likely will never return.
Physicists are called on to think about bombs and
rockets and fallout shelters and all the other frightful
paraphernalia of modern war. In general, they are not
very happy about this new responsibility, but they
reason that someone must think about these highly
technical and often enormously complicated matters,

and if the physicists don't, who will? The result of the publicity about bombs and rockets has been, on the one hand, to accord physicists an entirely new status in the community (the old joke "Help! Help! My son the doctor is drowning!" today might well go ". . . My son the nuclear physicist . . .") and, on the other, to obscure almost completely what physics really is—the discovery of laws of nature, or, if you will, natural philosophy. There are actually no new physical principles involved in the production of bombs and rockets, though the technology is extremely subtle; indeed, to confuse rocketry with physics is something like equating the invention of the long-playing record with the writing of a symphony. Nonetheless, it must certainly be said that the interaction of government and physics has been profitable to physics (i.e., natural philosophy) as well as to government (i.e., rocketry).

Of the greatest importance to the development of physics has been government support of basic, or pure, research. Entire laboratories, like the Brookhaven National Laboratory, at Upton, Long Island, have been established through coöperation between universities and the government. When it became clear after the war, that some scientific projects would be simply too big for a single university to handle, nine Eastern universities banded together to form a center for research. In 1947, they founded Brookhaven. The Laboratory utilizes what remains of Camp Upton, an old Army base, and visitors to the site are often struck by the somewhat military nature of the architecture. The money for the Laboratory comes from the Atomic Energy Commission, but the Laboratory is administered by the member universities. On the reservation are two very large particle accelerators, the AGS (alternating-gradient synchrotron) and the cosmotron, the latter having been completed in 1953 and the former in 1961; a nuclear-research reactor; a research hospital; and many other scientific facilities. The Laboratory is devoted to research in practically every branch of pure science. A particle accelerator like the AGS costs about thirty million dollars to build. In this case, the A.E.C. supplied the money and then made the AGS available to physicists from the nine universities. However, individual experiments in which it is used may themselves represent investments of hundreds of thousands of dollars in special equipment—electronic computers, bubble chambers, and so on. This money also comes from the A.E.C. No university can hope to maintain high-level research in contemporary physics without government support. The sheer bigness of it all is bound to affect the attitudes of individual physicists. A man who is responsible for a research instrument like a large bubble chamber, which costs about a million dollars to build, does not, and cannot, have the same relation to it that he would have to a small homemade device put together with his own hands. Dr. Arthur Roberts, now of the Argonne National Laboratory, outside Chicago, who is a musician and a writer of verse as well as a distinguished physicist, has managed to capture a bit of the dismay and nostalgia that the new physics has inspired in many physicists who grew up in the prewar, or string-and-sealing-wax, era. However, after composing the ballad quoted below, he himself went on to do research with the big machines:

> . . . at an ancient Army base
> the best electro-nuclear
> machine at any place.
> It will cost a billion dollars.
> Ten billion volts 'twill give.
> It will take five thousand scholars
> seven years to make it live.
>
> . . . .
>
> This machine is just a model
> for a bigger one, of course.

That's the future course of physics,
as I'm sure you'll all endorse.

. . . .

Take away your billion dollars.
Take away your tainted gold.

. . . .

Take, oh, take your billion dollars.
Let's be physicists again.

As things have worked out, in a laboratory like Brookhaven there are really three groups of physicists. First,
there are the theorists, who do mathematical physics—who
attempt to predict or interpret the results of experiments
by using the techniques of mathematical calculation in the
same spirit (though normally with vastly less success) as
that of Newton when he analyzed observations on planetary motion in terms of the law of gravitation. Then, there
are the experimentalists, who actually do the experiments.
Finally, there is a group that might be called the instru-
mentalists, who design and build the complicated equipment, like the AGS, that is used in many experiments. In
Newton's era—and, indeed, until rather recently—an individual was often able to perform all three functions himself. Now everything is just too complicated. As a rule, an
experimentalist does not have the time or the mathematical training to do theory, and a theorist does not know
enough electronics to do experiments, and so on. Of
course, these boundaries are not absolute, but a physicist
who can cross even one of them successfully is quite a
rarity. In fact, the only contemporary physicist to make
numerous contributions of the first magnitude to both
experiment and theory was the late Enrico Fermi. Fermi,
who was born in 1901, in Rome, and came to the United
States in 1939, worked in essentially every branch of modern physics. In 1938, he won the Nobel Prize for his
experimental work in neutron physics, but by that time he

had also done great pioneering work in several fields of theoretical physics, and it would be impossible to say which of the contributions was more significant. Fermi spent the war years working on the development of the atomic bomb and the nuclear reactor. After the war, he joined the faculty of the University of Chicago, where he remained until his death, in 1954. Besides being both a theoretical and an experimental physicist, he was one of the great teachers of physics, and he attracted to Chicago a whole postwar generation of physicists, who are now playing a major role in the field. Fermi was equally at home with experimental equipment and with mathematical calculations. He was unique in his time, and as physics has been getting steadily more complicated since his death, it seems unlikely that the future will produce a physicist quite like him.

In all the good work in physics, a perpetual colloquy goes on between experiment and theory. Theoretical proposals suggest experiments, and vice versa. One of the best illustrations of this process in modern times took place in the years 1956 and 1957. It has led to a very great advance in pure physics, although one which, as far as anybody can tell now, has no technological applications or implications. This discovery involved two theoretical physicists, Chen Ning Yang and Tsung-Dao Lee, and in October of 1957 they were together awarded the Nobel Prize in physics for, in the language of the Swedish Royal Academy, "their penetrating research into the laws of parity, which has led to major discoveries concerning the elementary particles." Yang was then thirty-five and Lee thirty-one, which puts them among the youngest Nobel laureates; they are also the only Chinese who have so far won the prize. The award was the climax of what was certainly the most exciting year in postwar physics.

In modern physics, there has been nothing quite like the collaboration between Lee and Yang. It is true that collaboration is the rule in experimental physics; indeed, owing to the complexity of the experiments, it is absolutely essential. Hence, there are experimental teams that have worked together for many years. Theoretical physicists, however, are notoriously independent. Some never collaborate. Most of them work occasionally with others (two people making the same calculation independently are much more efficient than one person making the same calculation twice) but are likely to change partners frequently. Lee and Yang are theoretical physicists exclusively. (As a graduate student, Yang tried some experimental work in the laboratory of Professor S. K. Allison, at the University of Chicago, but, to judge by reports I have heard from his fellow-students, he was not altogether at home in the laboratory—"Where there's a bang, there's Yang" was a local rhyme—and after a short time he switched to theory. Lee has avoided laboratory work entirely, though both he and Yang find much pleasure in learning about the inner workings of experimental equipment.) While each has done outstanding work alone and now and then with other collaborators, much of the work they have done, including all the work leading to the Nobel Prize, was done by the two of them together.

In 1945, both Lee and Yang were students at the Southwest Associated University, in Kunming, a city in pre-Communist China, and within a few months—Yang that year and Lee the next—both of them came to this country on fellowships. Yang, who was twenty-three, had completed the equivalent of a Master's degree in physics. His father, Professor K. C. Yang, is a mathematician, so Yang had grown up with mathematics and physics, and by the time he came to the United States he had had a very thorough preparation in both. He was, in fact, considerably more advanced than the other graduate students at the University of Chicago, where he eventually found himself. While Yang was still in China, he read Benjamin Franklin's autobiography, and Franklin made a tremendous impression on him both as a person and as a scientific figure. Upon coming to America, therefore, Yang decided to name himself after Franklin. Because he did not like the name Benjamin, he called himself Franklin, or Frank. The name caught on with the graduate students at the University of Chicago, and now he is known informally to physicists as Frank. Lee is known affectionately to physicists as "T. D." Yang arrived in New York, via India, the Suez Canal, and the Atlantic, in late November, 1945. He was already an admirer of Fermi, and, thinking that Fermi was still at Columbia University, where he had been a professor of physics until the atomic-bomb project took him to Los Alamos, he went to the Pupin Physics Laboratories at Columbia to find out when Fermi was to lecture. As Yang has since written, "I remember that one day, soon after my arrival in New York, I trudged uptown and went up to the eighth floor of Pupin to inquire whether Professor Fermi would be giving courses soon. The secretaries met me with totally blank faces. I learned that there were rumors of a new institute to be established at Chicago and that Fermi would join the institute. I went to Chicago, registered at the University, but did not feel completely secure until I saw Fermi with my own eyes when he began his lectures in January, 1946." Yang presently became a kind of assistant to Fermi, and was sometimes called on to serve as a substitute lecturer when Fermi was away. Yang was in this country on a Boxer Fellowship, which he had won in China on the basis of a nationwide examination. The history of the Boxer Fellowships is interesting, and in his address at the Nobel banquet Yang outlined some of it as follows:

"Your Majesties, Your Royal Highnesses, Ladies and Gentlemen:

"First of all, allow me to thank the Nobel Foundation and the Swedish Academy of Sciences for the kind hospitality that Mrs. Yang and I have enjoyed. I also wish to thank especially Professor Karlgren for his quotation and his passage in Chinese, to hear which is to warm my heart.

"The institution of the awarding of Nobel Prizes started in the year 1901. In that same year, another momentous event took place of great historical importance. It was, incidentally, to have a decisive influence on the course of my personal life and was to be instrumental in relation to my present participation in the Nobel festival of 1957. With your kind indulgence, I shall take a few minutes to go a little bit into this matter.

"In the latter half of the last century, the impact of the expanding influence of Western culture and economic system brought about in China a severe conflict. The question was heatedly debated of how much Western culture should be brought into China. However, before a resolution was reached, reasons gave way to emotions, and there arose in the eighteen-nineties groups of people called I Ho Tuan in Chinese, or Boxers in English, who claimed to be able to withstand in bare flesh the attack of modern weapons. Their stupid and ignorant action against Westerners in China brought in 1900 the armies of many European countries and of the U.S. into Peking. The incident is called the Boxer War and was characterized on both sides by barbarious killings and shameful lootings. In the final analysis, the incident is seen as originating from an emotional expression of the frustration and anger of the proud people of China, who had been subject to ever-increasing oppression from without and decadent corruption from within. It is also seen in history as settling, once and for all, the debate as to how much Western culture should be introduced into China.

"The war ended in 1901, when a treaty was signed. Among other things, the treaty stipulated that China was to pay the powers the sum of approximately five hundred million ounces of silver, a staggering amount in those days.

About ten years later, in a typically American gesture, the U.S. decided to return to China her share of the sum. The money was used to set up a fund which financed a university, the Tsinghua University, and a fellowship program for students to study in the U.S. I was a direct beneficiary of both of these two projects. I grew up in the secluded and academically inclined atmosphere of the campus of this university, where my father was a professor, and enjoyed a tranquil childhood that was unfortunately denied most of the Chinese of my generation. I was later to receive an excellent first two years' graduate education in the same university and then again was able to pursue my studies in the U.S. on a fellowship from the aforementioned fund.

"As I stand here today and tell you about these, I am heavy with an awareness of the fact that I am in more than one sense a product of both the Chinese and Western cultures, in harmony and in conflict. I should like to say that I am as proud of my Chinese heritage and background as I am devoted to modern science, a part of human civilization of Western origin, to which I have dedicated and I shall continue to dedicate my work."

T. D. came to Chicago by a rather different route. He was born in Shanghai, the third of six children of a businessman. His education was badly broken up by the war. In 1945, he went to Kunming and matriculated at the Southwest Associated University, where Yang had already received his Master's degree. Lee and Yang had only a nodding acquaintance at the time, and did not really come to know each other until they met again in Chicago. At Kunming, Lee studied with Professor Ta-You Wu, a well-known Chinese theoretical physicist, who is now working at the Canadian National Research Council, in Ottawa. Dr. Wu, a native of Canton, received his Ph.D. at the University of Michigan in 1933 and then went back to China to teach. After the war, he came again to this country to do research work, bringing with him two students. As one of them he chose Lee. At this time, Lee was still an undergraduate, so Dr. Wu's choice showed remarkable foresight. In a letter Dr. Wu then wrote to Professor S. Goudsmit, now of Brookhaven, who had been his teacher at Michigan, he included a description of Lee that in retrospect seems a notable piece of understatement: "He has had only three years in the university in China, but he is a very bright boy who thinks straight, is critical, and works very hard. I am sure he will make a good physicist if given the proper guidance." Upon arriving in America, Lee learned that the University of Chicago was the only university that would permit a student without an undergraduate degree to begin working for his doctorate, so he registered at Chicago.

Thus, in 1946, both Frank and T. D. found themselves living in the International House at the University of Chicago. One of their earliest collaborations had nothing to do with physics. It was in a puzzle contest being run in one of the Chicago newspapers. The puzzles were Scrabble-like, and the first prize was something in excess of fifty thousand dollars. This seemed like a nice sum, so they enlisted the help of a few of the other graduate students and entered the contest. One of their fellow-contestants was Dr. R. L. Garwin, who was then working in experimental physics under Fermi and is now the associate director of the I.B.M. Watson Laboratory and an adjunct professor of physics at Columbia University; he came to play an important role in the parity experiments in 1957. The entry required a cash outlay of about eight dollars, and in addition the group invested forty dollars in a two-volume unabridged Webster's New International Dictionary, which was the official dictionary of the contest. They solved the initial series of puzzles correctly, whereupon they were sent a succession of "tie-breaking" puzzles. They studied these tie-breakers exhaustively and, perceiving an ambiguity in the contest rules, submitted two sets of solutions, one for each interpretation. A few days later, they were outraged to learn that they had been disqualified for submitting too many solutions. They had beaten the eventual winner by several points, but to no avail.

Meanwhile, Yang and Lee had begun serious discussions of physics. In those days, Lee learned a great deal of physics from Yang, who had a three- or four-year head start in the subject. At the University of Chicago, the graduate students in general were expected to educate themselves and each other as much as possible. There were courses, but it was considered somewhat infra dig to rely on them very heavily. When he felt sufficiently prepared, the student took a stiff examination qualifying him to work on a doctoral thesis, generally under the supervision of a faculty member. Lee, who passed the exam in 1948, wrote his thesis on a problem in astrophysics (it concerned the theory of white dwarf stars), under Fermi. Yang worked on a problem in the theory of nuclear reactions, under Professor Edward Teller. Yang got his degree in 1948, and Lee got his in 1950. Their first joint paper, published in 1949, was written in association with M. Rosenbluth, another graduate student at the University of Chicago at that time, who is now a professor at the University of California at La Jolla and a research physicist at the General Atomic Company. Throughout their years in Chicago, Yang and Lee attended a series of informal night lectures that Fermi gave for some of the graduate students. Fermi kept a remarkable series of notebooks, in which he jotted down his ideas on a wide variety of topics in physics. At the evening lectures, either Fermi or one of the students would propose a topic for discussion, and then the notebooks would be searched until Fermi found something relevant, which he would present. His discussions were always given on an elementary, almost intuitive level, with great emphasis on the simple principles that underlie mathematical derivations. The quality and variety of these lectures made a lasting impression on both young men. Yang has written of them, "We learned that physics should not be a specialist's subject; physics is to be built from the ground up, brick by brick, layer by layer. We learned that abstractions come *after* detailed foundation work, not before. We also learned in these lectures of Fermi's delight in, rather than aversion to, simple numerical computations with a desk computer."

In 1950, Lee joined the Physics Department of the University of California at Berkeley as a lecturer. The year before, Yang had gone to the Institute for Advanced Study, at Princeton, where he became a permanent member in 1952. There are usually about a hundred people at the Institute who are called temporary members, but there are only twenty permanent members, representing various disciplines, and very few of the permanent members are physicists. Lee joined Yang at the Institute for two years—from 1951 to 1953—and then accepted a position at Columbia. The distance between New York and Princeton being not very great, they worked out a schedule whereby each would visit the other once a week. In the course of these visits, they discussed anything that seemed important in physics at the time. In 1953, too, Yang began spending summers at Brookhaven. The Laboratory holds a very active summer session, with visitors from all over the world, who divide their time between their offices and laboratories in Upton and the many nearby beaches. The summer at Brookhaven provides scientists who are widely separated during the academic year with an opportunity to meet and discuss common problems. A good deal of excellent physics has come out of these summers, some of it being done on the beach. In 1956, Yang returned to Brookhaven in April, and he and Lee began visiting back and forth between Upton and New York. Until then, they had been pursuing rather different lines of inquiry, but now they were both concentrating on a single problem, and in June, Lee joined Yang at Brookhaven.

What Yang and Lee were preoccupied with that spring was a mystery known as "the theta-tau puzzle," which was plaguing physicists concerned with the study of elementary particles. Elementary particles are the building blocks of which all matter is composed. For the Greeks and, by and large, for everyone else up until 1911, when Ernest Rutherford discovered the atomic nucleus, the elementary particles were thought to be the atoms; indeed, the word "atom" means "indivisible." After 1911, it was discovered that the atom was divisible, into a massive interior called the nucleus, and a more loosely composed, electrically charged exterior, which nowadays is called the electronic cloud. At first, it was held that the nucleus itself was made up of protons and electrons. The proton, a relatively heavy, positively charged particle, was thought to give the nucleus its massive character. However, the idea that electrons were present in the interior of the nucleus turned out to be untenable. In any case, in 1932 J. Chadwick discovered the neutron, the electrically neutral partner of the massive proton, and it became clear that the nucleus was in fact composed of protons and neutrons. Also in 1932, C. D. Anderson, of the California Institute of Technology, in Pasadena, confirming a brilliant theoretical speculation by the English theorist P. A. M. Dirac, discovered a positive counterpart of the electron, called the positron. The electron and the positron were the first example of a particle-and-antiparticle pair to be found in laboratory experiments. Now it is known that each kind of particle has an antiparticle equivalent of the same mass, and that when the two are brought together they annihilate each other, becoming transformed into energy of various kinds. This transformation is an illustration of Einstein's discovery of the equivalence of mass and energy, which can be expressed in the formula $E = mc^2$. By the end of 1932, five elementary particles were known, the fifth being the photon, the particle of which light is composed. (Some particles, such as the photon, are identical with their antiparticle.) Now the known total has risen to somewhere in the hundreds, depending a little on what one means by "elementary," and it is by no means clear that the list has been exhausted. Many of these particles were discovered after the war, mainly as a result of the continuous improvement in experimental techniques. Large accelerators, like the AGS, were constructed, and as the energy of the accelerators has been increased they have been able to produce particles of greater and greater mass. The positrons on which Anderson experimented were found in cosmic radiation—the name given to the natural radiation (exclusive of light) that comes to us, in small amounts, from outer space. It is obviously vastly more efficient for an experimentalist to have available a beam of particles of some desired kind, produced at will in an accelerator, than it is to wait until one appears by chance in cosmic rays. Of course, Anderson did not know he was going to find the positron beforehand, and cosmic rays have been an extremely fruitful source of unexpected particles.

By the mid-nineteen-fifties, an entirely new class of particles had been discovered. They had not been predicted by any theory; they were simply there. For that reason, they were named "strange particles." The study of strange particles constitutes one of the most active branches of contemporary physics. The first of these particles was discovered in cosmic rays, in 1947, when G. D. Rochester and C. C. Butler, two English experimentalists, observed its track in a cloud chamber. The connection between strange particles and ordinary matter is very remote indeed. Ordinary matter can be thought to be composed of protons, neutrons, and electrons, for most practical purposes. However, when matter is bombarded at high energies by, say, protons, the strange particles are produced in the debris of the collision. It is the fact that the same peculiar objects are produced again and again in such collisions which gives physicists confidence in their existence. An experimenter looking at a photograph of a nuclear collision can tell what particles are produced by observing how the tracks look. He has usually seen the same kind of tracks dozens or even hundreds of times before.

The theta meson and the tau meson were two—or at least seemed to be two—of the strange particles. They decayed—that is, disintegrated—spontaneously into more familiar particles, called pi mesons, or simply pions. The puzzle lay in the fact that the theta and the tau had apparently identical properties, especially in respect to mass and lifetime, but that one of them (the theta) decayed into two pions and the other (the tau) into three. It seemed extremely odd that there should exist in nature two such similar objects differing only in this decay. It was much more appealing to postulate *one* particle with two decay modes. In fact, physicists would have been happy to put the theta and the tau down as identical. However, an extensive analysis of tau decays in 1954–55 by Dr. R. H. Dalitz, an Australian physicist who is now at Oxford, seemed to show that this was impossible. The Dalitz analysis was based on the physical principles that were generally accepted at that time. One of the most important of these was called the law of parity conservation. This law seemed at the time to be one of the most firmly established laws of physics, and one that was not to be tampered with lightly. After the Dalitz analysis demonstrated there there was a problem, many theorists, including Yang and Lee, went to work on it. At first, there was some hope that the theta and the tau might prove to have slightly different masses, which would have permitted a rather simple explanation of the two decay modes. But during the fall and winter of 1955 the measurements of their masses became more and more precise, and as a result it became more and more evident that the theta and the tau had (within experimental error) exactly the same mass. Hence, any simple explanation was ruled out. By the spring of 1956, it was certain that physicists were faced with a genuine paradox.

That April, when the Sixth Annual Rochester Conference on High Energy Nuclear Physics was held at the University of Rochester, in upstate New York, the theta-tau puzzle was high on the agenda. A number of suggestions of ways to escape the dilemma were made during the proceedings, but all of them proved unsatisfactory. Following a summary talk on strange particles by Yang, there was a discussion period. The conference reporters kept notes of the discussion, and one particular section is worth quoting: "Yang felt that so long as we understand as little as we do about the theta-tau degeneracy, it may perhaps be best to keep an open mind on the subject. Pursuing the open-mind approach, Feynman brought up a question of Block's: Could it be that the theta and tau are different parity states of the same particle, which has no definite parity; i.e., that parity is not conserved? That is, does nature have a way of defining right- or left-handedness uniquely? Yang stated that he and Lee looked into this matter without arriving at any definite conclusions. . . . So perhaps a particle having both parities could exist. . . . Perhaps one could say that parity conservation . . . could be violated. Perhaps the weak interactions could all come from this same source, a violation of space-time symmetries." There was more discussion and speculation, and finally, just before closing the session, Professor J. Robert Oppenheimer, who was chairman, remarked, "It is clear that the tau meson will have either domestic or foreign complications." It was a prophetic statement.

At that moment, the general feeling was one of bafflement and frustration. Yang has since written, "The situation the physicist found himself in at that time has been likened to a man in a dark room groping for an outlet. He is aware of the fact that in some direction there must be a door which would lead him out of his predicament. But in which direction?" He and Lee went back to work. Finally, seeing no other way out, they decided to make a detailed study of the experimental foundations of parity conservation itself. Surprisingly, this turned out to be the door.

What is parity conservation, and why were physicists so reluctant to question it? Parity conservation—or, as it is sometimes called, mirror symmetry—is the symmetry between a physical system and its so-called mirror system. It is well known that when an object is examined in a mirror, the mirror reflects right into left, and vice versa. In physics, all experience up to the recognition of the theta-tau puzzle seemed to show that a physical system and its mirror in which left and right are exchanged behave identically, follow the same laws. This identity of behavior between a left-handed physical system and a right-handed one is mirror symmetry. However, it could be proved, using complicated mathematical reasoning, that to identify the theta and the tau meant abandoning mirror symmetry—that is, the law of parity conservation—in the description of their decays. In his Nobel address, Yang tried to convey some of the connotations of this law. He said, "The symmetry principle between left and right is as old as human civilization. The question whether nature exhibits such symmetry was debated at length by philosophers of the past. Of course, in daily life, left and right are quite distinct from each other. Our hearts, for example, are on our left sides. The language that people use both in the Orient and the Occident carries even a connotation that right is good and left is evil. However, the laws of physics have always shown complete symmetry between the left and the right, the asymmetry in daily life being

attributed to the accidental asymmetry of the environment, or initial conditions in organic life. To illustrate the
point, we mention that if there existed a mirror-image
man with his heart on his right side, his internal organs
reversed compared to ours, and in fact his body molecules
—for example, sugar molecules—the mirror image of ours,
and if he ate the mirror image of the food that we eat,
then, according to the laws of physics, he should function
as well as we do."

The question that Lee and Yang asked themselves in
May, 1956, was: How do we know that this law is true?
What they discovered, much to their astonishment, was
that previous experiments proved the law only for strong
forces, such as those that hold the nucleus together, and
the chemical forces that are responsible for chemical
reactions; there simply were no experiments testing the
law for weak forces, such as those that cause particles
like the tau and the theta, or the famous radioactive
isotopes, to decay. There had been plenty of experiments on weak forces, but none of them (with one remarkable exception, unknown at the time to Lee and
Yang and to most other physicists) were relevant to the
question of parity conservation. Yang has described the
effect that this insight had on them at the time: "The fact
that parity conservation in the weak interactions was believed for so long without experimental support was very
startling. But what was more startling was the prospect
that a space-time symmetry law that the physicists had
learned so well might be violated. This prospect did not
appeal to us. Rather, we were, to to speak, driven to it
through frustration with the various other efforts that had
been made to understand the theta-tau puzzle."

In retrospect, a discovery like the one made by Lee and
Yang may look easy, but to the discoverers it almost never
is. I once discussed this with Yang, and he tried to describe
the psychological process one goes through at such a time.

He said that because, in dealing with something like the theta-tau puzzle, one just has no idea where to look for a solution, it is difficult to concentrate on any single approach. Once one has a clue to the solution, one can focus all one's efforts on the task of working it out, but until that time one's mind darts here and there without lighting on anything solid. Yang did not remember precisely how the idea of examining the previous experiments on weak interactions came to him and Lee, but he remembers when and where. It was early in May, and it occurred just after he had driven into New York from Upton to visit Lee. He had picked up Lee at his Columbia office and was having difficulty finding a parking place near Columbia. He and Lee were driving around looking for one and talking. They finally parked the car temporarily in front of a Chinese restaurant near the corner of Broadway and 125th Street. The restaurant was not yet open, so they went into the White Rose Café nearby. They sat down at a table and resumed their conversation, and it was then that the idea struck them. It was suddenly clear to them that the results of one weak-interaction experiment after another had to be examined to see if they gave any information on parity non-conservation.

This Yang and Lee did, in three weeks of intensive work, Yang at Brookhaven and Lee at Columbia. Their method was to pick a given experiment and to work out the theory for it, allowing for the fact that parity might not be conserved. For example, they computed the rates for various weak-decay processes. In the mathematical formula for the rate, the terms that might have reflected parity non-conservation just cancelled out. Thus, no experiment on the rates, however well done, could show the effect of parity non-conservation. And so it went with all the other experiments that had been done prior to 1956. For several weeks, they were at a loss to find a guiding principle that would enable them to say in advance of detailed calculation which experiments would be sensitive to parity non-conservation and which would not. Sometime in early June, they discovered how to do this, and it then became relatively simple to draw up a list of experiments that would, in principle, exhibit parity-conservation-violating effects.

Late in June, at Brookhaven, Yang and Lee wrote a paper called *Question of Parity Conservation in Weak Interactions,* which is now a classic. The opening section, which summarized the situation, is a model of scientific prose. It reads: "Recent experimental data indicate closely identical masses and lifetimes of the theta and tau mesons. On the other hand, analyses of the decay products of tau strongly suggest on the grounds of angular momentum and parity conservation that the theta and tau are not the same particle. This poses a rather puzzling situation that has been extensively discussed. One way out of the difficulty is to assume that parity is not strictly conserved, so that theta and tau are two different decay modes of the same particle, which necessarily has a single mass value and a single lifetime. We wish to analyze this possibility in the present paper against the background of the existing experimental evidence of parity conservation. It will become clear that existing experiments do indicate parity conservation in strong and electromagnetic interactions to a high degree of accuracy, but that for weak interactions (i.e., decay interactions for the mesons and hyperons and various Fermi [it was Fermi who first proposed the basic theory of the weak decays, in 1934] interactions) parity conservation is so far only an extrapolated hypothesis unsupported by experimental evidence. (One might even say that the present theta-tau puzzle may be taken as an indication that parity conservation is violated in weak interactions. This argument is, however, not to be taken seriously because of the paucity of our present knowledge concerning the nature of strange particles. It supplies rather an incentive for an examination of the question of parity conservation.) To decide unequivocally whether parity is conserved in weak interactions, one must perform an experiment to determine whether weak interactions differentiate the right from the left. Some such possible experiments will be discussed." In the rest of the paper, they gave a detailed outline of the experiments to be done.

Having challenged the experimentalists to go and have a look, Lee and Yang could do nothing but wait, and while they were waiting they started working at Brookhaven, in an entirely different branch of physics—statistical mechanics. Statistical mechanics is the study of systems, such as gases, that are composed of very large numbers of particles. In describing such a system, one does not try to analyze the behavior of individual atoms or molecules but attempts to make a statistical theory of large numbers of particles. It is an interesting branch of physics, and at one time or another Lee and Yang have made major contributions to it. A marvellous document has survived this waiting period— a sheet from Lee's scratch pad at Brookhaven. Another physicist working at the Laboratory found it and decided to save it as a souvenir, and after the excitement of the following fall and winter it was reproduced on the December, 1957, cover of *Physics Today*, a trade journal published by the American Institute of Physics. The sheet is covered with symbols and formulas in Lee's neat script, and an occasional ink blot is to be seen. The interesting thing is the subject matter. About half the formulas deal with statistical mechanics, and the other half deal with weak interactions and the non-conservation of parity. There was nothing for a theorist to do while the experimenters were measuring but wait and doodle, and Lee was waiting and doodling.

I think it is fair to say that in the summer and fall of 1956 most physicists regarded the possibility of the non-conservation of parity as something of a long shot. It was felt that if there were non-conserving effects they would probably be very small. The arguments that Yang and Lee had presented in their paper were unimpeachable, but it was hard to understand why the weak interactions alone should not conserve parity. (It is, by the way, still hard to understand.) Among the experimental groups that took up the challenge was one representing a Columbia University–National Bureau of Standards collaboration. They recognized that, in the tradition of good physics, an experiment to check a general principle *should* always be done, even if the anticipated chance of spectacular results is small. They therefore went at it with full strength. Of the various physicists involved in the group, the one who worked most closely with Yang and Lee was Mme. C. S. Wu, a professor of physics at Columbia. Mme. Wu (Mrs. Luke Chia-liu Yuan), like Lee and Yang, was born in China, and her scientific career, like theirs, had been pursued in the United States. She had long been a friend of both men, and was also a colleague of Lee's at Columbia. She was already world-famous for her highly accurate experiments on weak interactions. It was she who formed the collaboration with a group at the National Bureau of Standards, in Washington—experimentalists who were experts on techniques involving extremely low temperatures. These techniques were needed in the experiment, and when the final paper appeared, it was signed by Mme. Wu, representing Columbia, and E. Ambler, R. W. Hayward, D. D. Hoppes, and R. P. Hudson, representing the Bureau. Independently of the Columbia-Bureau experiment, a group at the University of Chicago, under the direction of Professor V. L. Telegdi, had started at about the same time another of the experiments suggested in the Lee and Yang paper. By December, there were strong hints in the data from the Columbia-Bureau experiment that in weak interactions parity was not conserved. The group was composed of excellent experimentalists, as well as cautious ones, and, realizing that they might be on the brink of one of the major discoveries in twentieth-century physics, they were very eager to make sure that everything was exactly right before publishing their results. However, Yang and Lee were in more or less daily communication with Mme. Wu, and as the evidence piled up they became convinced that parity conservation was out.

On Friday, January 4th, the physicists at Columbia assembled for a "Chinese lunch." Chinese lunches have been a tradition in the Columbia Physics Department since 1953, when Lee arrived on the scene. They still go on. These lunches usually take place on Friday—Friday being the day on which various departmental seminars are held—in one of several excellent Chinese restaurants near Columbia, and consist of ten or eleven dishes. Lee is rather a gourmet (this may stem from a wartime sojourn in the refugee camps, when he lived for a year on rice and peppers), so he usually takes charge of the menu. On this particular Friday, Lee brought in the important news he had just learned from Mme. Wu—that it seemed almost certain that parity was not conserved in the Columbia-Bureau experiment. He went on to describe the lines along which he and Yang had been thinking. Professor Leon Lederman, an experimentalist at Columbia, was among the Friday Chinese-lunch enthusiasts. He was then studying another weak decay, that of the pi meson. The pion decays into another meson, the muon, which in turn decays into an electron and two neutrinos. (The neutrino is a massless particle that is emitted in many weak decays. It interacts only very weakly with ordinary matter, and not until 1953 was the neutrino actually seen to react with matter, in a beautiful experiment performed at Hanford, Washington, by two Los Alamos scientists, F. Reines and C. L. Cowan, Jr.) It occurred to Lederman that with a little luck one might devise an experiment to show up parity non-conservation in both decays if it turned out that parity was not conserved. That night, at nine o'clock, he got in touch with Dr. R. L. Garwin, who was then at Columbia, and the two of them began working on the problem. By ten-fifteen, they had figured out how to do the experiment, and by 2 A.M. had started to take data on the Columbia accelerator. In fact, they thought they saw the effect they were looking for, but at that moment something in the equipment burned out. The weekend was spent repairing the damage (Garwin surprised his colleagues by turning out the new part himself on a machine-shop lathe), and on Monday afternoon the equipment was back in operation. By early Tuesday morning, their experiment had left no doubt whatever that parity conservation was dead in the weak interactions. At 6 A.M. Tuesday, Lederman phoned Lee to announce the news. This was the first of many such phone calls between physicists, and I think it is not much of an exaggeration to say that by the end of the week every physicist in the United States who was active in high-energy physics had heard about the experiments. I remember that on Wednesday or Thursday I was with a group of physicists at Harvard who were discussing rumors then circulating outside the Bureau of Standards. (We had no direct contact with any of the groups.) Professor Julian Schwinger, the leading theoretical physicist at Harvard, was urging us not to jump to conclusions before the final results were known. Then he was called to the telephone. It was Professor I. I. Rabi, at Columbia, with the final results. Schwinger came back and said, "Gentlemen, we must bow to nature."

The following Tuesday, January 15th, the Columbia University Physics Department did something until then unprecedented: it held a press conference on the new discoveries. Rabi was quoted as saying, "In a certain sense, a rather complete theoretical structure has been shattered at the base and we are not sure how the pieces will be put together." It was a fair statement. And parity non-conservation was now official. The next day, the *Times* ran an editorial, under the title "Appearance and Reality," in which it made a pass at explaining the significance of the experiments. The last paragraph will surely strike anyone currently active in the elementary-particle field as sadly ironic, because the gap between theory and experiment in most areas has, if anything, widened since 1957. The *Times* wrote, "This [the discovery of parity non-conservation], it is believed, has removed the principal roadblock against the building of a comprehensive theory about the fundamental building blocks of which the material universe is constituted. What the theory will be may take another twenty years in the making, but physicists now feel confident that they have at last found a way out of the present 'cosmic jungle.' "

As late as January 17th, Professor Wolfgang Pauli, at the Eidgenössische Technische Hochschule, in Zurich, expressed skepticism about parity non-conservation in a letter to Professor V. F. Weisskopf, at M.I.T. Pauli, a Viennese by birth, was one of the most productive theorists of the twentieth century (he died in 1958) and one of the most acute critics of theoretical physics who ever lived; it was he, by the way, who, in 1931, postulated the existence of the neutrino in the first place, as an explanation of a *then* current mystery in the weak forces, involving the conservation of energy. The weak forces have been a gold mine of new ideas in physics. Weisskopf, another Viennese, had been a professor in the United States since Hitler's rise in Germany and is now Director-General of the international nuclear laboratory CERN (Conseil Européen pour la Recherche Nucléaire), in Geneva. He had been one of Pauli's favorite students in the early nineteen-thirties and was in frequent correspondence with his old teacher. Pauli wrote, "I do *not* believe that the Lord is a weak left-hander, and I am ready to bet a very large sum that the experiments will give symmetric results." On January

27th, after news of the experimental results reached Zurich, Pauli wrote to Weisskopf again, and this letter illustrates as well as anything could, perhaps, how deeply the notion of parity conservation was embedded in the minds of physicists. "Now, after the first shock is over, I begin to collect myself," he wrote. "Yes, it was very dramatic. On Monday, the twenty-first, at 8 P.M. I was to give a lecture on the neutrino theory. At 5 P.M. I received three experimental papers [the reports of the two experiments at Columbia and the one at Chicago that had been finished at about the same time]. . . . I am shocked not so much by the fact that the Lord prefers the left hand as by the fact that He still appears to be left-right symmetric when He expresses Himself strongly. In short, the actual problem now seems to be the question: Why are strong interactions right-and-left symmetric?"

The American Physical Society holds an annual meeting in New York late in January, between the fall and spring academic terms. The programs for these meetings, which are published in advance, are ordinarily an excellent index to the subjects that are of the greatest current interest to physicists, for any member of the Society may give a ten-minute talk, provided he sends an abstract of the talk to the secretary of the Society, and physicists who have done something particularly outstanding are invited to give longer talks. However, if one looks back at the program for the 1957 meeting, which began on January 30th, one finds nothing at all about the non-conservation of parity; indeed, to judge by the program, the 1957 meeting was quite routine. In reality, it was anything but that. The subject of parity non-conservation was not included in the program simply because all entries had had to be in by late November, when the experiments were still under way. By the time the meeting began, the first experimental results were known and the experimenters, as well as everyone else, were eager to have them presented in public. Although rumors had been circulating for some time, and the press conference had taken place a short while before, few physicists working in other fields had had access to any of the details. Besides, there had been new results almost daily. Hence, a special session was organized for the last day of the meeting, Saturday. The meeting itself, which was held in the New Yorker Hotel, drew a record crowd of about three thousand physicists. In the words of Dr. Karl K. Darrow, the Society's long-standing secretary, who generally manages to illumine the otherwise rather opaque Physical Society Bulletins with his literary style, "the figure of registration ascended to the stately value 3110, pressing hard upon the record 3206 set by the joint convention of the American Institute of Physics with ours and all of its other founder societies just one year ago." And Dr. Darrow continued, "Even more astonishing was the smash hit scored for the first time in history by the post-deadline session, during which—and on Saturday afternoon to boot—the largest hall normally at our disposal was occupied by so immense a crowd that some of its members did everything but hang from the chandeliers. This was because the blackboards and the grapevine had spread the news that some of the post-deadline papers would be devoted to the issue of the non-conservation of parity, which had burst into public view exactly two weeks before." It was a great occasion. The meeting was scheduled for two o'clock, and by one-fifteen the largest room in the hotel was jammed with physicists. I had arrived at twelve-thirty bringing my lunch, and managed to find a seat. Lee was not so fortunate, and for a while it looked as if he were not going to be able to get into the hall at all. Then some physicists recognized him and made way. Yang, Lederman, Telegdi, and Mme. Wu spoke. Some of the experimental data were so new that on the graphs illustrating them the points and the curved lines connecting them had been only roughly sketched in. When the evidence against parity conservation was thus marshalled in a single place, in a single room, it was absolutely convincing, and one had a feeling of witnessing a turning point in scientific history. There was no opportunity to ask questions during the meeting, and afterward, in the lobby, I caught a glimpse of Lee and Yang surrounded by a crowd of eager physicists, who were trying to get more information.

Stimulated by the new results, Lee and Yang dropped statistical mechanics entirely and set to work to see what could be made of the situation, and, from January on, things happened so fast that neither man gave any further thought to statistical mechanics for over a year. Lee had a strange experience that winter, and he once described it to me. He and Yang were invited to a conference on statistical mechanics at Stevens College, in Hoboken. In the course of it, Weisskopf asked Lee a question about a formula that he and Yang had derived. Lee said that, try as he would, he couldn't remember a single thing about it. As he put it, "Nothing would come out." At that time, he and Yang were completely absorbed in the weak interactions, and all thoughts about statistical mechanics had vanished. In fact, after the post-deadline session of the conference had made it common knowledge among physicists that parity conservation was violated, no one in physics who understood what was happening could think of much else.

By the time of the spring meeting of the Physical Society, held during the Easter vacation, "parity" had become a recognized field. At this meeting, there was a *scheduled* parity symposium, addressed by Lee, Mme. Wu, Garwin, Telegdi, and K. M. Crowe. The addition of Crowe's name is interesting, because he was from Stanford University and his presence on the program was indicative of the fact that by the spring of 1957 most of the major laboratories in the United States—and elsewhere as well— were doing intensive work on parity and weak-interaction experiments. As Lee puts it, "There was an avalanche effect." Once it was seen that the conservation of parity was violated in *some* weak decays, it became obvious that *all* weak decays had to be studied from this point of view. Hence, there was work for laboratories of every size. Places like Berkeley and Brookhaven, which had accelerators capable of producing strange particles, studied parity non-conservation in their decays, and the people who were used to working with the more conventional radioactive isotopes studied those. The next few months were a happy and constructive time in physics. In October of 1957, Lee and Yang were awarded the Nobel Prize. By the next New York meeting of the Physical Society, in January, 1958, it was not only known but just about taken for granted that parity was not conserved in all well-established weak decays. The first inklings of the theta-tau puzzle in the Dalitz paper of 1955 had reaped a whirlwind.

A remarkable historical sidelight on the parity story was recently turned up by Dr. L. Grodzins, a physicist then working at Brookhaven. On looking through some of the older physics literature, he noted that parity-non-conserving effects had actually been discovered in experiments with radioactive isotopes as early as 1928. In that year, R. T. Cox, C. G. McIlwraith, and B. Kurrelmeyer, three American physicists working at New York University, discovered in their data on the decay of a radioactive isotope of radium an effect that was, in terms of today's concepts, a clear violation of parity symmetry. Then C. T. Chase, a student of Cox's, carried out further experiments along these lines, but with improved techniques, and by 1930 was able to conclude that "not only in every run, but even all readings in every run, with few exceptions, show the effect." However, at this time the study of weak interactions was in its infancy, and there was just no theoretical context in which to put the results. In fact, it was only in 1927 that a Hungarian-born physicist, Eugene Wigner (now a professor at Princeton University) , had devised the first real mathematical formulation of parity symmetry in quantum theory. Therefore, it was not as if the results had challenged an existing theory that was well understood. They were, rather, a kind of statement made in a void. It took almost thirty years of intensive research in all branches of experimental and theoretical physics, and, above all, it took the work of Lee and Yang, to enable physicists to appreciate exactly what those early experiments implied.

What has all this meant for physics? The issue is still in doubt, but some things have become clear. In the Columbia-Bureau experiment, parity non-conservation was not the only discovery made. Another long-standing invariance principle, which physicists call "charge-conjugation invariance," was also shattered. "Charge conjugation" refers to the mathematical operation indicating the transformation of particles into antiparticles—for example, an electron into a positron. Until 1957, physicists had believed that, say, a galaxy made up of antimatter would be identical in all its physical characteristics (such as the emission of light) with a galaxy made up of matter. If the two galaxies collided, the matter and the antimatter would annihilate each other, into radiation, for example (a process that has been observed many times on a small scale in the laboratory) . However, as long as the matter and antimatter were kept apart, someone observing the two galaxies from the outside could not tell which was which—so the belief ran. The new experiments showed this not to be true. The weak forces distinguished between particles and antiparticles in principle. It was a quite unexpected result, and one that had not been remotely suggested by the theta-tau puzzle. After these two apparently well-established symmetry principles had fallen, the question was: Do the weak forces show any symmetries of this type at all? Actually, during the summer of 1956 Yang and Lee had envisioned the possibility that more than one symmetry at a time might be violated by the weak forces. Their thinking along these lines had been stimulated by a letter they received that August from Reinhard Oehme, a theorist at the University of Chicago. He raised the question whether some of the ideas in the first Lee and Yang paper might be regarded in a more general context. After studying this question in some depth, Lee and Yang speculated that it was possible in principle to imagine a situation in which the weak forces violated parity, P, and charge conjugation, C, separately but in which the two symmetries taken together in a multiplication, CP, might be valid. In the CP symmetry, one first replaces the system by its mirror image and then replaces particles by their antiparticles. Until the summer of 1964 it appeared as if CP invariance were universally valid for all forces. However that summer a group from Princeton, J. H. Christenson, J. W. Cronin, U. L. Fitch, and R. Turlay, working at Brookhaven found a small CP violating effect in theta-meson decays. The significance of this very important discovery is still not clear. As Pauli clearly foresaw in 1957, the relation of the symmetries between the weak forces and the strong has turned out to be a major theoretical problem, and thus far rather little progress has been made toward its solution.

Another very important result that emerged from the parity year was a clarification and simplification of the theory of the neutrino, the particle whose existence Pauli postulated to save the theory of energy conservation in the weak processes. In 1929, the late Professor H. Weyl, a German-born mathematician and physicist (who worked at the Institute for Advanced Study from 1933 to 1955), noticed that a remarkably simple and beautiful mathematical theory that has since been applied to the neutrino was available, but only if parity conservation was abandoned. For many years, the theory was ignored. After the developments of 1956, this theory was revived by Lee and

Yang, and also by a Russian, L. Landau, and a Pakistani, A. Salam, each working independently. It has now survived all the experimental tests presented to it and has become the commonly accepted mathematical description of the neutrino. Weyl himself once remarked to Professor F. J. Dyson (another permanent member in physics at the Institute for Advanced Study), "My work always tried to unite the true with the beautiful, but when I had to choose one or the other I usually chose the beautiful." It is an irony that his death, on December 9, 1955, just preceded the developments that led to the revival of his theory. Because of the excitement of 1956 and 1957, the attention of many physicists who had been working in other fields was focussed on the study of weak interactions. Consequently, important advances have been made. Still, the connection between the weak and strong forces is almost as mysterious as it ever was.

Eventful though the year was for physics, it did not bring any great change in the lives of Lee or Yang. In 1960, Lee moved from Columbia to the Institute at Princeton. He has now returned to Columbia, while Yang has left Princeton for Stony Brook University near Brookhaven. In recent years they have been working on a variety of problems.

They both live quietly with their families. Each has an attractive and charming wife. Yang's wife, Chih-Li Tu, was a pupil of his when he was teaching high school in China in 1945; Lee met his wife, Jeannette Chin, in 1948, when she was visiting Chicago. The Lees have two sons, and the Yangs have two sons and a young daughter. They try to pass on to their children as much of their rich Chinese heritage as possible. The children are growing up in homes filled with magnificent Chinese art objects—though, of course, as they get older they are tending strongly toward the usual interests of American children. Jeannette Lee's father is an artist living in China, and some of the loveliest wall decorations in the Lees' apartment are scroll paintings of birds and flowers that he has done for them. Lee has a great love of Chinese art. This enthusiasm comes just after his enthusiasm for physics, and one of the great delights of knowing Lee is to hear him discuss art. I remember especially one discussion we had in the cafeteria at CERN during the summer of 1961. It was early in the morning, and the room was almost empty. Lee had just learned that the Metropolitan Museum was about to display a number of works from the Chinese Imperial Palace collection, which had been taken from Peking to Taiwan in 1948 and 1949. I was quite ignorant of the history of Chinese art, and he began outlining it for me. Soon several pages in my notebook were filled with important dates and examples of calligraphy. Lee uses his hands very expressively when speaking (both he and Yang, when they are doing calculations away from a blackboard or without paper and pencil, tend to write in the air with a finger; Lee has told me that this was a habit he acquired during the war, when there was an acute paper shortage in China) , and as he got more and more carried away by the subject, we gradually attracted a small group of physicists, who naturally assumed from his enthusiastic manner that he was announcing a new discovery in physics. Our discussion then turned into a debate on the pros and cons of various aspects of Oriental art, which lasted, on and off, for most of the day. Yang, too, is fascinated by Chinese art, as well as by Chinese philosophy, and on occasion he also enjoys outdoor sports. He has tried mountain-climbing and skiing. The former almost led to a disaster in the summer of 1952, when he visited the University of Washington, in Seattle, and did some climbing there. The physicists at the university, many of whom are experienced mountaineers, have said that Yang's instinctive grace and balance make him an excellent natural climber, but on this particular climb one member of the party, a woman, fell on a steep ice slope, pulling Yang with her. Fortunately, they were held on the rope by Dr. E. A. Uehling, a well-known theoretical physicist at the university and a skilled climber, and the incident was only minor.

Ultimately, however, Yang and Lee are dedicated to physics. When they are working on a problem, it is a day-and-night affair, with little time for anything else. From time to time, they do give special lectures at American Physical Society meetings and elsewhere. These are characterized by great clarity and great charm of presentation. What Yang once wrote about Fermi's lecture style is equally applicable to his own and to Lee's: "As we all know, Fermi gave extremely lucid lectures. In a fashion that is characteristic of him, for each topic he always started from the beginning, treated simple examples and avoided as much as possible 'formalisms.' (He used to joke that complicated formalism was for the 'high priests.') The very simplicity of his reasoning conveyed the impression of effortlessness. But this impression is false. The simplicity was the result of careful preparation and of deliberate weighing of different alternatives of presentation."

Doing science at the level at which Lee and Yang do it requires considerable self-confidence, yet at the same time the very scale of the problems imposes a profound humility on those who undertake to solve them. Lee expressed this feeling of humility before the complexity and depth of the problems in a characteristic way on the occasion of the awarding of the Nobel Prize. This ceremony always culminates in a grand dinner and ball, to which students from the Swedish universities are invited. It is customary for one of the laureates to address the students. The students decided, because he was so near their age, that they wanted to hear Lee, and he was drafted to speak. He had not been warned, and was not quite sure what to say. Then he thought of a lovely Chinese parable, and spoke as follows:

"I would like to tell you a little tale, taken from a

Chinese novel called *Hsi Yiu Chi*. It's about a monkey. This monkey, unlike other monkeys, was born out of a rock, and consequently he was very, very intelligent. He happened to realize this himself—and that's how the whole thing started. He began to grow ambitious. First he wanted to become the King of the Monkeys. This he achieved with no difficulty at all. But soon he grew tired of being a monkey—of being even the King of the Monkeys. Now he wanted to learn the ways of men. After years and years of studying human habits and behavior, he was able to dress like a man and talk like a man—indeed, he even managed to look like a man. But again he was dissatisfied. Now he wanted to learn the ways of the gods. He went to the holy mountain, and after centuries and centuries of hard study and difficult research he did learn the ways of the gods. Indeed, he was able to acquire great magic power. He knew, for instance, how to travel one hundred and eight thousand miles by one single jump. So he decided to jump for Heaven—and he reached it in half a jump. There he demanded the position of a god. The Emperor of the Gods at first tried to ignore him, but the monkey was so persistent that the Emperor yielded and granted him the position of a god, together with the title 'The Great Saint.' But again the monkey grew dissatisfied. Now he wanted to be not only a god but the King of Heaven. The Emperor of the Gods had no choice. He was forced to fight the monkey—and he did. But the monkey defeated the whole Army of Heaven. As a last resort, the Emperor of the Gods asked the help of the great Buddha. The Buddha came. He told the monkey that in order to become the King of Heaven one ought to have some special qualifications. The Buddha opened his hand and said to the monkey, 'If you want to be the King of Heaven, you must be able to jump into my palm—and then out again.' The monkey looked at the Buddha, who was, say, one hundred feet tall. 'I can travel one hundred and eight thousand miles in one jump,' he said to himself, 'and this will be an easy way indeed of becoming the King of Heaven.' So he jumped into the Buddha's palm—and then made a big jump trying to get out. To be on the safe side, he kept on jumping. After millions and millions of years of jumping, the monkey began to feel a little tired. Finally, he reached a place which had five huge, pinkish columns. He thought that this must certainly be the boundary of the universe—the columns marking its very limit. He was very excited about this, and at the foot of the middle column he wrote, 'The King of Heaven was here,' and, very gay and very happy, he started to jump back. At long last, he reached the place from which he had started, and he proudly demanded to be the King of Heaven. The Buddha then, with his other hand, lifted the monkey up, pointed down into the open palm, and showed him, just where his middle finger began, some tiny, tiny little words in the monkey's writing: 'The King of Heaven was here.' Since then there is in Chinese a saying: 'Jump as you may, it is not possible to jump out of the Buddha's palm.'

"In our search for knowledge, we may be making rapid progress. But we must remember that even at the bottom of the Buddha's finger we are still very far from absolute truth."

Among physicists, there are many views on what the future of elementary-particle physics may hold. Some feel that it may be a hundred years before the next real break-through comes. They point out that between the rise of Newtonian mechanics and quantum mechanics a period of nearly three hundred years elapsed, during which there were all sorts of mathematical and technological advances; for example, most of the mathematics needed to formulate the quantum theory was not invented until the nineteenth century. As other physicists see it, the enormous accelera-tion that has taken place in the development of physics in the twentieth century may serve to compress the waiting time between breakthroughs. There are probably more physicists at work today than there were in the whole history of the science before 1900. It may not be an accident that the two greatest conceptual advances in physics since Newton's day, the theory of relativity and the quantum theory, occurred within about twenty years of each other—the former in 1905 and the latter in the late nineteen-twenties.

From time to time, Yang and Lee speculate on this question. In dealing with such problems, they take great pleasure in drawing on one of the most profound sources of Oriental wisdom, *I Ching,* or *The Book of Changes.* In its earliest form, *The Book of Changes* dates from about 2000 B.C. It has been in a state of continuous development ever since, with generations of Oriental scholars contributing to its interpretation. The present version of the book probably owes most to the work of Confucius, who made a major revision of it around 500 B.C. *I Ching* consists of a series of rather abstract prophetic verses—sometimes accompanied by commentaries—that are associated with a system of mathematical symbols. The user formulates a question and then takes three coins. (In the more traditional version, fifty stalks of the white flowering yarrow plant are used. "One is put aside and plays no further part," and the rest are arranged in a fairly complicated pattern outlined in the ritual.) In the past, these were the traditional Chinese bronze coins, with a square hole in the middle, but in the consultations that have taken place at Princeton use has been made of United States currency of various denominations, and a system of heads and tails has been devised. The head counts as a yin, with a numerical value of two, and the tail as a yang, with the value three. After tossing the three coins, one adds up the numbers, which can come to nine, eight, seven, or six. These numbers correspond to symbols in the book, and these symbols are built into hexagrams consisting of long and short lines. There are sixty-four basic hexagrams, which are the keys to the oracles. The results are usually quite beautiful and occasionally rather startling. As Lee once told me, "The prophecies sometimes set your mind off into new directions." On November 26, 1959, he and Yang asked *I Ching*, "Is there going to be a breakthrough in elementary-particle physics in the next two years?" They obtained, in part, the following:

Development. The maiden
Is given in marriage.
Good fortune.
Perseverance furthers.

On the mountain a tree,
The image of DEVELOPMENT.
Thus the superior man abides in dignity and virtue
In order to improve the mores.

The wild goose gradually draws near the plateau.
The man goes forth and does not return.
The woman carries a child but does not carry it forth.
Misfortune.
It furthers one to fight off robbers.

The wild goose gradually draws near the cloud heights.
Its feathers can be used for the sacred dance.
Good fortune.

The wild goose gradually draws near the summit.
For three years the woman has no child.
In the end nothing can hinder her.
Good fortune.

On June 21, 1961, Professor A. Pais, a Dutch-born colleague of Lee's and Yang's then at the Institute, asked *I Ching*, after a careful study of the methods, "Does there exist one universal principle that unifies strong, electromagnetic, and weak interactions?" He obtained, in part, the following answer:

Waiting. If you are sincere,
You have light and success.
Perseverance brings good fortune.
It furthers one to cross the great water.

Clouds rise up to heaven,
The image of WAITING.
Thus the superior man eats and drinks,
Is joyous and of good cheer.

    Commentary. When clouds rise in the sky, it is a sign that it will rain. There is nothing to do but wait until the rain falls. It is the same in life when destiny is at work. We should not worry and seek to shape the future by interfering in things before the time is ripe. We should quietly fortify the body with food and drink and the mind with gladness and good cheer. Fate comes when it will, and thus we are ready.

Lee and Yang are waiting and working with gladness and good cheer.

3

CERN

SHORTLY after the Second World War, when the normal international life of science was resumed, a physicist who had just listened to several hours of technical lectures at a large conference remarked that the international language of physics had become a combination of mathematics and broken English. Today, almost all scientific journals, including the Russian—and even the Chinese journals, such as the *Acta Mathematica Sinica,* and *Scientia Sinica,* published in Peking—give at least the title of each article, and often an abstract, in English. From the title and the equations and the graphs, a specialist in the field can usually reconstruct the general theme of the article. The exchange of articles and journals among scientists of different countries is one of the oldest and best traditions of science. It goes on independently of the political climate. During the darkest days of the

Stalinist period in Russia, scientific papers went back and forth across the Iron Curtain, and Western physicists could follow the work of such Russians as Lev Landau (the most distinguished Russian theoretical physicist, who won the Nobel Prize in 1962), despite the fact that he was under house arrest in Moscow, in part because of his liberal ideas and in part because he is a Jew.

With the death of Stalin and the relaxation of some of the tensions between East and West, it became possible for scientists to travel in and out of the Eastern countries. The so-called Rochester Conference in High-Energy Physics (it gets it name from the fact that the first seven conferences, starting in 1950, were held in Rochester, New York) now meets one year in the United States, one year in Geneva, and one year in the Soviet Union. Several American universities have regular exchange programs with Soviet universities, and it is no longer a novelty to find a Russian physicist giving a series of lectures in an American university, and vice versa.

The ultimate in international scientific coöperation is, of course, the international scientific laboratory, in which scientists of many countries can actually work together. In fact, it is becoming increasingly clear that such laboratories are not only desirable but necessary. Research in a field like high-energy physics—in a way, the most basic of all the sciences, since it is the study of elementary particles, the ultimate constituents of all matter—has become so expensive that many people have come to believe that pursuing it as a purely national enterprise is difficult to justify. A recent editorial in the New York *Times* pointed out that "high-energy physicists . . . use the most elaborate and most expensive equipment employed in any branch of terrestrial basic research," and went on to say, "These are the particle accelerators, which today cost tens of millions of dollars each, and which will in the future be priced in the hundreds of millions. The Atomic Energy Commission's operating and construction costs in this field are already expected to aggregate $165 million in the next fiscal year, and one authoritative estimate places the annual bill by the end of the next decade at $370 million, reaching $600 million by 1980. . . . Nuclear physicists are already talking about far more powerful—and much more expensive—atomic-research instruments. The case for building these machines is an impressive one, but the case for building them only with the resources of one country is not convincing."

The editorial concluded by pointing out that there already exists an excellent working example of an international atomic laboratory; namely, CERN (standing for Conseil Européen pour la Recherche Nucléaire), which is operated jointly by almost all the Western European countries and is situated in the Swiss town of Meyrin, a suburb of Geneva that is almost on the French frontier. CERN itself sprawls along the frontier, and recently, when it needed room for expansion, the French government gave it a ninety-nine-year lease on a hundred acres of French land, matching the hundred acres of Swiss territory that the center now occupies. This makes CERN the only international organization that actually straddles a frontier. Its facilities include two accelerators (the larger, a proton synchrotron, accelerates protons to energies up to twenty-eight billion electron volts, and shares with its slightly more powerful twin, the alternating-gradient synchrotron at Brookhaven National Laboratory, the distinction of being the largest accelerator now operating), several electronic computers, and a vast collection of bubble chambers, spark chambers, and other paraphernalia necessary for experimenting with the particles produced in the accelerators—to say nothing of machine shops, a cafeteria, a bank, a travel agency, a post office, a large library, and a multitude of secretarial and administrative offices. It costs about twenty-five million dollars a year to run. This money is contributed by thirteen European member states —Austria, Belgium, Great Britain, Denmark, France, Greece, Italy, the Netherlands, Norway, Spain, Sweden, Switzerland, and West Germany. Neither the United States nor Russia is eligible to become a member, since neither is "Européen," but there are Americans and Russians who work at CERN. An exchange agreement exists between CERN and DUBNA, a similar laboratory near Moscow, where physicists from the Iron Curtain countries work together. Each year, DUBNA sends two or three physicists to CERN for several months at a time. American physicists at CERN have been supported by sabbatical salaries, by fellowships like the Guggenheim and the National Science Foundation, or by money from Ford Foundation grants (totalling a bit over a million dollars) that were given to the laboratory explicitly for the support of scientists from non-member countries. (The grants have now been discontinued, following the Ford policy of "pump-priming," and the laboratory is looking for other sources of money.) There are usually twenty or twenty-five Americans at CERN. In addition, the laboratory has contingents of Japanese, Indians, Poles (a very active and scientifically strong group of about a dozen), Yugoslavs, Turks, Israelis (there is an exchange agreement with the Weizmann Institute, in Rehovoth), and Hungarians. All the permanent personnel at CERN—about sixteen hundred people, of whom about three hundred are physicists and engineers—are drawn from the member states. (Their average age is thirty-two.) As one might imagine, all this produces a tutti-frutti of languages, national types, political attitudes, and social mannerisms, and everyone accepts and enjoys the chaos of national flavors as part of the working atmosphere of the laboratory. As an American physicist and a perennial summer visitor to CERN, I have had fairly typical experiences there. One summer, for example, I worked with an Italian physicist in an attempt to extend some work done by a German-born American physicist who was visiting the laboratory on a Guggenheim Fellowship. This work was itself an extension of another Italian physicist's work, which, in turn, was based on the work of an American physicist who is a frequent visitor to CERN. (I also helped a Yugoslav physicist with the English translation of a short book written by a well-known Russian physicist whom I met when he visited CERN to attend the Rochester Conference of 1962, which was held in Geneva.) My working language with the Italian physicist was English (and, of course, mathematics) . Most of the people at the laboratory are polylingual. All scientific lectures are given in English, and almost all the technical personnel have a good command of the language. However, the language one hears most often is French; the secretaries, postmen, bank clerks, mechanics, and telephone operators speak it among themselves, and so do many of the European physicists. Secretaries must be able to type technical manuscripts in English, since almost all the publications that come out of CERN each year (several hundred of them) are in that language.

Because nuclear physics has become so closely associated (at least in the public mind) with its military applications, many people have wondered how a laboratory that intermingles physicists from the East and the West—and, indeed, from all over the world—can possibly operate without running into all sorts of problems of military security and national secrecy. The answer is that nuclear physics is a very broad subject. It ranges from the study of nuclear energy—fission, fusion, reactors, and the like—to the study of the interior structure of the nucleus, and even to the study of the structure of the very neutrons and protons and other particles that compose the nucleus. This latter study is the frontier of modern physics. Because high-energy particles are necessary in order to probe deeply into the interior of the nucleus, this branch of physics is called "high-energy," as opposed to "low-energy," or "classical"— "classical" in that the laws governing the behavior of the nuclei in, say, the fission process in a reactor are now pretty well understood, and have been for some time. The military and technological applications of nuclear physics are based on these latter laws, whereas the study of the interior structure of the nucleus has no technological applications at present; more than that, it is difficult now to imagine any such applications in the future. However, the example of Einstein's special theory of relativity— one of the most abstract theories in physics—which has been the basis of the entire development of nuclear energy, shows that theoretical speculations that may at the moment seem far removed from reality can very quickly change all of technology.

The very fact that high-energy physics does not have military applications was among the reasons it was chosen as the discipline for an international laboratory. In the late nineteen-forties, when a number of prominent physicists— including the late H. A. Kramers, of Holland; Pierre Auger and Francis Perrin, of France; Edouardo Amaldi, of Italy; and J. Robert Oppenheimer, of the United States— began informally discussing the prospects for creating an international laboratory in Europe, they set out to look for a field that would be sufficiently close to recent developments in atomic energy for European governments to be interested in supporting the project financially, and yet far enough removed from immediate applications of atomic energy for military security not to be a problem. They also realized that it would be necessary to engage the support of the European diplomats who were then promoting attempts to create a United Europe. One of the most influential of these diplomats was François de Rose, of France. (He is now the French Ambassador to Portugal.) De Rose became interested in the possibilities of atomic research just after the war, and in 1946 he met with Oppenheimer in New York at the United Nations Atomic Energy Commission. Out of the resulting friendship between the two men an important link developed between the scientific and diplomatic communities. Dr. L. Kowarski, a French nuclear scientist and one of the pioneers of CERN, has written a semi-official history of the origins of the laboratory, in which he notes:

> The first public manifestation of this new link occurred in December, 1949, at the European Cultural Conference held in Lausanne. A message from Louis de Broglie [de Broglie, the most distinguished French theoretical physicist of modern times, was awarded the Nobel Prize in 1929 for his work on the wave nature of electrons] was read by Dautry [Raoul Dautry was at that time the administrator of the French Atomic Energy Commission and one of the leaders of the movement for a United Europe], in which the proposal was made to create in Europe an international research institution, to be equipped on a financial scale transcending the individual possibilities of the member nations. . . . At that time [a dilemma] was besetting the scientists' aspirations: atomic energy was attracting public readiness to spend money, but atomic energy invited security-mindedness and separatism. The way out of the dilemma was clear enough. The domain of common action should be chosen so as not to infringe directly the taboos on uranium fission, but [to be] close enough to it so as to allow any successes gained internationally in the permitted field to exert a beneficial influence on the national pursuits.

The ultimate choice—high-energy physics—was a perfect compromise; although it is a branch of nuclear physics, it is one that is far removed from military applications.

In June of 1950, the American physicist I. I. Rabi initiated the first practical step toward the creation of such a pan-European laboratory. As a member of the United States delegation to UNESCO he was attending the UNESCO conference held that year in Florence. Speaking officially on behalf of the United States, he moved that UNESCO use its good offices to set up a physics laboratory (he had high-energy physics in mind) with facilities that would be beyond those that any single European country could provide, and that would be comparable to the major American facilities at Brookhaven and Berkeley. It was an important step, because it placed the prestige and influence of American science behind the project. The implementation of Rabi's motion became the work of Pierre Auger, of France, a distinguished physicist who was the UNESCO scientific director. As a result of his efforts, various cultural commissions of the French, Italian, and Belgian governments donated about ten thousand dollars for a study program, and CERN was under way. (In the course of the discussions held at that time, Rabi stressed the desirability of not having any nuclear reactors at CERN, since they have both military and commercial applications—and, in fact, there are none.) Dr. Kowarski writes:

> Two objectives were suggested: a longer-range, very ambitious project of an accelerator second to none in the world [this resulted in the construction of the proton synchrotron, which was completed in 1959] and, in addition, the speedy construction of a less powerful and more classical machine in order to start European experimentation in high-energy physics at an early date and so cement the European unity directed to a more difficult principal undertaking.

At the end of 1951, an organizational meeting was held in Paris; all the European members of UNESCO were invited, but there was no response from the countries of Eastern Europe. Then, at a meeting held in Geneva early in 1952, eleven countries signed an agreement pledging funds and establishing a provisional organization. There was something of a tug-of-war among the member countries to decide where the new laboratory should be built. The Danes, the Dutch, the French, and the Swiss all had suitable territory for it, but in the end Geneva was chosen, partly because of its central location, partly because of its long tradition of housing international organizations (there are, for example, all sorts of multilingual elementary schools in the city) —and, it is said, partly because some of the physicists involved in the decision were avid skiers. The Swiss government gave, free, the site near Meyrin, and in June, 1953, the Canton of Geneva formally ratified, by popular referendum, the government's invitation to CERN to settle there; in addition, the laboratory was given the same political status as that of any of the other international organizations in Geneva. At the same time, a formal CERN Convention was prepared for the signature of the member states, which then numbered twelve; Austria and Spain joined later, and Yugoslavia, an original signatory, withdrew in 1962, because of a lack of foreign currency. Article II of the Convention stipulates: "The Organization shall provide for collaboration among European States in nuclear research of a pure scientific and fundamental character, and in research essentially related thereto. The Organization shall have no concern with work for military requirements, and the results of its experimental and theoretical work shall be published or otherwise made generally available." The Convention also set up a formula for CERN's financial support. Roughly speaking, each member nation pays each year a certain percentage (a fraction of one per cent) of its gross national product. This means, in practice, that Great Britain, France, and West Germany pay the largest shares. The CERN Council, the governing body of the laboratory, was set up, with two delegates from each country—one a scientist and the other a diplomat, like de Rose. The Council meets twice a year to pass on such matters as the budget and the future development of the laboratory. (During my last visit to CERN, there was a Council meeting in which the question of constructing a still larger international machine—a machine capable of accelerating protons to three hundred billion electron volts, or about ten times the capacity of the present machine—was discussed.) The Council also, by a two-thirds majority, appoints the Director-General of the laboratory. The Director-Generalship of CERN is a very complex job, and few people are really qualified for it. In the first place, the Director-General can have no special national bias. As the Convention puts it, "The responsibilities of the Director and the staff in regard to the Organization shall be exclusively international in character." In the second place, the Director must clearly be a physicist, for, among other things, he must decide which of various extremely expensive experiments the laboratory should concentrate on. The first Director, chosen in 1954, was Professor Felix Bloch, of Stanford University—a Swiss by origin and a Nobel Prize winner in physics. Professor Bloch returned to Stanford in 1955 and was succeeded by C. J. Bakker, a Dutch cyclotron builder. (Professor Bakker was responsible for the construction of the cyclotron, the smaller of the accelerators at CERN.) He held the post from 1955 to 1960, when he was killed in an airplane accident on his way to Washington, where he had intended to deliver a report on the operation of the large accelerator, the proton synchrotron, which had gone into operation in 1959.

If any one individual was responsible for the successful construction of the large accelerator, it was John B. Adams, an Englishman, who took over the Director-Generalship on Bakker's death. Adams was born in 1920 in Kingston, Surrey, and received his education in English grammar schools. At eighteen, he went to work for the Telecommunications Research Establishment, and when the war broke out he joined the Ministry of Aircraft Production. He had received some training in electronics with the Telecommunications Establishment, and in the M.A.P. he became involved with the problem of installing

the first radar in fighter planes. It soon became evident
that he had a gift both for engineering and for the complex job of directing a large technical project. In fact, the
war produced a whole generation of young scientists and
engineers who not only were technically competent but
had acquired considerable practical experience in running
large-scale and costly scientific enterprises. These men
moved readily into the various atomic-energy programs
that were started after the war, and Adams joined the
nuclear laboratory at Harwell, the principal British center
for experimental work in nuclear physics. At this time, the
people at Harwell were beginning work on a hundred-and-
seventy-five-million-volt proton accelerator, and Adams
became an important member of the project. The machine
was finished in 1949, and Adams spent the next three years
working on the design of special radio tubes needed in
connection with accelerators. Then he was released by the
Ministry of Supply to go to Geneva and join the new
accelerator project at CERN.

By that time, the CERN group, which had been at work
since 1951, had inherited a technological windfall in the
way of accelerator design. A particle accelerator can accelerate only those particles that carry an electric charge.
Advantage is taken of the fact that when a charged particle
passes through an electric field it is accelerated by the force
that the field exerts on it. In modern accelerators, trans-
mitting tubes generate the electromagnetic fields, in the
same way that radio transmitters generate radio waves.
These accelerating stations are placed at intervals along
the path of the particles in the machine, the simplest
arrangement being along a straight line. This layout results in what is called a linear accelerator, or LINAC. The
particles move faster and faster in a straight line and are
finally shot out the other end into a target of some sort.
The energy that such particles can acquire is limited by
the length of the straight line, as well as by the power of

the transmitters. At Stanford University, there is a nearly completed straight-line accelerator, known among physicists as "the monster," that will accelerate electrons over a path almost two miles long; the emerging electrons will have an energy of about twenty billion electron volts. Most accelerators, however, are circular. The accelerating stations are arranged along the perimeter, and as the particles go around and around they acquire more energy in each orbit. This arrangement saves space and greatly reduces the number and size of the accelerating stations. The problem that naturally arises is how to maintain the particles in circular paths while they are being accelerated, since a particle will move in a circle only if a force acts on it to keep it from flying off at a tangent. In circular accelerators, this force is supplied by electromagnets. The magnets are deployed along the path of the particles, and the magnetic fields they produce hold the particles in orbit. The drawback to this system is that the more energy a particle acquires, the more strongly it resists staying in a circular orbit and the larger the magnet required to keep it so. In fact, as the postwar accelerators became more and more powerful, the size of their magnets began to get out of hand. The Brookhaven cosmotron, a proton accelerator producing protons with an energy of three billion electron volts, has a magnet of four thousand tons; the Berkeley bevatron, with six-billion-electron-volt protons, has a magnet weighing ten thousand tons; and, most striking of all, the Russian phasotron at DUBNA, which produces protons of ten billion electron volts, has a magnet weighing thirty-six thousand tons.

This was where things stood in 1952, when the CERN group planned to make an accelerator of at least ten billion electron volts. By using a somewhat modified and more economical design than the one for the DUBNA machine, the new accelerator could have been made with a magnet weighing from ten to fifteen thousand tons, but even this seemed monstrous at the time. That year, however, a group at Brookhaven consisting of E. Courant, M. S. Livingston, and H. Snyder, in the course of solving a problem put to them by a group of visiting accelerator experts from CERN, invented a principle of magnetic focussing that altered the situation completely. (It turned out later that their method had been independently invented a few years earlier by an American-born Greek named N. Christofilos, who was employed in Greece selling elevators for an American firm and was a physicist in his spare time. Christofilos had sent a manuscript describing his invention to Berkeley, where it was forgotten until news of the work at Brookhaven reminded somebody of it. Christofilos is now at the Livermore Laboratory of the University of California.) The magnet in a circular accelerator not only bends the particle trajectories into circles but applies a force that focusses the beam and keeps it from spreading out indefinitely as it goes around and around. The magnets in the old machines could supply only very weak focussing; thus the beam was pretty thick, and the vacuum pipe it circulated in and the magnet surrounding it also had to be large. (At Berkeley, a man can crawl through the vacuum chamber.) It was known, however, that magnets could be made that would give much stronger focussing forces, but only in one direction at a time; that is, if the beam was kept confined horizontally it would expand vertically, and vice versa. What the Brookhaven people found was that if an accelerator-magnet ring was built up of alternate sections that provided strong focussing and defocussing forces, the net result was a focussing much stronger than anything that had previously been achieved. (In the new machines, the beam can be contained in a vacuum pipe only a few inches in diameter.) This meant that the magnets could be much smaller in size, with a great saving of weight, power, and cost. The CERN magnetic system weighs only three thousand tons, although the proton energies achieved are nearly three times those generated by the old Russian machine, which had a magnet weighing over ten times as much. The focussing works so well that the final beam of particles, which consists of about a thousand billion protons per second, is only a few millimetres wide when it emerges from the machine. The ring around which the protons race is about two hundred metres in diameter. The protons are injected into the main circular track by a small linear accelerator, and in the single second that they remain in the machine they make about half a million revolutions. The entire ring must be kept at a fairly high vacuum, since otherwise the protons would knock about in the air and be scattered. There is also a delicate question of timing. The accelerating fields must deliver a kick to each bunch of protons at just the right instant in its orbit. As the protons move faster and faster, approaching the speed of light, the synchronization of the fields and the particles must be constantly changed. However, according to Einstein's special theory of relativity, no particle can go faster than light, so that near the end of the cycle the protons will be gaining energy but not speed (the particles, again according to the relativity theory, get heavier and heavier as they move faster and faster), which simplifies the timing problem somewhat. Indeed, high-energy-accelerator design, which uses the theory of relativity extensively, and which clearly works, is one of the best-known tests of the theory itself. That all these factors, complex as they are, can be put together to make a reliably operating machine is an enormous triumph of engineering physics.

Needless to say, the Brookhaven people were eager to build a machine operating on the principle they had invented. However, the cosmotron had only recently been finished, and they could not get immediate support for the construction of an even larger machine—especially one that would use a principle still untested. The CERN people, however, were in a much more advantageous position, and in 1953 they began designing the laboratory's present machine, the CPS (CERN proton synchrotron). About six months later, influenced partly by the progress at CERN, the Brookhaven people got under way with the construction of a similar but slightly larger machine—the AGS, or alternating-gradient synchrotron. A friendly race developed between the two groups, with CERN finishing in November, 1959, and Brookhaven about six months later.

In order to construct the CERN accelerator, Adams gathered around him a superb international team of engineers and physicists interested in accelerator construction. Not only is he a brilliant engineer himself but he has the ability to organize other engineers into effective groups with physicists, so that very new ideas can be effectively realized on an industrial scale. In fact, working on the accelerator at CERN came to be a considerable distinction for an engineer, and CERN got almost the pick of the European engineers, even though the laboratory could not compete financially with the salaries that were being offered by European industry. The machine was so well designed that it worked better than had been generally anticipated. It became available to the physicists at CERN early in 1960, and Adams stepped into the gap caused by Bakker's death to become Director-General of the laboratory for a year. He also received an honorary degree from the University of Geneva, which he accepted on behalf of the group that had worked with him. He is now back in England directing a laboratory that is studying the problem of controlling nuclear-fusion energy for general application. (Nuclear-fusion energy arises when nuclear particles are fused to make a heavier nucleus. The heavier nucleus actually weighs less than the sum of its parts, and—again according to Einstein's relativity theory—the excess weight is liberated as energy. The hydrogen bomb is an unfortunate application of this principle.)

After Adams's departure the Director-General became Professor Victor F. Weisskopf, who was given leave of absence from M.I.T. to take over in 1961. (Very recently he was succeeded by Bernard Gregory, a French physicist.) Professor Weisskopf, whom I got to know when I was a student at Harvard in the nineteen-fifties, was born in Vienna, so although he is an American citizen, he can be counted as a European. He is one of the world's leading theoretical physicists, as well as one of its most likable. A large, friendly man, he is known to almost everybody at CERN as Viki, and despite a recent and very serious automobile accident he remains a devoted skier and hiker. During my summers at CERN, I had several talks with him about its development. One of the most interesting observations he made had to do with the evolution of the present generation of European physicists. At the end of the war, he said, European physics, which had been the finest in the world, was greatly damaged. Many of the best European physicists were more or less permanently settled in either England or the United States and had no desire to come back to Europe and relive a very unpleasant experience. In particular, the tradition of experimental physics, which requires complicated equipment, had greatly suffered on the Continent during the years of deprivation. Consequently, when the big accelerator at CERN was ready, there was a shortage of highly trained European experimenters to use it. On the other hand, the war had greatly strengthened physics in the United States, not only because so many Europeans had come here to live but because physicists had been working all through the war at places like Los Alamos on subjects that were not entirely dissimilar to their peacetime research. Thus, the postwar generation of American physicists was highly trained and ready to continue along the line of research that had made the development of high-energy physics the frontier of physics. (Many of the early research papers written at CERN during this period were done by Europeans in collaboration with Americans at the laboratory, some of whom had been born in Europe and were back on visits.) Of even greater importance, most of the European physicists who currently have important positions at CERN spent time in the United States, where they received training in the then novel techniques of experimental physics. As Weisskopf pointed out, a new generation of excellent and inventive physicists has by now grown up in Europe. They are producing scientific work at the forefront of modern physics that is of the first quality and the equal of anything being done in the United States or Russia. These physicists are now training young Europeans, to say nothing of American postdoctoral visitors. Originally, some European university professors were opposed to the creation of CERN on the grounds that it would draw too many scientists away from the universities at a time when there was a desperate shortage of them. Weisskopf remarked that it has worked out almost the other way—that European physicists have come to Geneva for a few years of advanced training and then gone back to their own countries to teach and do research in universities. In fact, according to many of the young European physicists I have spoken to, it is now quite hard to find good jobs in European universities, and CERN offers an opportunity to continue working until a suitable position opens up somewhere.

For me, one of the most interesting experiences at CERN was the contact with some of the Russian physicists at the laboratory. As a rule, the Russians who come to Geneva are about equally divided between experimental and theoretical physicists. Because high-energy experimental physics is done by teams, the experimental physicists join a group of other experimenters, while the theorists work pretty much alone. As it happened, one of the Russian experimenters—Vitaly Kaftanov, from the Institute for Experimental and Theoretical Physics, in Moscow—was working on an experiment that was of special interest to me, since I had been studying some of its theoretical implications. This experiment—one of the most elaborate and active at CERN—involves the study of reactions induced by neutrinos. The neutrino is almost impossible to detect directly, for it has no charge and no mass, and it interacts very weakly with ordinary matter. Indeed, someone has estimated that if one took a single neutrino produced in the accelerator at CERN or the one at Brookhaven (where the first high-energy neutrino experiments were done) and shot it through a layer of lead about as thick as the distance from here to Pluto, it would undergo only one collision during its entire passage. Fortunately, however, the experimenter is not limited to one neutrino; an accelerator produces millions of them a second, and some are bound to make a collision in a target of reasonable size. These collisions produce particles that *can* be seen, so that neutrino reactions can be studied. Since the collisions are so rare, the whole experimental area must be carefully shielded from cosmic rays and other annoying background that could be confused with the few events that one is looking for. In the experiments both at CERN and at Brookhaven, this required literally thousands of tons of heavy shielding material. (The shielding in the Brookhaven experiment was made from the remnants of an obsolete battleship, while at CERN it consists of steel ingots lent to the laboratory by the Swiss government from its strategic stockpile.) At both CERN and Brookhaven, neutrino events have been successfully detected; in fact, in the Brookhaven experiment it was first shown that there are two quite distinct species of neutrino. Until that experiment, the neutrino was generally taken to be a single, unique particle (although there were some theoretical conjectures to the contrary). The fact that precision experiments can now be done with neutrinos is a very impor-

tant breakthrough in the technology of experimental physics, and it is only natural that a physicist like Kaftanov is
eager to work on the project.

Kaftanov, who is married and has a young son, first came
to CERN alone. This past summer, he was joined by his
family. He has a warm, friendly personality and a good
command of English. (He told me that when he was young
his parents agreed to allow him to give up music lessons,
which he hated, on condition that he study English.)
Many of our conversations concerned the progress of the
experiment, but as we got to know each other better we
talked a good deal about a physicist's life in the United
States and in Russia. In his country, physicists and engineers are at the very top of the social and economic scale,
and the disciplines themselves are characterized by a
highly didactic style. There is a great deal of sharp, sometimes quite personal criticism at all levels. Among European physicists, by contrast, there is still some feeling of
deference toward the professor or the senior scientist; in
fact, some of the European physicists have told me that
they were quite taken aback to see Americans and Russians
going at each other hammer and tongs in all-out scientific
debate at international meetings. The Russians have a very
active high-energy-physics program, and are well along
with the construction of a seventy-billion-electron-volt accelerator at Serpukhov, which will be the largest in the
world. All the physicists I have spoken with at CERN, including Kaftanov, are very eager for increased East-West
coöperation, and hope that the existing political situation
will continue to permit it.

Ultimately, the most important process in a scientific
laboratory is the process of constant reciprocal education.
At CERN, this is facilitated by the layout of the buildings,
which are low and long and are joined by a maze of
passageways. (The buildings are mostly white with a blue
trim, which gives them a clean-cut Swiss look.) As one

walks down the halls, one hears a continual buzz of multi-lingual conversations about physics. There are often knots of physicists in the halls or in the library, which has a few special soundproof rooms with blackboards for informal discussions. Everywhere, one gets the impression of people working and arguing with each other, and this extends even to the cafeteria. There is a long lunch period at CERN (the working day is from eight-thirty to five-thirty, and for many of the experimenters, who work in shifts on the accelerator, it runs into the evenings and weekends), and during it everything closes down—the bank, the post office, the machine shops, and the rest. But the talk goes on. The cafeteria is furnished with long tables, and by some sort of informal tradition the technical personnel tend to eat at noon, while the physicists eat at one. Usually, the experimental groups eat together and the theorists, too, form groups, sometimes according to language and sometimes according to common interests in physics. After lunch, dessert and coffee are served at a small bar, and everyone spends the rest of the lunch hour in the lounge over coffee or, on sunny days, on the broad terrace in front of the cafeteria, from which one has a fine view of Mont Blanc. Everywhere one looks, there are people discussing physics, sometimes with paper and pencil, sometimes with elaborate gesticulations, and usually in two or three languages. It is the time of day when one hears the latest technical gossip, both from CERN and from laboratories around the world.

In addition to this informal process of education, there are more formal lecture courses and seminars. The summer before last, I attended a lecture series, given especially for physicists, on using electronic computers. Surprisingly, most of the computer use at CERN and at other high-energy-physics laboratories is not by theoretical physicists but by experimenters. A typical experiment involves placing a target, such as a bubble chamber filled with liquid hydrogen or liquid helium, in front of the beam of particles emerging from the accelerator. The particles leave tracks in the liquid, and these tracks are photographed—a process likely to involve photographing hundreds of thousands of tracks from several angles. Then the photographs, which often look like examples of abstract art, must be "scanned"; that is, the events of special interest must be distinguished from the inevitable chaotic background. Much of this scanning is done—visually, in the first instance—by a large group of people, mostly women. The scanners do not have to be physicists, since picking out events of interest is a question of pattern recognition and can be taught to almost anyone. After the events have been roughly selected, they must be "measured." The curvature and thickness of the tracks as well as the angles between them are determined, to see whether the event in question is really what one is looking for or is perhaps something that looks similar but is really quite different. These distinctions are made with the help of a computer, which is programmed to correlate the results of the measurements, try to fit the event with various hypotheses, and then report back. Without a computer, this procedure would be enormously time-consuming, since many possibilities must be explored in each photograph, and there are thousands of photographs to study. Moreover, some devices that make possible a partial automation of the measuring process are now in use—an operator sets a crosshair on a track, and the machine does the rest of the measuring automatically, feeding the results into the computer—and there are systems under development that in certain cases will do the pattern recognition automatically. Hence, one can imagine a time when computers will study all the pictures and deliver carefully analyzed experimental curves to the researcher. The amount of computing required for such work is tremendous. CERN has recently bought the largest computer in the world to replace its old equipment, which was completely saturated.

I also attended two courses given by theoretical physicists especially for the experimenters at the laboratory. There is a communication problem between experimental and theoretical physicists that arises from the increasing need to specialize in a single aspect of physics because of the complexity of the field. The old-fashioned romantic notion of the experimenter coming into the physics laboratory in his white coat, with his mind unburdened by preconceptions or theoretical fancies, and saying to himself, "Well, what am I going to discover today?" just doesn't apply to experimental high-energy physics. The probable theoretical implications of experiments are carefully considered in advance. Recently, in an editorial in *Physical Review Letters,* a journal that specializes in the rapid publication of important new results in physics, Dr. S. A. Goudsmit commented, somewhat ironically, "At present, most experiments are only undertaken to prove or disprove a theory. In fact, some experimental teams employ a theorist somewhat in the role of a court astrologer, to tell them whether the stars in the theoretical heavens favor the experiments they are planning."

In any case, an experimenter must have a knowledge of the latest theoretical results and how they bear on his work. Thus, one of the jobs of the theoreticians at CERN is to explain what is happening in their fields. One of the special courses, given by Professor Leon Van Hove, a Belgian physicist (formerly of Utrecht, Holland) who directs the theoretical group at CERN, presented an especially lucid review of general aspects of reactions at high energies, but this course was finishing for the summer when I arrived, so I could attend only the last few lectures. The other course, given by Professor Bernard d'Espagnat, a French theorist from Paris, was concerned with some of the most exciting ideas that have come along in elementary-particle physics for several years. These ideas have to do with what is known as "unitary symmetry," or, less accurately, "the eightfold way." To understand what they signify, one must go back into the history of the subject a bit.

In the past few years, more and more new particles have been discovered in experiments with the accelerators. These particles are characterized by, among other properties, their masses, their electric charges, and—because they are in general unstable—their lifetimes. The major problem the particles have presented has been whether they have any interconnections or are completely independent units. In this area, atomic physics furnishes an especially encouraging example, since a superficial look at the array of chemical elements and their diverse properties might lead one to conclude that they could have no connections with one another. However, it is well known that all atoms are composed of only three distinct types of particle—the proton and the neutron, which form the atomic nucleus, and the electron, the light, negatively charged particle that generates a cloud of negative charge around the nucleus. The number and distribution of the electrons determine the chemical properties of a given atom, and the protons and neutrons determine its mass. In the case of the so-called elementary particles, one may ask the same sort of question: Is there a simple basic set of elementary particles from which all the others can be constructed? Or, as the question has sometimes been phrased: Are some elementary particles more elementary than others, and can the rest be made up of the most elementary ones? It is quite possible that this question has no real answer. Observations made with the aid of bubble chambers and other detection devices show that, in accordance with certain general rules, elementary particles can be transformed into one another in high-energy reactions. For example, if a pi meson from an accelerator bombards a liquid-hydrogen target, there can be reactions in which the pi meson and the proton that composes the liquid-hydrogen nucleus disappear and out come a so-called K-meson and another particle, called a lambda. Thus, the system of pi meson and proton is transformed into K-meson and lambda. In accounting for this transformation, one may think of the proton as being made up of a K-meson and a lambda, or one may think of the lambda as being made up of a proton and a K-meson, or one may think of all these particles as elementary. Many physicists have come to believe that the choice among these possibilities is a matter of convenience, to be decided only by which choice leads to the simplest and most beautiful theory. It has recently become clear that all known particles can be thought of as being made up of three basic particles, and this way of looking at them appears to be the simplest possible. The basic set has not yet actually been seen, and one of the great tasks of high-energy experimental physics in the next few years will be to search for new particles that may be candidates for the basic ones. The search has already started at CERN and Brookhaven. The term "eightfold way" derives from the fact that the particles composed of the basic threes fall naturally into groups of eights (in some cases, into groups of tens) that have closely interconnected properties. There is now very solid evidence that these groupings exist, and if the basic set of threes is identified, this will close one of the most fascinating investigations of elementary-particle physics.

After one of Professor d'Espagnat's lectures, on a particularly warm and lovely summer's day, I decided to take a walking tour of the CERN site. At different times over the years, I had visited most of the installations, but for the fun of it I thought I would make the whole round in one swoop. The laboratory is surrounded by gentle rolling fields leading off to the Jura, the wooded, glacially formed foothills of the Alps; in fact, during the winter, people from CERN often spend their lunch hour skiing in the Jura, which are only a few minutes away by car. When I left the building where the theoreticians have their offices, the first thing that struck me was the construction work going on everywhere—laborers (most of them Spaniards and Italians, as is the case in all of Switzerland) were enlarging roads and erecting new buildings. Alongside one of the roads I saw a striking silvered bubble—a safety tank for holding hydrogen. Hydrogen, which is the most popular target for experiments, because of its simplicity, is also one of the most difficult gases to handle, because of its explosive nature, and there is a whole complex of installations at CERN devoted to processing and handling it, all of them plastered with multilingual signs telling one not to smoke. A little farther on, I came to one of three "halls" in which experiments are actually done. As the proton beam runs around its track, it produces particles in targets, and these can be siphoned off at various stages and directed into one of the halls; this was the East Hall. I am not very enthusiastic about attempts to romanticize science and scientists, but there is something romantic about a high-energy experimental laboratory. Its attraction lies partly in the complexity and diversity of the equipment—giant magnets, trucks filled with liquefied gases, wonderful-looking electronic devices that flash lights of every color—and partly in the knowledge that what is being studied lies at the very heart of the composition of the world. There was almost total silence in the East Hall, broken only by the rhythmic booming of the main magnet of the accelerator and the constant hum of electric motors. (CERN uses almost ten per cent of Geneva's entire power supply.) I stood in awe until someone came up and asked if I was looking for something. For want of anything better, I told him that I had got lost while trying to find the road leading to the center of the accelerator ring. He gave me some directions.

I walked outside and quickly found it. The ring is buried, and one can see its outline as a slight circular mound raised above the fields. The center of the ring is guarded by fences and signs warning against radioactivity and barring entry to anyone without permission. This day, though, I noticed a number of men inside the ring cutting the grass; the machine was undoubtedly off while they were working. I crossed over and went below ground into the central building. Inside, equipment sprawled everywhere, and there was a faint smell of resin, which is used in soldering electrical circuits. Dozens of men in laboratory coats were working at one job or another with great concentration. As I watched them, the title of a book on mountain-climbing came to mind—*Les Conquérants de l'Inutile*. In a way, high-energy physics is *"la conquête de l'inutile,"* but it is also one of the most exciting, benign, and revealing intellectual disciplines that man has been able to devise.

4

I Am This
Whole World :
Erwin Schrödinger

o

o

o

THERE is a parlor game often played by my colleagues in physics. It consists of trying to decide whether the physicists of the extraordinary generation that produced the modern quantum theory, in the late twenties, were intrinsically more gifted than our present generation or whether they simply had the good fortune to be at the height of their creative powers (for physicists, with some notable exceptions, this lies between the ages of twenty-five and thirty-five at a time when there was a state of acute and total crisis in physics—a crisis brought about by the fact that existing physics simply did not account for what was known about the atom. In brief, if our generation had been alive at that time, could we have invented the quantum theory?

It is a question that will never be answered. But there is no doubt that the group of men who *did* invent the theory was absolutely remarkable. Aside from Max Planck and Einstein (it was Planck who invented the notion of the quantum—the idea that energy was always emitted and absorbed in distinct units, or quanta, and not continuously, like water flowing from a tap—and it was Einstein who pointed out how Planck's idea could be extended and used to explain a variety of mysteries about matter and radiation that physicists were contending with), who did their important work before 1925, the list includes Niels Bohr, who conceived the theory that the orbits of electrons around atoms were quantized (electrons, according to the Bohr theory, can move only in special elliptical paths— "Bohr orbits"—around the nucleus and not in any path, as the older physics would have predicted); Prince Louis de Broglie, a French aristocrat who conjectured in his doctoral thesis that both light and matter had particle and wave aspects; Werner Heisenberg, who made the first breakthrough that led to the mathematical formulation of the quantum theory, from which the Bohr orbits can be derived, and whose "uncertainty relations" set the limitations on measurements of atomic systems; P. A. M. Dirac, who made basic contributions to the mathematics of the theory and who showed how it could be reconciled with Einstein's theory of relativity; Wolfgang Pauli, whose "exclusion principle" led to an explanation of why there is a periodic table of chemical elements; Max Born and Pascual Jordan, who contributed to the interpretation of the theory; and, finally, Erwin Schrödinger, whose Schrödinger Equation is in many ways the basic equation of the quantum theory, and is to the new physics what Newton's laws of motion were to the physics that went before it.

While Heisenberg, Pauli, and Dirac were all in their early twenties when they did their work, de Broglie and Bohr were older, as was Schrödinger, who was born in Vienna in 1887. In 1926, he published the paper in which his equation was formulated. Oddly, just a few years before, he had decided to give up physics altogether for philosophy. Philipp Frank, who had been a classmate of Schrödinger's in Vienna, once told me that just before Schrödinger began his work on the quantum theory he had been working on a psychological theory of color perception. Schrödinger himself writes in the preface of his last book, *My View of the World* (Cambridge), published posthumously (he died in 1961), "In 1918, when I was thirty-one, I had good reason to expect a chair of theoretical physics at Czernowitz. . . . I was prepared to do a good job lecturing on theoretical physics . . . but for the rest, to devote myself to philosophy, being deeply imbued at the time with the writings of Spinoza, Schopenhauer, Ernst Mach, Richard Semon, and Richard Avenarius. My guardian angel intervened: Czernowitz soon no longer belonged to Austria. So nothing came of it. I had to stick to theoretical physics, and, to my astonishment, something occasionally emerged from it."

The early quantum theoreticians were a small group, mainly Europeans, who knew each other well. There was among them a sense of collaborating on one of the most important discoveries in the history of physics. In his *Science and the Common Understanding*, Robert Oppenheimer wrote, "Our understanding of atomic physics, of what we call the quantum theory of atomic systems, had its origins at the turn of the century and its great synthesis and resolutions in the nineteen-twenties. It was a heroic time. It was not the doing of any one man; it involved the collaboration of scores of scientists from many different lands, though from first to last the deeply creative and subtle and critical spirit of Niels Bohr guided, restrained, deepened, and finally transmuted the enterprise. It was a period of patient work in the laboratory, of crucial experiments and daring action, of many false starts and many untenable conjectures. It was a time of earnest correspondence and hurried conjectures, of debate, criticism, and brilliant mathematical improvisation. For those who participated, it was a time of creation; there was terror as well as exaltation in their new insight. It will probably not be recorded very completely as history. As history, its re-creation would call for an art as high as the story of Oedipus or the story of Cromwell, yet in a realm of action so remote from our common experience that it is unlikely to be known to any poet or any historian."

However, as the outlines of the theory became clearer, a sharp division of opinion arose as to the ultimate significance of it. Indeed, de Broglie, Einstein, and Schrödinger came to feel that even though the theory illuminated vast stretches of physics and chemistry ("All of chemistry and most of physics," Dirac wrote), there was fundamentally something unsatisfactory about it. The basic problem that troubled them was that the theory abandons causation of the kind that had been the goal of the classical physics of Newton and his successors: In the quantum theory, one cannot ask what one single electron in a single atom will do at a given time; the theory only describes the most probable behavior of an electron in a large collection of electrons. The theory is fundamentally statistical and deals solely with probabilities. The Schrödinger Equation enables one to work out the mathematical expressions for these probabilities and to determine how the probabilities will change in time, but according to the accepted interpretation it does not provide a step-by-step description of the motion of, say, a single electron in an atom, in the way that Newtonian mechanics projects the trajectory of a planet moving around the sun.

To most physicists, these limitations are a fundamental limitation, in principle, on the type of information that can be gathered by carrying out measurements of atomic systems. These limitations, which were first analyzed by Heisenberg and Bohr, are summarized in the Heisenberg uncertainty relations, which state, generally speaking, that the very process of making most measurements of an atomic system disturbs the system's behavior so greatly that it is put into a state qualitatively different from the one it was in before the measurement. (For example, to measure the position of an electron in an atom, one must illuminate the electron with light of very short wave length. This light carries so much momentum that the process of illuminating the electron knocks it clear out of the atom, so a second measurement of the position of the electron in the atom is impossible. "We murder to dissect," as Wordsworth has said.) The observer—or, really, his measuring apparatus—has an essential influence on the observed. The physicists who have objected to the quantum theory feel that this limitation indicates the incompleteness of the theory and that there must exist a deeper explanation that would yield the same universal agreement with experiment that the quantum theory does but that would allow a completely deterministic description of atomic events. Naturally, the burden of finding such a theory rests upon those who feel that it must exist; so far, despite the repeated efforts of people like de Broglie, Einstein, and Schrödinger, no such theory has been forthcoming.

Schrödinger, who was a brilliant writer of both scientific texts and popular scientific essays, summarized his distaste for the quantum theory in an essay entitled *Are There Quantum Jumps?* published in 1952: "I have been trying to produce a mood that makes one wonder what parts of contemporary science will still be of interest to more than historians two thousand years hence. There have been ingenious constructs of the human mind that gave an exceedingly accurate description of observed facts and have yet lost all interest except to historians. I am thinking of the theory of epicycles. [This theory was used, especially by the Alexandrian astronomer Ptolemy, to account for the extremely complicated planetary motions that had been observed; it postulated that they were compounded of innumerable simple circular motions. Reduced to the simplest terms, a planet was presumed to move in a small circle around a point that moved in a large circle around the earth. The theory was replaced by the assumption, conceived by Copernicus and Kepler, that the planets move in elliptical orbits around the sun.] I confess to the heretical view that their modern counterpart in physical theory are the quantum jumps." In his introduction to *My View of the World*, Schrödinger puts his belief even more strongly: "There is one complaint which I shall not escape. Not a word is said here of acausality, wave mechanics, indeterminacy relations, complementarity, an expanding universe, continuous creation, etc. Why doesn't he talk about what he knows instead of trespassing on the professional philosopher's preserves? *Ne sutor supra crepidam.* On this I can cheerfully justify myself: because I do not think that these things have as much connection as is currently supposed with a philosophical view of the world." There is a story that after Schrödinger lectured, in the twenties, at the Institute of Theoretical Physics, in Copenhagen, in which Bohr was teaching, on the implications of his equation, a vigorous debate took place, in the course of which Schrödinger remarked that if he had known that the whole thing would be taken so seriously he never would have invented it in the first place.

Schrödinger was too great a scientist not to recognize the significance of the all but universal success of the quantum theory—it accounts not only for "all of chemistry and most of physics" but even for astronomy; it can be used, for example, to make very precise computations of the energy generated in the nuclear reactions that go on in the sun and other stars. Indeed, Schrödinger's popular masterpiece, *What Is Life?* deals with the impact of quantum ideas on biology and above all on the molecular processes that underlie the laws of heredity. The two striking features of the hereditary mechanism are its stability and its changeability—the existence of mutations, which allow for the evolution of a biological species. The characteristics that are inherited by a child from its mother and father are all contained in several large organic molecules—the genes. Genes are maintained at a fairly high temperature, 98°F., in the human body, which means that they are subject to constant thermal agitation. The question is how does this molecule retain its identity through generation after generation. Schrödinger states the problem brilliantly: "Let me throw the truly amazing situation into relief once again. Several members of the Habsburg dynasty have a peculiar disfigurement of the lower lip ('Habsburger Lippe'). Its inheritance has been studied carefully and published, complete with historical portraits, by the Imperial Academy of Vienna, under the auspices of the family. . . . Fixing our attention on the portraits of a member of the family in the sixteenth century and of his descendant, living in the nineteenth, we may safely assume that the material gene structure responsible for the abnormal feature has been carried on from generation to generation through the centuries, faithfully reproduced at every one of the not very numerous cell divisions that lie between. . . . The gene has been kept at a temperature around 98°F. during all that time. How are we to understand that it has remained unperturbed by the disordering tendency of the heat motion for centuries?"

According to the quantum theory, the stability of any chemical molecule has a natural explanation. The molecule is in a definite energy state. To go from one state to another the molecule must absorb just the right amount of energy. If too little energy is supplied, the molecule will not make the transition. This situation differs completely from that envisaged by classical physics, in which the change of state can be achieved by absorbing any energy. It can be shown that the thermal agitations that go on in the human body do not in general supply enough energy to cause such a transition, but mutations can take place in those rare thermal processes in which enough energy is available to alter the gene.

What Is Life? was published in 1944. Since then the field of molecular biology has become one of the most active and exciting in all science. A good deal of what Schrödinger said is now dated. But the book has had an enormous influence on physicists and biologists in that it hints how the two disciplines join together at their base. Schrödinger, who received the Nobel Prize jointly with Dirac, in 1933, succeeded Max Planck at the University of Berlin in 1927. When Hitler came to power, Schrödinger, although not a Jew, was deeply affected by the political climate. Philipp Frank has told me that Schrödinger attempted to intervene in a Storm Trooper raid on a Jewish ghetto and would have been beaten to death if one of the troopers, who had studied physics, had not recognized him as Germany's most recent Nobel Laureate and persuaded his colleagues to let him go. Shortly afterward, Schrödinger went to England, then back to Austria, then to Belgium, when Austria fell, and finally to the Dublin Institute for Advanced Studies, where he remained until he returned to Vienna, in 1956. By the end of his life, he must have mastered as much general culture—scientific and non-scientific—as it is possible for any single person to absorb in this age of technical specialization. He read widely in several languages, and wrote perceptively about the relation between science and the humanities and about Greek science, in which he was particularly interested. He even wrote poetry, which, I am told, was extremely romantic.

(The pictures of Schrödinger as a young man give him a Byronic look.) What kind of personal metaphysics would such a man derive from his reading and experience? In *My View of the World,* he leaves a partial answer.

My View of the World consists of two long essays—one written in 1925, just before the discovery of the Schrödinger Equation, and one written in 1960, just before his death. In both essays he reveals himself as a mystic deeply influenced by the philosophy of the Vedas. In 1925 he writes, "This life of yours which you are living is not merely a piece of the entire existence, but is in a certain sense the *whole;* only this whole is not so constituted that it can be surveyed in one single glance. This, as we know, is what the Brahmins express in that sacred, mystic formula which is yet really so simple and so clear: *Tat tvam asi,* this is you. Or, again, in such words as 'I am in the east and in the west. I am below and above, *I am this whole world,'*" and in the later essay he returns to this theme. He does not attempt to derive or justify his convictions with scientific argument. In fact, as he stresses in his preface, he feels that modern science, his own work included, is not relevant to the search for the underlying metaphysical and moral truths by which one lives. For him, they must be intuitively, almost mystically arrived at. He writes, "It is the vision of this truth (of which the individual is seldom conscious in his actions) which underlies all morally valuable activity. It brings a man of nobility not only to risk his life for an end which he recognizes or believes to be good but—in rare cases—to lay it down in full serenity, even when there is no prospect of saving his own person. It guides the hand of the well-doer—this perhaps even more rarely—when, without hope of future reward, he gives to relieve a stranger's suffering what he cannot spare without suffering himself."

In 1960, I had the chance to visit Schrödinger in Vienna. I was studying at the Boltzmann Institute for

Theoretical Physics, whose director, Walter Thirring, is the son of Hans Thirring, a distinguished Austrian physicist, also a classmate of Schrödinger. Schrödinger had been very ill and he rarely appeared at the Institute. But he enjoyed maintaining his contact with physics and the young physicists who were working under Walter Thirring. Thirring took a small group of us to visit Schrödinger. He lived in an old-fashioned Viennese apartment house, with a rickety elevator and dimly lit hallways. The Schrödinger living room–library was piled to the ceiling with books, and Schrödinger was in the process of writing the second of the two essays in *My View of the World*. Physically he was extremely frail, but his intellectual vigor was intact. He told us some of the lessons that modern scientists might learn from the Greeks. In particular, he stressed the recurrent theme of the writings of his later years—that modern science may be as far from revealing the underlying laws of the natural universe as was the science of ancient Greece. It was clear from watching and listening to him that the flame that illuminated his intellectual curiosity throughout his long life still burned brightly at the end of it.

5

Einstein and Bohr : A Debate

A SCIENTIST writing for the general reader has at least one obvious advantage over the non-scientist; he is writing about something that he presumably knows from within. In fact, for him the process of popularizing a scientific idea does not differ greatly from the process of explaining his ideas to a colleague or a student. The fundamental difference lies in what he can assume that his listener already understands; the bridge between the boundary of the layman's knowledge and the scientific idea is much longer, and crossing it requires a great deal of patience on both sides. On the other hand, a scientist writing about science and scientists, especially if they are his colleagues and contemporaries, is in a certain respect at a disadvantage. Scientific work, as is true of any other creative discipline, usually reflects the personality of the scientist. While it is definitely possible to understand and appreciate a scientific development without knowing anything about the men who created it and the atmosphere in which they worked, just as it is possible to enjoy a Mozart symphony without knowing anything about Mozart, such an understanding may lack perspective. A scientist writing about the work of his colleagues and his predecessors feels a restraint that he is invading his friend's privacy when it comes to correlating ideas and personalities. For this reason, I suspect, there are almost no books by physicists about modern physics that attempt to link the ideas expressed to the people who invented them and to the atmosphere in which they were invented. The major exception I know is Philipp Frank's wonderful *Einstein: His Life and Times.* Professor Frank knew Einstein, both as colleague and as friend, from the beginning of his scientific career. He understood Einstein's physics about as well as it can be understood and he shared much of Einstein's European background; Professor Frank was Einstein's successor at the University of Prague. His book presents a magnificent picture of Einstein, his ideas, and his life. However, Frank told me that the very fact that he knew Einstein so well and was in frequent contact with him while the book was in progress obligated him to make his portrait incomplete. It was not that he knew any scandalous secrets about Einstein; it was simply that he knew that Einstein would criticize whatever portrait he created. After Einstein's death, Frank often thought of redoing parts of his book, but he felt that his memory at the end of his life was no longer reliable (when I first met him, he had essentially total recall) and he hesitated to begin such an ambitious project. It is with a feeling of tragedy that one watched such a chance slip away. Future generations may well call our era the Age of Einstein, just as we now call the seventeenth century the Age of Newton, and they will regret the lack of a full contemporary portrait of Einstein as we regret the lack of a full contemporary portrait of Newton.

It is with the same feeling that physicists watch the inventors of the quantum theory slip away without leaving behind, in tangible form, the splendid collection of stories and insights into the creative process in science that went along with the birth of the theory. As Oppenheimer wrote, "For those who participated, it was a time of creation; there was terror as well as exaltation in their new insight. It will probably not be recorded very completely as history. As history, its re-creation would call for an art as high as the story of Oedipus or the story of Cromwell, yet in a realm of action so remote from our common experience that it is unlikely to be known to any poet or any historian." The American Physical Society and the American Philosophical Society have been attempting to persuade the inventors of the quantum theory to record, for future historians, their impressions of how it came about. But men like Wolfgang Pauli died before the project got under way, and, saddest of all, Niels Bohr, the figure around whom the quantum theorists revolved as they crystallized and formulated their ideas, died just after he had begun to record his recollections.

As Oppenheimer suggested, it is unlikely that any single individual will be able to tie together all the strings of the story and give not only a complete account of the physics involved but a real sense of the color and poetry of its creators. Many books will no doubt be written on the subject, and from them one will be able to piece together the history; a certain number of books and articles have already been published. But the first book I have read that appears to me to offer some understanding of the physics and, above all, of the physicists concerned is, perhaps not surprisingly, by a non-scientist, Barbara Lovett Cline—a book called *The Questioners: Physicists and the Quantum Theory* (Crowell) . Mrs. Cline, a professional science writer and editor, spent five years preparing her book, and her list of acknowledgments makes it clear that she has discussed her subject with innumerable physicists, including Oppenheimer and Bohr's son Aage, who succeeded his father as director of the Institute for Theoretical Physics, in Copenhagen. I do not think Mrs. Cline will claim that she has produced a complete description of the quantum theory—that is not possible in a non-technical book—but her description is adequate and basically sound. Moreover—and in this respect her book is quite unique—she has succeeded in bringing the physicists alive without any of the meaningless and irrelevant adulation that occurs when one tries to characterize personalities as rich and complex as those of Einstein and Bohr by stating they were men of genius and letting it go at that. The *were* men of genius, but they were full of life as well, full of sorrows and joy, full of human qualities that were expressed in their work.

The quantum was the invention of the German physicist Max Planck. At the beginning of this century, physicists studying the spectrum of the radiation emitted from a heated oven developed a simple empirical physical law that such a spectrum obeyed, but no one had been able to *deduce* this law from first principles—first principles then being Newtonian mechanics, electromagnetic theory, and thermodynamics. In 1900, Planck managed to deduce the law, but only by making what appeared to be the completely arbitrary assumption that the radiation in the oven consisted of indivisible packets of energy—quanta of energy. In other words, he held that the radiation from the oven had a kind of atomic (i.e., indivisible) structure, although the classical theory on which the science of the phenomenon had up to then been based assumed that these units of radiation were infinitely divisible. (A rough analogy would be a fluid conceived of as a continuous substance instead of—in accordance with molecular theory —being composed of tiny molecules packed so close together as to appear unseparated.) According to Planck's hypothesis, the energy in a quantum is proportional to its frequency; for example, violet light, which has a higher frequency than red light, is composed of quanta of greater energy. He could not demonstrate the validity of this assumption, and regarded his use of it as simply a trick that enabled him to get the right answer. Indeed, he spent some fruitless years trying to derive a formula for the spectrum by using classical physics. (Einstein later proved that such a derivation was impossible.)

Mrs. Cline gives a fascinating description of Planck, some of it based on a series of brilliant articles by Martin Klein, a physicist at Case Institute of Technology. The great historic physics papers are a little like the great historic works of literature—they are more often quoted than read. Klein actually set out to read carefully the early papers of Planck and Einstein, which are in German and employ rather archaic and sometimes clumsy mathematical notation. This absorbing study enables one to realize, in the light of our present knowledge, just how much the great pioneers in physics foresaw and how much they didn't. Mrs. Cline notes that when Planck began his career in physics, in 1875, he was told by the head of the Physics Department of the University of Munich, where his father taught law, that "physics is a branch of knowledge that is just about complete. The important discoveries, all of them, have been made. It is hardly worth entering physics any more." This is a lament that one sometimes hears today from the elder statesmen of science, and when one hears it it is worth keeping in mind that within thirty years of this prediction Planck and Einstein had discovered, between them, the relativity theory (Einstein,

1905) and the quantum (Planck in 1900 and Einstein about 1905) .

Planck's introduction of the concept of the quantum eventually led to the fall of the whole edifice of classical physics and brought about one of the great revolutions in the history of science, yet he was by temperament one of the least revolutionary figures imaginable, and, indeed, he could never completely accept the most revolutionary implications of his own discovery. Planck came from an academic Prussian family. His life was governed by strict rules and traditions. Mrs. Cline writes:

> A young physicist who was staying in Max Planck's home during a visit to Berlin gradually became aware of a certain regularity in the Planck household. The visitor's curiosity was aroused; he made an observation: stationing himself by the door of his room he waited to see what would happen as the clock in the hall struck the hour. Sure enough, while the clock still was sounding, Planck emerged from his room, proceeded down the stairs, and then out the front door. Further observation confirmed the regularity of his comings and goings; as the big hall clock struck a certain hour, invariably there Max Planck would be, on his way down the stairs.

> Systematically, part of Planck's day was allotted for a walk, just as thirty minutes regularly were devoted to playing the piano. And when this highly organized scientist worked in the study among his treasured collection of scientific volumes, he worked standing up. His desk was a high one like those used in Dickens' time by clerks, who sat on high stools. But Planck did not use a stool.

Unlike Planck, Einstein, the second important figure in the history of the quantum, had the anarchistic temperament of a genuine revolutionary. He was twenty-one in 1900, the year Planck invented the quantum. By any standards, he was a total academic failure. A few years before, he had succeeded in dropping out of the *Gym-*

nasium in Munich, where he had been left by his father when a business failure forced him to move to Italy. Einstein hated the regimentation of the German educational system, and he got a doctor to say that he was suffering from "nervous exhaustion," which would respond to a six-month stay in Italy. But before he could present his doctor's note to the authorities he was asked to leave school because his negative attitude had made the other students disrespectful of their teachers. Einstein's father could support him for no more than a few months in Italy, but then, with the aid of a relative, he was sent to Zurich, only to fail the entrance examination in mathematics for the Polytechnic Institute. He went to a Swiss *Gymnasium* to get a diploma, and a year later he finally entered the Institute. There he fared almost as poorly. He simply could not learn what he was supposed to. In his sixties, he wrote a brief biography, which appears as the introductory essay in a marvellous collection entitled *Albert Einstein: Philosopher-Scientist,* edited by P. A. Schilpp. About his school days, during which, instead of studying the required courses, he was already formulating the ideas that eventually resulted in the relativity theory, he wrote:

> I soon learned to scent out that which was able to lead to fundamentals and to turn aside from everything else, from the multitude of things which clutter up the mind and divert it from the essential. The hitch in this was, of course, the fact that one had to cram all this stuff into one's mind for the examinations, whether one liked it or not. This coercion had such a deterring effect [upon] me that, after I had passed the final examination, I found the consideration of any scientific problems distasteful to me for an entire year. In justice I must add, moreover, that in Switzerland we had to suffer far less under such coercion, which smothers every truly scientific impulse, than is the case in many another locality. There were altogether only two examina-

tions; aside from these, one could just about do as one pleased. This was especially the case if one had a friend, as I did, who attended the lectures regularly and who worked over their content conscientiously. This gave one freedom in the choice of pursuits until a few months before the examination, a freedom which I enjoyed to a great extent and have gladly given into the bargain the bad conscience connected with it as by far the lesser evil. It is, in fact, nothing short of a miracle that the modern methods of instruction have not yet entirely strangled the holy curiosity of inquiry; for this delicate little plant, aside from stimulation, stands mainly in need of freedom; without this it goes to wreck and ruin without fail.

Mrs. Cline notes that Einstein graduated from the Polytechnic Institute and became a tutor, but he soon lost his job because he wanted his charges to leave the *Gymnasium,* where he thought their curiosity was being smothered; their father, a *Gymnasium* teacher, wanted no such thing. What occurred next can be described only as a scientific miracle. Einstein, through an acquaintance, got a job in the patent office in Bern examining patent applications and inventions (throughout his life, he retained a fondness for inventions, especially if there was some quackery in them or if they illustrated a nice point in physics), and while he was working on this job (one can only wonder how many hours a day) he wrote and published three physics papers that transformed twentieth-century science and, ultimately, our way of life. The first paper contains an explanation of Brownian motion—the motion of tiny, almost invisible particles suspended in a liquid, a motion named for the biologist Robert Brown, its discoverer. Einstein pointed out that if one assumed that the liquid was a mass of invisible molecules that were bombarding the suspended objects, the motion of these objects was explained. In his brief biography, he notes that he had not heard of Brown's work, but he realized that the motions of molecules would produce such an effect, and the experiments he proposed to establish this point had, unknown to him, already been carried out by Brown. This may seem a minor point, but at the time there was great doubt, among even the leading scientists, that atoms actually existed, and Einstein's paper, taken in connection with Brown's experiment, was one of the first convincing arguments that they did. The second paper presents the "special theory" of relativity—as opposed to the "general theory," which deals with gravitation and which was also invented, some ten years later, by Einstein. (Just after his first paper on special relativity, he published a very brief note in which he used the theory to derive the formula $E = mc^2$.) He often remarked in later years that the special theory of relativity, on which he had been working more or less since the age of sixteen, would have eventually been invented anyway by someone or other, for many of the ideas it embodies were in the scientific atmosphere of that period. What is most remarkable about this paper is its complete lucidity. The arguments, based on a profound but fundamentally simple analysis of the meaning of space and time measurements, sweep one along, and reading it is one of the greatest experiences anyone with scientific training can have. The third paper has to do with quanta, and it was for this paper that Einstein received the Nobel Prize in 1921.

From the beginning, Einstein realized that Planck's invention of the quantum was not simply a mathematical device but a far-reaching statement (if it was true) about the nature of light. Until the beginning of the nineteenth century, there had been a controversy as to whether light consisted of particles or of waves. Newton had developed a particle theory of light, but it was discredited when experiments showed that light rays could interfere with each other—a phenomenon that could be explained only if the rays had wave properties. (The interference of waves is a familiar phenomenon. If one drops two stones close together in a pond, the two systems of waves that are created will, when they meet, interfere with one another and create a completely different wave formation. On the other hand, if two hard particles collide, they simply bounce off each other, retaining their identity as particles.) But Einstein realized that Planck's hypothesis meant that in certain circumstances light must behave as if it were made up of particles instead of waves, and he pointed out that this phenomenon had already been observed. (The early experiments were quite crude, and part of Einstein's genius was his ability to intuit the real significance of imperfect and apparently conflicting experimental results.) He was speaking of what is known as the photoelectric effect—the shining of light, or X-rays, an energetic form of light (that is, electromagnetic radiation), on a metal plate, which results in the emission of a stream of electrons from the plate. It was, he said, as if the quanta of light were bombarding the plate, like billiard balls, and releasing the electrons from it by simply knocking them out of the metal. (According to the Planck assumption, the more violet the light was, the more energetic the light quanta would be, and thus the more energetic the electrons would be when they were knocked out of the metal; in fact, merely by changing the frequency of the light, one could control the energy of the outgoing electrons.) The theory turned out to be absolutely correct, but it presented physicists with a paradox—the paradox that light sometimes exhibited itself as a wave phenomenon and sometimes as a particle phenomenon. This paradox has become the cornerstone of the quantum theory. In the nineteen-twenties it was proved, as had been suggested by the French theoretical physicist Louis Victor de Broglie (the suggestion, for which he received the Nobel Prize, was the basis of his Ph.D. thesis), that matter, too, has wave properties. The electron microscope is based on the fact that electrons have wave properties, like light and X-rays, and the great value of the electron microscope is that the wavelength of electrons is much shorter than characteristic X-ray wavelengths, so that one can explore smaller structures with electron microscopes than one can with X-ray microscopes. The particle-wave duality, in fact, runs through all of nature, and classical physics offers no explanation of it.

Einstein's explanation of the photoelectric effect was not universally accepted. Physicists are frequently reluctant to accept radically new ideas; when, in 1913, Einstein, at Planck's invitation, became a professor in Berlin, where Planck was the leading scientific figure, Planck wrote that "he may sometimes have missed the target . . . as, for example, in his hypothesis of light quanta" but that this "cannot really be held against him." However, Mrs. Cline points out, Planck was one of the first physicists to recognize the importance of Einstein's theory of relativity, about which he wrote, in 1910, that if it "should prove to be correct, as I expect it will, he will be considered the Copernicus of the twentieth century." The relativity theory could be fitted comfortably into the mold of classical physics, while the quantum could not.

The story of the quantum now shifts scene—to England, and Manchester, and the laboratory of Ernest Rutherford, a New Zealander. Mrs. Cline's chapters on Rutherford are among the best in her book. He was a gruff, brilliant man of limitless energy. Out of his laboratory came the discovery that the atom had a massive nucleus, which we now know is made up of neutrons and protons. Rutherford pictured the atom with the outer electrons moving like planets around the massive nuclear interior. It was a fine concept and it accommodated itself with many of the known facts, but it, too, soon led to conflict with classical physics. Electrons carry an electric charge, and according to classical physics they should have radiated away energy, in the form of light or X-rays, as they moved about the nucleus, and should have collapsed into the nucleus as they lost this energy. Therefore, the Rutherford atom was extremely unstable, whereas the actual atom is extremely stable. Indeed, it is the stable building block out of which all matter is constructed.

What accounts for the stability of the atom? It was to this problem that Niels Bohr, a shy, unknown Danish student who had come to Rutherford on a fellowship (Rutherford wrote, to a friend, "Bohr, a Dane, has pulled out of Cambridge and turned up here to get some experience in radioactive work"), turned his genius. Bohr is the heroic figure of the quantum theory and the hero of Mrs. Cline's book. Her description of his life and his work does justice to the grandeur of both. She notes:

> Niels Bohr did not look intelligent. Also, unlike Einstein, who possessed a flair for using words and expressed his thoughts easily, clearly, and vividly, Bohr spoke tentatively and it was hard at times to make out his meaning. This was only partly due to the fact that his voice was soft and that he had a slight speech impediment. There was also the fact that he did not necessarily try to express his thoughts in the clearest possible way. For Bohr words were tools: in doing physics he used words almost as much as he used mathematical symbols. Often when he talked he was not reporting a conclusion but working toward it as he spoke. Once one got to know Bohr and understand his way of using words, conversation with him could be exciting, especially if one questioned his ideas. In argument he was at his best.

From the beginning, Bohr felt that the solution to the problem of reconciling the theories of the stable atom and the Rutherford one lay with the quantum. He began thinking about this in Manchester, but in 1912 his fellowship money ran out and he returned to Denmark to teach. In the spring of 1913, he was discussing his problem with a colleague, who suggested that he might find a clue in the physics literature dealing with the light spectra emitted when atoms in, say, a gas are excited after an electric spark has been passed through the gas. It was known that each gas emits a characteristic spectrum of light, in the form of lines of different colors—lines that, when one looks at them, appear to be distributed in orderly patterns—and that no two gases emit exactly the same spectrum. (In contrast, the seemingly white light of an incandescent lamp is, when analyzed in a prism, seen to be composed of a continuum of light of every color.) The study of these spectral lines had been under way for many years. In 1885, a Swiss schoolteacher, Johann Jakob Balmer, worked out an extremely simple mathematical formula for describing some of the patterns of frequencies of the lines of the spectrum of hydrogen gas, which is the simplest atomic system (since it consists of one proton and one electron), and these lines are now known as the Balmer Series. Bohr had not been aware of the existence of Balmer's formula, for spectroscopy was a rather isolated branch of physics, and no one had realized its relevance to the problem of atomic structure, but now the Balmer Series provided the clue for him. The fact that atoms emitted light at only certain frequencies contradicted classical physics, which held that when an electron emitted light, as it spiralled into the nucleus, it emitted light of every frequency. According to classical physics, atoms should emit—like the incandescent lamp—a chaos of light of all colors.

Bohr used this knowledge, roughly, as follows: An electron loses energy when it emits light. This is true in both classical and quantum physics. In losing energy, it drops from the orbit it has been following to one closer to the nucleus, and according to classical physics it could, and would, drop all the way into the nucleus. But in an atomic spectrum only certain frequencies show up, which meant to Bohr that only certain orbits were allowed to the electron. The electron, in Bohr's theory, cannot make arbitrary changes of orbit, as it could according to classical physics; it can jump only from one allowed orbit to another. Bohr argued that there must be a smallest allowed orbit to which the electron ultimately descends after it has finished cascading down from the higher orbits, and once it reaches this lowest orbit it remains there (it cannot move closer to the nucleus) unless it is knocked back up to a higher orbit by a collision with, say, another atom, and (again in contradiction of classical physics) it cannot radiate away energy, once it is there, since there is no lower orbit for it to drop to. The problem of finding the energy of the observed quanta became the same as finding these orbits—now known as Bohr orbits. By a marvellously ingenious argument, Bohr succeeded in determining these orbits and in deriving the Balmer formula from first principles.

In March, 1913, Bohr sent a manuscript off to Rutherford, who replied that he found it too long. Indeed, Rutherford wrote Bohr, in a letter that Bohr treasured and quoted from for the rest of his life, "There is one criticism of minor character which I would make in the arrangement of the paper. I think in your endeavor to be clear you have a tendency to make your papers much too long, and a tendency to repeat your statements in different parts of the paper. I think that your paper really ought to be cut down, and I think this could be done without sacrificing anything to clearness. I do not know if you appreciate the fact that long papers have a way of frightening readers, who feel that they have not time to dip into them." This embarrassed Bohr, who had already sent him a version that was even longer, but, after a trip to England, during which he had a chance to discuss his ideas with Rutherford, the paper was finally published. It is now recognized as one of the pivotal papers in modern science. Mrs. Cline notes that, characteristically, Einstein was one of the first physicists to understand its significance: "A colleague [the Hungarian physicist and chemist Georg von Hevesy] who told him of some new evidence in support of Bohr's theory said that as he listened, 'the big eyes of Einstein looked still bigger.' 'Then,' Einstein said, 'it is one of the greatest discoveries.' "

Physics never stands still. The principal features of the Bohr theory were confirmed by many experiments in the nineteen-twenties, but it became increasingly clear that the theory was not complete. In the first place, in an atomic spectrum some of the lines are brighter than others. While Bohr's theory, and subsequent refinements of it, predicted the positions of many of the lines, it could not make real predictions about the relative degrees of brightness. Moreover, the theory did not take proper account of the spectra of atoms like helium, in which two or more electrons move around the nucleus. Bohr's theory worked for hydrogen, which has a single electron, and for ionized helium, in which one of the two outer electrons has been knocked out. But it failed for neutral helium, in which two electrons are present. There was a feeling of frustration among physicists of that time—a feeling that they were on the verge of a fundamental insight into nature but that it was constantly eluding them. Wolfgang Pauli, one of the most brilliant physicists working with Bohr, wrote, in 1925, during the height of the confusion, to a colleague, "*Die Physik ist momentan wieder sehr verfahren; für mich ist sie jedenfalls viel zu schwierig und ich wollte ich wäre Filmkomiker oder so etwas und hätte nie etwas von Physik gehört!*" ("Physics is once again very fouled up, and for me it is so difficult that I wish I were a film comedian or something like that and had never heard of physics in the first place!")

In 1920, some Danish businessmen donated money for a building for an Institute for Theoretical Physics in Copenhagen—an institute to be built for Bohr. (One of the principal investors in the Institute was the Carlsberg brewery. The Carlsberg people had already built a House of Honor, a lavish residence in Copenhagen meant to house the first citizen of Denmark. It was given to Bohr in the early nineteen-thirties.) It was in this institute that the quantum theory, which replaced Bohr's theory about the orbits of electrons and from which all of atomic and nuclear physics flows, took form. Not all the work, by any means, was done in Copenhagen. But physicists from everywhere in Europe travelled to and from the Institute, and Bohr acted as the critical conscience of the theory, sifting the true from the false and the superficial from the deep. In the words of a Copenhagen student song frequently sung at the Institute, *"Nobelmanden Niels Bohr, ved vej blandt alle vildspor"* ("Nobelman Niels Bohr knows the way among all false tracks"). The final synthesis of the different strands of the theory was hammered out around Bohr in Copenhagen, and it has become known as the Copenhagen Interpretation.

It is not possible to give a detailed account of the quantum theory in a brief essay. Explaining the theory in words is extremely difficult, and even physics students with a considerable background in mathematics find it difficult to master. The basic issue is a deeply philosophical one. We are conditioned, in our understanding of nature, by our everyday experience. This experience is concerned with medium-sized objects, with relatively large masses moving in perceptible orbits at velocities that are very much slower than the speed of light. The objects of atomic physics—the atoms, the electrons, the protons—belong to a completely different realm. The diameter of a typical atom is only 10^{-8} cm, which means that a hundred million such objects would together measure less than an inch across. Atomic masses are incredibly small, whereas any perceptible mass is composed of billions upon billions of atoms. Therefore, the language we use to describe our everyday life cannot be freely extrapolated into the atomic or sub-atomic world. To describe this world, a new language has to be invented. The original Bohr theory, with its picture of electrons moving around the nucleus in perceptible orbits like planets, is an attempt to carry into the atomic domain concepts of common sense and Newtonian physics.

The first real breakthrough that led to the new quantum theory came when physicists asked whether it made sense to talk about the orbits of electrons around a nucleus. The crucial reasoning, reasoning that is typical of the new quantum theory, can be put as follows: How would one determine an electron's orbit? By shining light on the electron. But the light's quanta have energy and momentum, and if one attempts to "see" an atomic electron by shining light on it, the light's quanta transfer so much momentum to the electron that it is knocked clear out of the atom. Therefore, the electron's orbit cannot be determined. If the orbit cannot be determined, then why speak of it at all? "Whereof you cannot speak, thereof you should be silent," in the words of Wittgenstein. The new quantum theory makes use of quantities that are amenable to measurement, and quantities that cannot be measured have no part in the theory. The measurable quantities that the new theory describes are probabilities. The theory predicts the probability that an atomic event will take place, but its occurrence cannot be predicted uncondi-tionally. (The use of probabilities in the theory was introduced in the late nineteen-twenties by the German physicist Max Born.) For instance, one can predict the likelihood that an atomic electron will be found in a certain place near its atom, but one cannot assert that it will be found there. (These probabilities behave mathematically like waves, in the sense that the probabilities associated with individual electrons add together and interfere with each other like waves. It was Schrödinger who, in 1926, discovered the equation that these probability waves obey. The de Broglie waves are simply special solutions of the Schrödinger wave equation.)

Mrs. Cline gives a delightful and illuminating picture of the atmosphere at Bohr's Institute in the nineteen-twenties, at the time when these new ideas were being created. Apart from Bohr, the most remarkable figures at the Institute were Wolfgang Pauli and Werner Heisenberg, both in their twenties. Pauli had been a child prodigy. When he was in his teens, he wrote a definitive treatise on the relativity theory. About that time, he attended a meeting at which Einstein spoke, and after Einstein's lecture Pauli began some remarks with the phrase *"Was Herr Einstein gesagt hat ist nicht so blöd"* ("What Mr. Einstein has said is not so stupid"). He was a superb scientific critic, combining an acidulous wit, a keen perception of relevance, and a complete lack of inhibitions about stating his opinions. Pauli made decisive contributions to the mathematics of the theory and its application to atomic structure. Heisenberg had immense energy (he excelled in mountain-climbing) and a superb intuition in physics. It was Heisenberg who took the first steps toward creating the new physics by rejecting the concept of the Bohr orbits and by employing in the theory only quantities that are measurable. His analysis led, under Bohr's critical guidance, to the formulation of the Uncertainty Principle, which is at the heart of the theory. Of the Uncertainty Principle, more below.

The atmosphere at the Institute was both serious and gay. Bohr was full of life. He had a beautiful Danish wife and a large family of boys. (There were five, but the oldest died, still a young man, in a sailing accident.) His wife was always concerned to see that the physicists in Copenhagen had an adequate social life. They even developed a quantitative system of rating the attractiveness of the local girls. According to Mrs. Cline, there were five principal categories:

1. You can't stop looking.
2. You can stop but it hurts.
3. It doesn't make any difference whether you look or not.
4. It hurts to look.
5. You couldn't look if you wanted to.

Over the years, a surprisingly large number of theoretical physicists have married Danish girls.

In 1926, Heisenberg and Bohr began formulating the Copenhagen Interpretation. Mrs. Cline, whose book has some wonderful photographs of Heisenberg and Bohr at work, quotes Heisenberg: "I remember discussions with Bohr which went through many hours till very late at night and ended almost in despair, and when at the end of the discussion I went alone for a walk in the neighboring park I repeated to myself again and again the question: Can nature possibly be as absurd as it seems to us in these atomic experiments?" By 1927, Heisenberg had succeeded in formulating the Uncertainty Principle.

The Uncertainty Principle is a summary of the limitations on the measurements that can be made of atomic systems. In classical physics there are theoretically no such limitations, although in any experiment carried out in a laboratory there are always errors—errors that arise simply because of the practical limitations on the accuracy of measuring quantities such as distances by using rulers and the like. The position and velocity, or momentum, of an object like a billiard ball can be measured as exactly as one pleases, in prequantum physics, if one has the patience to refine the experimental techniques. But is an electron like a billiard ball? Does the fact that the electron is so fantastically much smaller and lighter than a billiard ball change in an essential way the limitations on the measurability of its position and momentum? The answer is emphatically yes. Heisenberg's arguments in favor of this answer paralleled the argument involved in determining the Bohr orbits. If one tries to locate an electron with light, one inevitably changes its momentum, and to an extent that cannot be precisely predetermined. The billiard ball, on the other hand, is so heavy that the change in its momentum when one attempts to locate it, while important in principle, is negligible in practice, so the billiard ball's position and momentum can be determined with almost total accuracy. In the spirit of the Copenhagen Interpretation, one must be careful not to attribute a definite momentum to electrons in situations in which the momentum cannot be determined by experiment.

It was at this point that Einstein abandoned the quantum theory. Perhaps it was a question of age and generation. In 1926, Einstein was forty-seven years old. Forty-seven may be the prime of life, but not for physicists. The creators of the quantum theory, with very few exceptions, were men in their early twenties, and the older generation —Einstein, Schrödinger, and de Broglie—never really accepted the new physics. In his scientific autobiography Max Planck wrote, "A new scientific truth does not triumph by convincing its opponents and making them see the light but rather because its opponents eventually die, and a new generation grows up that is familiar with it." It is a harsh judgment, but there is a good deal of truth in it. In any case, Einstein became the Devil's advocate against the theory. He tried for years, unsuccessfully, to find examples that would show that the Uncertainty Principle was wrong. He and Bohr engaged in a series of debates on the theory that lasted until the end of Einstein's life. Mrs. Cline offers a moving account of the encounters, and they are wonderfully summarized by Bohr himself in another article in the Schilpp collection—an article entitled *Discussion with Einstein on Epistemological Problems in Atomic Physics.* Einstein would not accept the fact that a fundamental theory of physics could contain probabilities and indeterminacies ("God does not play dice with the world"), while Bohr insisted that in the new atomic domain the old concepts did not apply. The debate reached a high point in 1930, when, at a conference, Einstein produced yet another example of a measurement that he thought appeared to violate the Heisenberg relations. After a sleepless night, Bohr discovered that in his argument Einstein had neglected an essential point that depended on Einstein's general theory of relativity. Although he acknowledged his mistake, Einstein remained unconvinced, and Bohr said that for the rest of his life, in his mind, he was constantly arguing with Einstein. On the night before Bohr died, a photograph, which appears in Mrs. Cline's book, was taken of Bohr's blackboard in his home in Copenhagen. It shows a diagram, which he had just drawn, of Einstein's proposed experiment to violate the uncertainty relations—the experiment in which he had neglected his own relativity theory.

Mrs. Cline closes her book with a beautiful portrait of Bohr and Einstein at the end of their lives. It is taken largely from a moving tribute to Bohr's memory by a Dutch-born physicist, Abraham Pais, now of Rockefeller University. Pais had come to Copenhagen after spending several years in Holland in hiding from the Nazis. During this time he had continued to work on physics, and after the war he came to Copenhagen as the first postwar visitor to the Institute from abroad. Pais recalls the first time he had a chance to talk to Bohr about his work, at the House of Honor. Pais was asked to explain the problem he had been studying. He says: "While I was telling Bohr about this, he smoked his pipe looked mainly to the ground and would only rarely look up at the blackboard on which I was enthusiastically writing down various formulae. After I finished, Bohr did not say much, and I left a bit disheartened, with the impression that he could not care less about the whole subject. I did not know Bohr well enough at the time to realize that this was not entirely true. At a later stage I would have known right away that Bohr's curiosity was aroused, as he had neither remarked that this was very, very interesting, nor that we agreed much more than I thought" (two favorite Bohr euphemisms indicating that the work being described was probably wrong) .

Pais, a few years later, came to the United States and the Institute for Advanced Study, in Princeton. In 1948, Bohr came back to the Institute, of which he had been a visiting member in 1939. Schilpp asked him to write something for Einstein's seventieth-birthday volume, an article that inevitably turned into an account of his discussions with Einstein. Pais says:

At this point I wish to relate my own first direct experience of the impact of Einstein on Bohr. It happened a few weeks later that Bohr came to my office at the Institute for Advanced Study, of which I then was a temporary member. He was in a state of angry despair and kept saying, "I am sick of myself" for several times. I was concerned and asked what had happened. He told me he had just been downstairs to see Einstein. As always, they had gotten into an argument about the meaning of quantum mechanics. And, as remained true to the end, Bohr had been unable to convince Einstein of his views. There can be no doubt that Einstein's lack of assent was a very deep frustration to Bohr. It is our good fortune that this led Bohr to keep striving at clarification and better formulation, and not only that. It was Bohr's own good fortune too.

Pais goes on:

In the 1948 period I saw a lot of Bohr, as he and his wife lived at 14 Dickinson Street, the same house in which I occupied the top floor. When I came home at night, the following charming little comedy would often be re-enacted. As I opened the door, Bohr would always just be walking in the corridor, his back towards me, on his way to the kitchen. In that way he would let me notice him first. He would then turn around in apparent surprise and ask if I would not care for a glass of sherry. And then we would settle down to talk about political problems. For at that period Bohr had become disillusioned with the official reactions to the atom. It was now his desire to make a direct attempt to get his views considered by those in positions of responsibility, and he was preparing a memorandum to this effect which was discussed over and over during those evenings. It formed the basis for Bohr's open letter to the United Nations in 1950.

Then Pais writes:

Apart from this, Bohr spent most of his time by putting the finishing touches to his article in the Einstein volume, mentioned earlier. This paper is Bohr's masterpiece. Nowhere in the literature can a better access to his thinking be found, and it is a must for all students of quantum mechanics, now or later. During that period I was witness of an amusing moment which involved both Bohr and Einstein.

One morning Bohr came into my office and started as follows: *"Du er så klog. . . ."* ("You are so wise.") I started to laugh (no formality or solemnity was called for in the contact with Bohr) and said, "All right, I understand." Bohr would like me to come down to his office and talk. We went there, and it should be explained that Bohr at that time used Einstein's own office in Fuld Hall. At the same time, Einstein himself used the adjoining small assistant's office; he had a dislike of the big one, which he did not use anyway. (A photograph in the Einstein anniversary volume of the *Reviews of Modern Physics,* 1949, shows Einstein sitting in the assistant's office.) After we had entered, Bohr asked me to sit down ("I always need an origin for the co-ordinate system") and soon started to pace furiously around the oblong table in the center of the room,

Reading this, I was reminded of the time, at Columbia University, I saw Pauli and Bohr in discussion. Pauli had just finished presenting what purported to be a new fundamental theory of elementary particles, and when he was finished Pauli said that the theory might have appeared somewhat crazy upon first hearing. Bohr replied that, for a fundamental theory, it did not appear crazy enough, meaning that a really novel theory, at first, looks so odd as to appear all but irrational. Bohr simply could not sit still in intense discussion, and soon he and Pauli were walking, one after the other, at a furious pace around the large table in the lecture hall. Each time Pauli arrived at the front of the table he would announce to the audience that the theory was crazy, while, when it was Bohr's turn, he would say, "It is not crazy enough."

Pais continues:

> He then asked me if I could put down a few sentences as they would emerge during his pacing. It should be explained that, at such sessions, Bohr never had a full sentence ready. He would often dwell on one word, coax it, implore it, to find the continuation. This could go on for many minutes. At that moment the word was "Einstein." There Bohr was, almost running around the table and repeating, "Einstein . . . Einstein . . ." It would have been a curious sight for someone not familiar with Bohr. After a little while he walked to the window, gazed out, repeating every now and then, "Einstein . . . Einstein . . ."
>
> At that moment the door opened very softly, and Einstein tiptoed in.
>
> He beckoned me with a finger on his lips to be very quiet, his urchin smile on his face. He was to explain a few minutes later the reason for his behavior. Einstein was not allowed by his doctor to buy any tobacco. However, the doctor had not forbidden him to steal tobacco, and this was precisely what he set out to do now. Always on tiptoe, he made a beeline for Bohr's tobacco pot, which stood on the table at which I was sitting. Meanwhile Bohr, unaware, was standing at the window, muttering, "Einstein . . . Einstein . . ." I was at a loss what to do, especially because I had at that moment not the faintest idea what Einstein was up to.
>
> Then Bohr, with a firm "Einstein," turned around. There they were, face to face, as if Bohr had summoned him forth.

It is an understatement to say that for a moment Bohr was speechless. I myself, who had seen it coming, had distinctly felt uncanny for a moment, so I could well understand Bohr's own reaction.

So they stood, and Pais adds, "A moment later the spell was broken when Einstein explained his mission." And, Pais concludes, "Soon we were all bursting with laughter."

6

Whither the Universe? °
On Cosmology °

FOR scientists and philosophers, the temptation to speculate about origins—the origins of the planets, of the sun, of the entire cosmos—is irresistible. Such speculation is as ancient as science, but in the twentieth century, with the discovery of the quantum theory and the theory of relativity, and their application to nuclear physics, cosmological theories have been given a certain degree of precision. Cosmology, the study of the origin and evolution of the universe, is a hybrid branch of physics and astronomy, and it has interested a wide variety of scientists and science writers. The best-known prewar writers on the subject were Sir Arthur Eddington and Sir James Jeans, English astronomers who combined exceptional literary gifts with great scientific achievement. The most interesting popular postwar writing on cosmology has been done by three English astrophysicists—Hermann Bondi, Thomas Gold, and Fred Hoyle—and by the brilliant and delightful Russian-born American physicist George Gamow.

Since 1940, Professor Gamow, who is now in the Physics Department of the University of Colorado, has been writing and rewriting, as well as illustrating, a trilogy of popular books dealing with cosmology. *The Birth and Death of the Sun,* first published in 1940 (and soon to appear in a rejuvenated version as *A Star Called the Sun*), deals with the physics of the sun. *The Creation of the Universe,* which first appeared in 1952 and was revised in 1961, deals with cosmological theory, and Professor Gamow's latest book, *A Planet Called Earth* (Viking), a new version of his *Biography of the Earth,* deals with the evolution of the earth and the moon. All of the books exhibit his special blend of serious science and lively humor. He is a splendid cartoonist, and part of the fun of his books is looking at his illustrations.

At present there are two important rival cosmologies—the Big Bang (or Big Squeeze) theory and the Steady State theory. The Big Bang theory, of which Gamow is an enthusiastic supporter, holds that the universe has developed out of an enormous explosion that took place a few billions of years ago. The Steady State theory—maintained by, among others, Bondi, Gold, and Hoyle—holds, in the words of Bondi, that "on the large scale [the universe is] not only uniform in space, as other theories assume, but also unchanging in time." In particular, they maintain that there is no epoch in the history of the universe in which there could have been such an explosion. The two points of view are diametrically opposed. But each of them must come to terms with the same set of facts. One of the most important of these is that the universe—at least that portion that is visible to us—is expanding. This striking, and fundamental, fact is deduced in part from the discovery, by the American astronomer Edwin Hubble, in 1925, that the Andromeda Nebula, which was until then thought to be part of our own Milky Way galaxy, was really a distant and separate galaxy in itself. (Although Andromeda is usually known as the Andromeda Nebula, it is actually a galaxy. A nebula is an interstellar gas cloud; a galaxy is a collection of stars and, perhaps, nebulae. Astronomers often tend to use the two terms interchangeably.) Moreover, as Professor Gamow says, in *The Creation of the Universe,* "It had been known for some time that the spectral lines in the light emitted by spiral nebulae [i.e., galaxies such as the Andromeda] show a shift toward the red end of the spectrum"—a shift indicating that the source of the light is moving away from the observer. (An analogous phenomenon is the lowering of the pitch of a locomotive whistle as a train moves away from us.) Gamow adds:

> As long as these objects [the galaxies] were believed to be members of our stellar system, one had to conclude that they had some peculiar motion among the stars, being driven from the central regions of the Milky Way toward its periphery. With the new broadening of horizons a completely new picture emerged: *the entire space of the universe, populated by billions of galaxies, is in a state of rapid expansion, with all its members flying away from one another at high speed.*

That the universe is expanding both the Big Bang and the Steady State people and essentially all other astronomers and physicists agree, but there are differences of opinion about the conclusions to be drawn. The Big Bang cosmologists believe that if the universe is now expanding, it must at one time have been contracted. They maintain that after the explosion took place, the compressed matter began to expand, and expanded until the universe reached its present state. In fact, some of them think that the universe may undergo expansion and contraction every few billion years; "The Big Squeeze that took place in the early history of our universe was the result," says Gamow, "of a collapse which took place at a still earlier era, and the present expansion is simply an 'elastic' rebound which started as soon as the maximum permissible squeezing density was reached."

Bondi and Gold and Hoyle feel there is no certain astronomical evidence of such an explosion. They maintain that observation shows the numbers and types of stars and stellar galaxies are about the same in any region of the cosmos that is within the limits of visibility, no matter how distant. This last point is especially significant; the most distant objects are necessarily very old, for the light we see from them has been travelling toward us for many millennia. So if there was any residual effect of that explosion it should be observable in the distant galaxies. It may be that the very distant quasi-stellar sources—quasars—are residues of such an explosion. What these Steady State theorists consider to be the uniformity of the observable cosmos is elevated by them to a principle—the Perfect Cosmological Principle—stating, in essence, that the cosmos is unchanging. They argue that if matter is disappearing beyond the horizon (because the universe is expanding), then something must replenish the matter that is disappearing in the expansion. Otherwise the amount of matter visible to us would steadily decrease, and that would destroy the assumption of the Steady State. These theorists therefore suppose that throughout the universe matter is being continuously and spontaneously created, and from this created matter new galaxies are being formed to replace the ones that are disappearing. On a percentage basis, the quantity of newly created matter is small; the amount of new matter required per year to keep the Steady State would be about the equivalent of a single atom in each volume the size of a twenty-story building. This amount of matter is so small that no laboratory could directly detect its presence. In a fascinating book, *The Nature of the Universe*, published by Mentor, Hoyle describes what would happen if one could make a film of the expansion of the universe and run it backward—assuming that the Steady State theory, with the continuous creation of matter, is right:

> New galaxies would appear at the outer fringes of our picture as faint objects that come gradually closer to us. . . . The galaxies would come closer and closer to us until they evaporated before our eyes. First the stars of the galaxy would evaporate back into the gas from which they were formed. Then the gas in the galaxy would evaporate back into the general background from which it had condensed. The background material itself would stay at constant density, not through matter being created, but through matter disappearing. How far could we run our hypothetical film back into the past? Again according to the theory, forever. After we had run backward for about 5,000,000,000 years, our own Galaxy itself would disappear before our eyes. But although important details like this would no doubt be of great interest to us there would again be a general sameness about the whole proceeding. Whether we run the film backward or forward the large-scale features of the Universe remain unchanged.

Each of these theories has its loyal and outspoken adherents, and the lively debate that goes on between the two groups has been a source of great stimulation to astronomers and physicists in general. In view of the recent evidence on quasars many scientists, including Hoyle, have now abandoned the Steady State theory. But historical experience has shown that cosmological theories, like metaphysical ones, constantly recur in new forms.

Gamow's *A Planet Called Earth* deals with the origin and development of our world. It is probable that the planets were formed at a time, five billion years ago, when the sun was surrounded by a rapidly whirling disc of gas. (Astronomers have observed other stars, apparently in about the state of development that the sun was in then, that are surrounded by similar discs.) The planetary matter presumably condensed out of this gas. As the earth cooled, a solid rock crust was formed, and Gamow notes, "It is most likely that a heavy iron ore core occupies about one-eighth of the entire volume of our planet and accounts for about one-quarter of its total weight."

Life on the earth derives all of its energy from the sun. The sun's energy is the result of a continuing thermo-nuclear burning process in which hydrogen is fused into helium—an activity accompanied by the release of a good deal of energy. (Helium, as its name suggests, was first discovered in the spectral analysis of sunlight, by the English astronomer Joseph Lockyer, in 1868, twenty-seven years before it was found on the earth.) The sun will continue to produce light and heat at its present rate as long as its supply of hydrogen holds out. Gamow says, "One calculates that the total life span of the Sun must be about ten billion years. Since, according to astronomical and geological data, our Sun is about five billion years old, we conclude that it still has another five billion years to live, during which time it will remain in approximately the same state as today."

Afterward? Gamow goes on:

When, in that distant future, the hydrogen content in the sun's core is completely exhausted, very important changes are expected to take place in its structure. With all internal fuel burned, "nuclear fire" will spread out into outer layers which still have untouched amounts of hydrogen. Since that process will bring closer to the surface of the Sun the region where thermonuclear reactions take place, the body of the sun will begin to expand and the amount of light and heat radiated by it will steadily increase.

This means that the sun will become gradually (about 0.0002°F. every century) hotter before it finally uses up all of its nuclear fuel. Gamow asks:

Do we have observational evidence supporting this, at first glance, fantastic prediction? Yes, and plenty of it. As we have mentioned, stars bigger and brighter than our Sun evolve considerably faster and, while ours is still a middle-aged fellow, these stars have already reached their doomsday and are in various stages of dying. Stars known from antiquity under such names as Antares and Betelgeuse shine in the night sky like bright-red lanterns and are classified by modern astronomers as *red giants*. Recent studies have shown that, although these stars are only several times more massive than our Sun, their diameters exceed that of the Sun by a factor of several hundred. There is no doubt that the red giants are stars in which "nuclear fire" is spreading out from their center, blowing them into giant balls of red-hot rarefied gas. And there is every certainty that our Sun will come to that stage five billion years from now.

For those who like to think of the prospects for the human race in terms of billions of years, the outlook is not cheering—unless we can escape to the outer planets when the sun heats up, and then to other stellar systems when our own star burns out completely. Gamow remarks:

The poet Robert Frost wrote

Some say the world will end in fire,
Some say in ice. . . .

Both these forecasts are certainly correct!

A Planet Called Earth, like the rest of Gamow's books, is full of absorbing scientific facts and ideas. Many of the present generation of scientists (myself included) got their first taste of the endless possibilities for scientific speculation by reading his popular books. They remain a challenge and a delight.

Part II

SCIENCE AND SOCIETY : PAST AND PRESENT

1

The Discovery
of History :
The Theory of Evolution

○
○
○

A WONDERFUL story that involves the late Morris
Cohen, who taught philosophy and philosophy of
science at City College, illustrates the elusive, almost
absurd quality many of the most profound philosophical questions seem to have. During one of his lectures
a student raised his hand and asked, rather belliger-
ently, "Professor Cohen, how do I know that I exist?"
Cohen replied, "And who is asking?" In *The Discovery of Time,* an absorbing study (Harper & Row)
of the history and philosophy of science, the British
historian of science Stephen Toulmin and his wife,

June Goodfield, consider a philosophical question that at first sight seems equally absurd: How can we be sure that the world has had a history? And what elements of our present experience impel us to conclude that certain phenomena reflect events from the distant past? And how did the human race come to discover its place in time?

The Toulmins underline the logical issue involved:

> Let us merely suppose (to borrow an argument from Bertrand Russell) that the whole universe was created five minutes before the present moment, with all the things it contains—our memories included—in their present places and conditions; then every belief about past events remoter than five minutes would be mistaken. If our present evidence is taken in isolation, this may in fact be the case. Our beliefs about Queen Victoria, Julius Caesar, Neanderthal Man, and the Ice Ages may be deeply rooted but, compared with our beliefs about present and immediate events, their basis in experience is slender and indirect. Stated in this form, the moral of Russell's skeptical argument may appear somewhat trite; yet his point is surely made. Our knowledge of happenings in the distant past, especially from prehistoric times, is certainly *inferential*. We were not there ourselves, nor do we have the testimony of eyewitnesses. Our beliefs come to us, rather, as the conclusions of reasoned arguments —chains of inference linking data in the present back to the epochs and events in question.

Once one begins to think about it, one realizes that the simplest of such inferences, inferences that we take almost for granted, are reflections of scientific and philosophical points of view that have been acquired over centuries. The very nature of historical discovery changes with the development of science. An obvious example is the use of the lifetimes of radioactive isotopes to date ancient objects—a process inconceivable until these isotopes were analyzed, rather recently, by physicists and chemists. An even more striking example is astronomy, which became a historical science the instant it was realized that it takes a small but nevertheless non-zero amount of time for light to travel between even the closest two points. Thus the observation of distant astronomical phenomena becomes a chronology of events in the remote past. These are examples of how scientific discovery can enlarge historical awareness. The best way to untangle the ideas that have gone into the making of historical deduction is to trace the steps that led to their eventual acceptance as common belief. This is what the Toulmins attempt to do. They restrict themselves to the consideration of Western civilization, and it would be fascinating to have a companion book about the development of the Oriental sense of time and history, which was certainly completely different, since Oriental science developed in such a different way. The Toulmins deal with the major steps that led to Darwinian evolution (biological history), the study of the earth for clues to the past (geological history), and the development of cosmology (astronomical history). *The Discovery of Time* is not a large book—some three hundred pages—and specialists in various fields will no doubt disagree about the selection and interpretation of the material in it. But it is in my opinion a brilliant conception, remarkably well realized in view of the massive amount of material in the many fields it deals with.

The Toulmins begin their study with the Greeks and certain pre-Greeks. In reading early Greek science, one is at once taken by the modernity of the questions raised and by the fantastic naïveté, in so many instances, of the answers. The Greeks believed that the complexity of the observable universe could be explained if one assumed that there existed a substratum of physical phenomena, not directly observable, which obeyed simple laws and from which the behavior of the observed phenomena could be deduced. This is the fundamental idea of the Greek atomistic philosophy attributed to Democritus. Everything is made up out of basic, indivisible units—atoms—which obey simple laws. But the atoms of Democritus, which were presumed to have specific shapes (bitter substances were, for example, supposedly composed of jagged atoms) and other tangible properties, have nothing in common with the atoms of modern physics, which cannot be properly described at all in non-technical language. (They have no shape in the conventional sense and, unlike the Greek ones, *are* divisible.) Yet the underlying philosophical motivation of his atomic theory and our own is the same: a simple description of observed phenomena. The Greeks felt that the living beings and creatures they observed must have had a historical origin. But their notion of what it was seems completely naïve. Anaximander, who lived in Miletos in the sixth century B.C., believed that life originated in the water. (Miletos was on the Ionian coast, and its life was dominated by the sea.) This is a not unreasonable notion, and, in fact, modern biologists hold a similar one. But here is what he wrote about it:

> The first animals were generated in the moisture, and were enclosed within spiny barks. As they grew older, they migrated onto the drier land; and, once their bark was split and shed, they survived for a short time in the new mode of existence. Man to begin with was generated from living things of another kind, since, whereas others can quickly hunt for their own food, men alone require prolonged nursing. If he had been like that in the beginning he would never have survived. . . . Thus men were formed within these [fishlike] creatures and remained within them like embryos until they had reached maturity. Then at last the creatures burst open, and out of them came men and women who were already able to fend for themselves.

In Anaximander and the later Greek writers on evolution one detects a keen awareness of what needed to be explained, and often—as in Aristotle—a marvellous precision of observation of biological phenomena. What is missing is any detailed account of the mechanism that, step by step, brought about the evolution of a species. The Greeks were surrounded by many of the phenomena that we now realize are hints about the way in which the evolutionary process unfolds. But in the absence of a detailed conceptual scheme, a fossil embedded in a rock can easily be interpreted as something from the recent past instead of as a clue to the state of the world eons earlier.

The Old Testament attempts to provide an evolutionary timetable, and a mechanism, an omnipotent God, who has created the world in six days. Even the most devout readers of the Bible are now for the most part willing to agree that this timetable is allegorical. Indeed, by the time Christ was born, students of the Biblical version of the Creation were already emphasizing its allegorical character. The Toulmins quote the writings of Philo, an Alexandrian Jew born about 20 B.C., who made an extremely subtle investigation of the Biblical allegory:

> "And on the sixth day God finished his work which he had made." It would be a mark of great naïveté to think that the World was created either in six days, or indeed in Time at all; for Time is nothing but the sequence of days and nights, and these things are necessarily connected with the motion of the Sun above and below the Earth. But the Sun is part of the heavens, so that Time must be recognized as something posterior to the World. So it would be correct to say not that the World was created in Time, but that Time owed its existence to the World. For it is the motion of the heavens that determines the nature of Time.

As Christianity spread, the allegory came to be interpreted in terms that were more and more precise, and the Bible was scrutinized for specific indications of the timetable of Creation. The Toulmins trace the origins of the notion, almost universally accepted in Europe well into the seventeenth century, that the Creation took place in 4000 B.C. (4004 B.C., according to Archbishop Ussher). In the fourth century A.D., Eusebius made a count of the number of generations from Adam to the Flood and from the Flood to Abraham, and his figures sum up to, respectively, 1656 years and 292 years. A verse from the Psalms— "A thousand years in Thy sight are but as yesterday"—was interpreted to mean that the "six days of Creation" implied that the life span of the world was six thousand years. Luther, who fixed the date of Creation at 4000 B.C., declared that the moral state of the world had decayed to such an extent that it would not survive even to the year 2000. It was commonly accepted, in the seventeenth century, that the end of the world was in sight. In about 1630, Sir Thomas Browne wrote, "The World grows near its End. . . . The last and general fever may as naturally destroy it before six thousand, as me before forty," and then, "In seventy or eighty years a man may have a deep Gust of the World . . . a curt Epitome of the whole course thereof."

In the seventeenth century, the age of Newton, many of the ideas of modern science were given their present form. Newton represents the split between the scientific and religious points of view that the literal interpretation of the Bible inevitably led to. While he was publicly carrying out his investigations in physics, he was secretly working on alchemy and Biblical chronology. In fact, he attempted, since he believed that the earth had once been molten, to estimate how long it would take a ball of molten iron the size of the earth to cool, and concluded that fifty thousand years would be required to cool it to the temperature of the earth, but he decided that he could not accept this figure because it contradicted the Scriptural timetable. Descartes had already devised an explanation of how the planets could have originated without Divine implementation; he suggested that the earth might have originally been a small star that cooled and drifted into an orbit around the sun. He never made completely unambiguous what his attitude toward his speculations was, probably because he feared censure, but he certainly encouraged the idea that a more precise account of the evolutionary process than the Bible offered was possible. And, needless to say, scientists who came after Newton made use of Newtonian mechanics in their accounts of the phenomenon even though they might conflict with religious doctrines.

By the seventeenth century, both the earth and the stars were being studied for historical evidence. It was known that stars appeared and disappeared; novae and supernovae had burst into view and then faded. These observations cast doubt on the common belief, inherited from the Greeks, that the stars were immutable. Bernard de Fontenelle, a follower of Descartes, wrote an immensely popular cosmology that dealt with stellar evolution—*Conversations on the Plurality of Worlds*. His "conversations," along the lines of the great dialogues of Galileo, were held with an imaginary marquise, as they walked up and down in her gardens. He told her that there was an indefinite number of stars and thus an indefinite number of planetary systems. Finally, they discussed the creation and destruction of the stars:

> "What!" cried she, "are Suns extinguished?"
> "Yes, without doubt," answered I. "The Ancients saw in the Heavens certain Stars which have disappeared, and never been seen since." . . .
> "You make me tremble," said the Marquise. "Now that I know the consequences that may happen from the Sun's paleness, I believe, that instead of going in the morning to see in my glass, whether I am pale or not, I shall go and look in the Heavens to see if the Sun is pale."
> "Ah! Madam," answered I, "be assured, it will require a long time to ruin a World."
> "But it may in the end," replied she. "It only requires time."

The seventeenth-century English scientist Robert Hooke and the Danish scientist Steno, or Niels Stensen, both came to the correct conclusion that the fossil remains often found far inland represent animal life from ancient vanished seas. Hooke, saying that "a great part of the Surface of the Earth hath been since the Creation transformed and made of another Nature; namely, many Parts which have been Sea are now Land; and diverse other Parts are now Sea which were once a firm Land; Mountains have been turned into Plains and Plains into Mountains and the like," reconciled his discoveries with the Biblical account by deciding that these great transformations were a product of the Flood. But by the eighteenth century there had accumulated so much evidence that the cosmos had a history extending beyond the allotted six thousand years that many cosmologists gave up trying to reconcile their ideas with a strict interpretation of the Scriptures, although any scientific discovery could be reconciled with the Bible by postulating an indefinite number of Divine interventions or "accidents." The acceptance of "accidents" was, however, contrary to the mechanistic attitude that science had acquired since Newton, who was not a mechanist in this sense, since he was quite willing to admit the intervention of God as the explanation of the incompletenesses that he felt were inherent in his physics. The reigning mechanistic attitude was later characterized by the French mathematical physicist Laplace, who claimed that if he was given the positions and momenta of all the particles in the universe at a certain time he could, by applying Newton's mechanics, calculate the entire future evolution of the universe. Napoleon is said to have asked Laplace what the role of God was in his theory, to which Laplace responded, "Sire, I have no need of that hypothesis." The Scriptures represented the popular opinion of how the universe had evolved, but, as has happened time and again, when that opinion is no longer compatible with a new scientific discovery it is abandoned. In a few generations, the new scientific discoveries become assimilated into common thought, and the fact that their discovery brought about the often traumatic breakdown of previously accepted ideas is largely forgotten.

The Toulmins regard the German philosopher and cosmologist Immanuel Kant and the French polyhistor Georges Louis Leclerc, Comte de Buffon, as the two principal figures in the eighteenth-century change of attitude toward the Biblical timetable. Kant lived and worked in Prussia, and as long as he was under the protection of Frederick the Great he could publish his ideas without fear of censure. After Frederick's death, he was forced to retract many of his cosmological views. As a philosopher, he was concerned with the problem of trying to determine just how much scientific theory is derived by us from experience and how much is, in the phrase of Einstein, "free creation." If we ever establish communication with intelligent extraterrestrial beings, will we discover they have arrived at the same set of scientific laws we have, or—influenced by their environment and perhaps even a different brain structure—will they have created a completely different set of laws, which we will hardly be able to comprehend? But Kant was also a cosmologist. He guessed, correctly, that the nebular patches in the Milky Way are distant galaxies held together as a unit by the mutual gravitational attractions of the stars that compose them, and he decided that the galaxies were undergoing a constant process of evolution—a process that would take millennia. He wrote, with a great sense of poetry:

There had perhaps flown past a series of millions of years and centuries, before the sphere of ordered Nature, in which we find ourselves, attained to the perfection which is now embodied in it; and perhaps as long a period will pass before Nature will take another step as far in chaos. But the sphere of developed Nature is incessantly engaged in extending itself. Creation is not the work of a moment. . . . Millions and whole myriads of millions of centuries will flow on, during which always new Worlds and systems of Worlds will be formed, one after another, in the distant regions away from the Centre of Nature, and will attain to perfection. . . . This infinity and the future succession of time, by which Eternity is unexhausted, will entirely animate the whole range of Space to which God is present, and will gradually put it into that regular order which is conformable to the excellence of His plan. . . . The Creation is never finished or complete. It has indeed once begun, but it will never cease. It is always busy producing new scenes of nature, new objects, and new Worlds. The work which it brings about has a relationship to the time which it extends upon it. It needs nothing less than an Eternity to animate the whole boundless range of the infinite extension of Space with Worlds, without number and without end.

In Kant there is theology, but there is, above all, a dramatic rejection of the Scriptural chronology.

Buffon was interested in all the sciences, especially as they illuminated history. He repeated Newton's effort to calculate the time required to cool the earth and concluded that it would have "cooled to the present temperature" in 74,832 years, "approximately." He felt that the geology of the earth indicated that it had once been a molten mass, that it had solidified, and that it then had been largely covered by water, which—when it receded—had bared the land out of which the present continental structures were formed, and he attempted to determine how long each of these states had lasted. His findings were published in a many-volumed *Natural History*. But Buffon was mainly interested in giving an account of the origins and the development of life. His conception of "evolution" is not the present one. Yet what he had to say was of importance in creating the climate of thought that produced Darwin's subsequent contributions to science and to history.

Evolution, as the term is used today, refers to the way in which living species transform in the course of time. Darwin's theory has now passed from speculation to common acceptance and, like many accepted dogmas, it is widely misunderstood. The usual cliché about evolution is that it concerns the descent of man from some lower form of animal life—perhaps an ape. But man has in fact "ascended," because of his increasing complexity, from his forebears. His ancestors—who were certainly not apes—were simpler versions of the present creature, as the ancestors of all the animals that exist today were simpler. It is precisely in understanding the increase in complexity of evolving species that Darwin progressed beyond his predecessors. When Buffon and his contemporaries, among them the great Swedish biologist Linnaeus, began their investigations, the general belief was that all the species, in both their simplest and their most complicated versions, had been created at once and remained linked together, immutable, in what was described as the Great Chain of Being. Buffon and Linnaeus came to reject this idea in favor of a less static although still incorrect description of species. Linnaeus observed the phenomenon of mutation in plants by which a characteristic of a species abruptly changes, yet the mechanism by which the change was brought about was beyond him. Buffon imagined that life began spontaneously at a time when the earth was much warmer, but he assumed, incorrectly, that the species we know sprang into existence in almost their present form and that the poorer strains simply died off, so that the present species arose simply by a process of subtraction from the original population. The Toulmins note, "What neither of the great eighteenth-century naturalists imagined was that a primitive stock of extremely simple organisms could give rise progressively to a later population of more complex ones." Darwin showed, in a qualitative way, how this happened, and modern genetics has revealed the quantitative mechanisms.

The Toulmins' chapter on Darwin is a delightful one. They describe his all but totally successful resistance to formal education when he was a young man (in this he closely resembles Einstein) :

> Darwin began and remained, by both experience and temperament, a gentleman-naturalist. The accepted channels of entry into scientific work were twofold: mathematics, which included the physical sciences, and medicine, which embraced also physiology. Darwin mastered neither. The love of the countryside which he inherited from his mother and developed in his youth never left him; the standard classical education bored him; the dissecting theatres at Edinburgh turned his stomach. Putting aside all idea of following his father and grandfather into medicine, he inclined towards Holy Orders, and spent some years ostensibly training for the ministry. Yet, once he had got to Cambridge, his conversations with local naturalists and scientists distracted him from theology as effectively as they had done from medicine earlier, and much of the time that remained he passed on horseback.

Despairing of everything else, his father allowed Darwin, on the advice of a teacher, to sail as chief naturalist on the naval survey ship *Beagle,* which was making a five-year voyage to South America. Darwin took with him *Principles of Geology,* by Charles Lyell, which he was advised to read "but," he later wrote, "on no account to accept the views therein advocated." Yet the book was probably the crucial element in Darwin's intellectual development. Lyell was the leading advocate, in the early nineteenth century, of the Uniformitarian view of geology, whose fundamental principle was that "all former changes of the organic and inorganic creation are referable to one uninterrupted succession of physical events, governed by the laws of Nature now in operation." This was in direct opposition to the view, then held by Darwin and many geologists, that the present state of the earth could have been accomplished only by a series of violent catastrophes invoked by the will of the Divinity. Lyell believed that the world was gradually transforming because of the action of natural forces—a transformation that had gone on for eons and was still continuing. By the time the *Beagle* reached South America, Darwin had become a thoroughgoing Uniformitarian. Indeed, he began to search for evidence of such natural transformations in the flora and fauna of the lands he was seeing for the first time. He witnessed an earthquake in Chile, during which the foothills of the Andes were raised some dozens of feet, and he took this as evidence that mountains could be built and destroyed, without Divine aid, by the forces that were currently operating in the earth. He also noted the great ability of species to adapt to their environment. Birds had wings when it was useful for them to fly, and flippers, like the penguins, when it was not. But his greatest discovery was made in the Galapagos, a group of small, close-together islands six hundred miles off the coast of Ecuador. At first Darwin thought that the animals—mostly turtles and finches—on each of these islands were identical, but it soon became apparent to him that they were not. He was haunted by this observation. How could such a variation of species have occurred in these separated environments? He spent the rest of his life considering this question. The *Beagle* returned to England in 1836, and it was in October of 1838 that Darwin read, in Malthus' *Essay on the Principle of Population*, the argument that anything done to improve social welfare, such as reducing infant mortality, will usually increase the reproductive ability of the population. Lyell had maintained that the struggle for existence among plants, animals, and men would kill off the weaker ones. But this was a process of winnowing away species, while Darwin was searching for a process that generated new species. Malthus supplied the hint. If, Darwin decided, by some mechanism of mutation a new species was produced whose descendants could more readily reproduce themselves, the new variety would soon dominate the population. Darwin never understood how the mutations came about, and it has been left to modern genetics to uncover the underlying laws of heredity and mutation. But he did see that the key to the whole matter was in the production of variants that in a given environment breed more readily than their predecessors. It is "survival of the fittest," but of the fittest to reproduce.

It was not until 1859 that the first edition of *The Origin of Species* was sent to the printer. Darwin spent years gathering evidence and marshalling his arguments. He knew that they would arouse a violent reaction in religious people, who would see in his working out of evolution a denial of the force of God in determining the formation of man. (This argument is still used in the United States by fundamentalists who want to suppress the teaching of evolution to schoolchildren.) The Toulmins give an excellent summary of this reaction, and they sort out the objections that were based on pure prejudice from those that had scientific merit and that have been resolved only in the twentieth century, with the aid of scientific information unavailable to Darwin.

The Toulmins conclude their volume by noting that the process of expanding historical inference through scientific discovery is still an extremely active one, especially in astronomy. The huge astronomical telescopes—both those that detect light and those that detect radio signals—probe deeper and deeper into the remote stretches of the universe, or farther and farther back in time. Recently, new astronomical objects—quasars (quasi-stellar sources) have been found—objects that are capable of emitting energy in quantities never before observed and by mechanisms that are still not well understood. These objects, being so far away, are souvenirs from an all but unimaginably remote past, and their discovery indicates, perhaps, that the universe was completely different in the past. Perhaps it began with a giant explosion. The quasars may represent the debris. It is even possible that the universe is undergoing cyclic expansion and contraction—giant explosions, followed perhaps by a reënactment of the whole story of Creation. It is likely that these speculations will seem as naïve to future generations as the "spiny-barked" animals of Anaximander seem to us. But they raise, at least to the imagination, the prospect of the existence of future generations hidden entirely from us and unaware of our existence, working out their destinies, perhaps better than we seem to be able to work out ours, only to be eclipsed and forgotten by generations still farther in the future. As to the meaning of the whole evolutionary drama? One can lament, with Tennyson:

> O life as futile, then, as frail!
> O for thy voice to soothe and bless!
> What hope of answer, or redress?
> Behind the veil, behind the veil.

2

Written in the Stars :
The Rise of Science

°
°
°

The Scientific Renaissance, by Professor Marie Boas, of the University of Indiana (Harper), is part of an eight-volume series (hers is the first portion to be published) that will trace the rise of modern science in the West. Several historians of science are contributing to the project (the series is being edited by Professor A. Rupert Hall, also of the University of Indiana), and if the rest of the studies are as good as this one, they will make a major contribution to the history of ideas.

The period Professor Boas has chosen to write about begins in 1450 and ends with the trial of Galileo, in 1633. It was a fascinating era. Western European scholars were then in the process of rediscovering the Greeks. European science had not yet split away from the humanities, and the job of the scientific scholar was primarily the translation and interpretation of Greek thinkers like Aristotle and Ptolemy. Such experimental research as there was had for its original aim the verification of discoveries already made by the Greeks. It was the realization that many of these discoveries were inaccurate that set modern science on its way to becoming an independent discipline: "Endeavoring to see in nature what Greek writers had declared to be there, European scientists slowly came to see what really was there," says Professor Boas.

The best illustration of this process is probably the development of modern astronomy, and a large fraction of *The Scientific Renaissance* is devoted to this subject. The scholar of the period had inherited a complete astronomical world from the Greeks. It consisted in part of Plato's dictum that the motion of celestial objects must be "perfect" and therefore, in his view, uniform and circular; in part of Aristotle's idea that heavenly bodies could not be made of the stuff of which terrestrial objects were made—supposedly earth, air, fire, and water—and therefore must follow unique laws. Aristotle felt that the stars, the planets, and the moon must be made of a fifth essence—*quinta essentia*. (This is the origin of the word "quintessence.") The Greeks made astronomical observations, too. They had studied the trajectories of some of the planets and discovered that these planetary motions seemed far from regular in the Platonic sense. In fact, from time to time the planets even appeared to reverse direction and go backward, a phenomenon known as "retrograde motion." The key problem of Greek astronomy was the reconciliation of these imperfections in planetary motion with the Platonic axiom that these motions must be uniform and circular.

This problem was most effectively dealt with by Ptolemy, a Graeco-Alexandrian astronomer who flourished about 150 A.D. He assumed that the planets move in small circles (that is, epicycles) whose centers move in larger circles around the earth. The earth itself sits at rest at the center of the universe. Matching the observed planetary orbits often required the use of more than one epicycle, and the astronomical system that Ptolemy finally devised in his celebrated *Almagest,* one of the great scientific classics (in which epicycles are piled upon epicycles), is like a gigantic Rube Goldberg fantasy. However, by 1496, when Nicholas Copernicus was finishing his studies at the University of Cracow, in Poland, astronomers had begun to realize that the *Almagest,* despite its enormous value, was not the ultimate word in astronomical theory. But it was more in keeping with the humanistic temper of a fifteenth-century astronomer to consult other Greeks for guidance than to consult the stars themselves. Professor Boas remarks, "When Ptolemy failed to give the required assistance, it seemed reasonable that the next step should be the examination of those notions of earlier Greek astronomy which the Ptolemaic system had in its day rendered obsolete." The way in which Copernicus himself was led to the hypothesis that the sun, not the earth, is the focus of the planetary orbits is obscure, but it is fairly clear that he felt that he was simply reviving and amplifying Pythagorean doctrines. (Professor Boas is led to wonder why Copernicus did not instead feel in alliance with Aristarchus of Samos, the Greek astronomer who was the first to postulate that the earth made both a yearly revolution about the sun and a daily rotation around the polar axis.) The Copernican system was a tremendous simplification. For example, it offered a ready explanation of the phenomenon of retrograde motion without using epicycles. In the Copernican system, all the planets move in the same direction around the sun, but at different speeds. When the earth passes a planet like Jupiter (Jupiter, which has a larger orbit than our own, takes nearly twelve years to circle the sun), the planet will for a short time *appear* to be moving backward when viewed against the fixed stars. However, the idea that the earth itself was in motion made people profoundly uneasy; why aren't birds left behind in space when they fly up off the ground? And throughout the sixteenth century a debate raged between the Copernicans and the anti-Copernicans. Professor Boas quotes Donne's superb poetic statement of the anti-Copernican point of view, written as late as 1611:

And New Philosophy calls all in doubt,
The Element of fire is quite put out;
The Sun is lost, and th' Earth, and no man's wit
Can well direct him where to look for it.
And freely men confess that this world's spent,
When in the Planets, and the Firmament
They seek so many new; then see that this
Is crumbled out again to his Atomies.
'Tis all in pieces, all coherence gone;
All just supply, and all Relation.

She goes on to comment, "If this was the way in which the Copernican doctrine affected poets, no wonder they rejected it. Especially in an age when all was doubt, decay, and dissension in the religious and political spheres in any case. Why should they welcome chaos among the stars as well?" While the debate helped spread knowledge of the Copernican doctrine, it did not do much to secure its acceptance by the scholarly community.

Indeed, the next major advance in astronomy was the contribution of an anti-Copernican, the Danish Tycho Brahe (1546–1601), who had been given the island of Hveen by the King of Denmark. Tycho was fundamentally an experimenter, and his enduring contributions to astronomy were the painstaking studies of planetary orbits that he made in the observatory erected upon the island.

These studies were extremely accurate, considering that they were accomplished with the naked eye. Tycho had his own astronomical system, now largely a historical curiosity. He did, nevertheless, offer the remarkable supposition that comets might not be subject to the Platonic laws of planetary motion and might even follow non-circular orbits. "For it is probable that Comets, just as they do not have bodies as perfect and perfectly made for perpetual duration as do the other stars which are as old as the beginning of the World, so also they do not observe so absolute and constant a course of equality in their revolutions—it is as though they mimic to a certain extent the uniform regularity of the Planets, but do not follow it altogether."

This deceptively simple idea was the forerunner of one of the greatest discoveries in the history of science—the discovery, by Johannes Kepler, the German astronomer (1571–1630), that *planets* as well do not follow circular orbits but have elliptical ones. Kepler was an amazing man, part scientist and part mystic, and his mystical beliefs were as strange as those of an astrologer. Indeed, like other astronomers of the time, he devoted a certain amount of time to astrology. But he was an important scientist because he insisted upon correlating the results of his calculations of planetary orbits with the exacting astronomical data assembled by Tycho, who had been put in charge of an observatory near Prague and had asked Kepler to become his assistant. The odd combination of empiricism and mysticism that characterizes Kepler reminds one of Einstein, who was guided throughout his life by a deep mystic faith in the simplicity and rationality of nature: *"Raffiniert ist der Herrgott,"* he once said, *"aber boshaft ist Er nicht."* ("God is sophisticated, but not malicious.") Professor Boas remarks, "Of all the astronomers of the post-Copernican period, the most difficult to appraise and appreciate is Johannes Kepler. Not a great observational astronomer—poor eyesight would have hindered him had he tried to be one—he yet insisted upon closer agreement between theory and observation than any astronomer before his time. A passionately devoted mathematical computer, and an extreme neo-Platonist mathematical mystic, he cared only for those mathematical representations of the heavens which offered the possibility of interpretation in physical terms. Mystic and rational, mathematical and quasi-empirical, he constantly transformed apparently metaphysical nonsense into astronomical relationships of the utmost importance and originality." The exactness of Tycho's observations spurred Kepler to more and more precise calculations of his own, and finally he decided that the planetary trajectories were actually elliptical, not circular at all.

By the time Kepler was through with planetary astronomy, he had discovered most of the major empirical laws of planetary motion, and the stage was set for Newton, who synthesized all the Keplerian discoveries in a single law of universal gravitation. Between Kepler and Newton there was, of course, Galileo (1564–1642), who did not make major contributions to astronomical theory but who argued in favor of the Copernican doctrine so effectively that it became accepted fact. (Galileo was a born polemicist; he had a splendid literary style and he loved a good intellectual fight.) He did make a major contribution to the science of astronomy when, in 1609, he became the first astronomer to produce a workable telescope. With it he discovered that Venus has phases like the moon, that Jupiter has moons like the earth, and—still worse—that the moon itself, again like the earth, is an imperfect, pockmarked body. All this demolished the Aristotelian-Platonic theory that the physics and chemistry of celestial objects differ from the physics and chemistry of terrestrial ones.

In a sense, the invention of the telescope and the microscope marks the split between the sciences and the humanities. Greek scientific speculations were based on common-sense notions and the most primitive scientific instruments. A biologist with a microscope has an incalculable advantage over one without any. Professor Boas comments, "One of the most noticeable changes in the period between 1450 and 1630 is the change in attitude towards the ancients. In 1450 men attempted no more than comprehension of what the ancients had discovered, certain that this was the most that could be known; by 1630 things had so changed that the works of the ancients were available in various vernacular translations, and even the barely literate who read these versions were aware that the authority of the Greek and Roman past was under attack. Ancient learning was increasingly old-fashioned; what had been new in 1500 was outmoded by 1600, so relatively rapidly had ideas changed. In 1536, Petrus Ramus as a wildly daring young man could, perhaps prematurely, publicly defend the thesis that everything Aristotle had taught was false; forty years later, Aristotle's philosophy was still a university subject, but bright undergraduates like Francis Bacon were already saying that the study of Aristotle was a great waste of time. By 1630 it was obvious that the way was clear for a new physics, as it was for a new cosmology; only Aristotle's zoological work still, precariously, survived."

It was a restless and brilliant age, and Professor Boas has written a lucid and delightful book about it—a book that helps construct a historical platform from which we may try to contemplate our own restless and richly scientific epoch.

3

To Find a Planet :
On Neptune

For most scientists, Newtonian mechanics and the law of universal gravitation are a model of what a scientific theory should be. Employing a few general principles of mechanics and the postulate that all the massive bodies in the universe attract each other by a force of universal strength that diminishes as the square of the distance between them increases, Newton was able to account for the known regularities in the motion of planets, as well as of the moon. To the philosophers and scientists who understood his theory, the workings of the solar system came to seem like the machinery of a giant clock. Newton did not claim to have provided a metaphysical explanation of the laws of physics, and he once dismissed such metaphysical speculation with the phrase *"Hypotheses non fingo"* ("I do not make hypotheses"). But his successors used his physics and astronomy as the basis of an entire mechanistic world view. They held that *all* the phenomena in the universe were not only explicable but predictable in terms of the laws of mechanics. A striking statement of this philosophy was made by the Marquis Pierre Simon de Laplace, in 1814:

> We ought then to regard the present state of the universe as the effect of its anterior state and as the cause of the one which is to follow. Given for one instant an intelligence that could comprehend all the forces by which nature is animated and the respective situation of the beings who compose it—an intelligence sufficiently vast to submit these data to analysis—it would embrace in the same formula the movements of the greatest bodies of the universe and those of the lightest atom; for it, nothing would be uncertain and the future, as the past, would be present to its eyes. The human mind offers, in the perfection which it has been able to give to astronomy, a feeble idea of this intelligence. Its discoveries in mechanics and geometry, added to that of universal gravity, have enabled it to comprehend in the same analytical expressions the past and future states of the system of the world.

Most contemporary scientists would reject such a starkly deterministic philosophy of science because of the quantum theory and the breakdown of Newtonian mechanics when applied to atomic phenomena. However, in the time of Laplace nothing was known of atomic physics, and the mechanistic world view was at its zenith. The discovery of the planet Neptune, in 1846, shortly after Laplace's death, appeared to be a profound confirmation of the validity of the deterministic world view. For, using the laws of Newtonian physics and extensive mathematical calculation, the French astrophysicist Urbain Leverrier and the English astrophysicist John Couch Adams had independently made predictions of the exact position of Neptune a short time before it was actually sighted. Their predictions were confirmed. The history of this discovery is a remarkable one, and it is told with great clarity and charm in *The Discovery of Neptune* (Harvard) by Dr. Morton Grosser, a university professor who has temporarily withdrawn from academic life to pursue an independent course of study.

Dr. Grosser begins his history of Neptune on March 13, 1781, when the German-born English astronomer William Herschel, who was making a new map of the stars, noticed a peculiar object in the neighborhood of the star H Geminorum:

> Increasing the power of his eyepiece he found that the object had a magnifiable disc; continued observation convinced him that it was in motion relative to nearby stars. Although he did not realize it at the time, Herschel had discovered the seventh planet. [This was Uranus.] . . . The possibility that his discovery was a planet, though perfectly compatible with the visual evidence, did not occur to Herschel initially. His lapse was understandable. For more than 2000 years, as far as anyone knew, there had been only six planets; their number remained constant despite frequent disagreements about their size and distance.

However, by the summer of 1781 the combined evidence of several astronomers left little doubt that Herschel's discovery was a planet. Its name was suggested by the German astronomer Johann Bode, who, in Dr. Grosser's words, "pointed out that if the new planet was named 'Uranus' the solar system would represent a coherent mythological family: Uranus, the god of the sky and husband of Earth, was the father of Saturn and the grandfather of Jupiter, who, in turn, fathered Mars, Venus, Mercury and Apollo (or the Sun) ."

The principal concern then was to determine the orbit of Uranus, which, according to Newton's laws, should be a simple ellipse if the only force acting on it was the gravitational attraction of the sun. Uranus, because of its great distance from the sun, takes about eighty-four years to complete a tour around it. Since it moves so slowly, determining its orbit was a difficult task. (During the periods when the planet is visible from the earth, it traces only a very brief path among the fixed stars.) So the astronomers began examining the records of observations prior to 1781 to see whether the planet had unwittingly been seen by astronomers before Herschel. They were not disappointed, and by the turn of the century the records of a number of earlier observations of Uranus had been uncovered. (The astronomers who had seen the planet had simply recorded it as a star.) A study of these data made it clear that the pre-Herschel orbit did not correspond to the post-Herschel orbit. Faced with this problem, many astronomers of the period decided that the earlier observations were inaccurate and should be ignored. This turned out to be a poor decision.

In 1820 the French astronomer Alexis Bouvard published what he thought to be a definitive table of the planet's orbit. In constructing his table Bouvard disregarded no less than seventeen earlier observations of Uranus. This aroused considerable criticism, and, furthermore, it soon became apparent that Bouvard's orbit didn't fit with the current observations, either. There were a variety of attempts to explain the discrepancy, and it was even suggested that Newton's law of gravitation be discarded. But Newton's law admits the possibility that the strong gravitational attraction of a neighbor can disturb the orbit of a planet. Such a disturbance is called a "perturbation." Many celebrated mathematicians of the eighteenth and nineteenth centuries had worked on the perturbation theory, and there was a school of European astronomers who felt that the disturbances in the orbit of Uranus were caused by other planets, although it did not seem that any of the *known* planets could produce a perturbing force strong enough to explain the irregular motion of Uranus. Dr. Grosser quotes a letter written by the Reverend Dr. Thomas John Hussey, a British amateur astronomer, in 1834:

The apparently inexplicable discrepancies between the ancient and modern observations suggested to me the possibility of some disturbing body beyond Uranus, not taken into account because unknown.

This was one of the first suggestions that an as yet unobserved astronomical body might be perturbing Uranus. Unfortunately, Dr. Hussey sent this letter to the British Astronomer Royal, George Biddell Airy, whose frigidity toward new astronomical speculations bordered on the incredible. Typically, Airy discouraged Dr. Hussey from beginning a telescopic search for the unknown object. But by 1840 the possibility that an unknown astronomical body was responsible for the perturbations of Uranus was widely accepted. However, no one had attacked the tremendously difficult problem of determining the properties of the unknown body that could account for the orbit of Uranus.

At this point two young astrophysicists, the Englishman Adams and the Frenchman Leverrier, came on the scene. They were from remarkably similar backgrounds. Leverrier was born in Saint Lô, in 1811, to a relatively poor family. His father was a minor government official. Adams, who was born in 1819, came from a poor farming family. The parents of both boys had great intellectual ambitions for their sons, who, after some initial setbacks, compiled brilliant academic records. Adams was senior wrangler at Cambridge, and Leverrier graduated near the top of his class at the Ecole Polytechnique in Paris. Leverrier began his scientific career as a chemist, but the only faculty job available to him at the Ecole Polytechnique was in astronomy, so he became an astronomer. By 1845, when he began the study of the movements of Uranus, he had already made a reputation as a mathematical astronomer. Unknown to him, Adams had been at work on the same problem for two years and had made definite predictions about the properties of the missing planet. (In guessing at its distance from the sun, both men used a peculiar empirical formula known as Bode's law, after Johann Bode. Bode's law is a simple algebraic equation that gives correctly the distances of most of the planets from the sun. It also appears to predict a planet between Mars and Jupiter. There is no planet there, but there is a band of small planetoids that are believed by many astronomers to be the result of the prehistoric disintegration of a major planet. There is no explanation, even now, of why the law works as well as it does.)

Between 1843 and 1845 there occurred a series of almost farcical mishaps, centering on the intractable personality of Airy, that prevented any effective search by British astronomers for the new planet. Dr. Grosser goes into splendid detail about them, and the result is almost a Gilbert and Sullivan operetta. Airy, on the advice of his doctor, had dinner at exactly three-thirty every afternoon. His butler made sure that he was never disturbed, and one day he turned away Adams, who had gone to the observatory in Greenwich to take Airy the results of his latest calculations on the planet.

Airy also felt an extreme distrust for the work of younger men. He tyrannized over his assistants and often treated them like children. Dr. Grosser quotes a contemporary of Airy:

> As an example of the . . . detail of the oversight which he exercised over his assistants, it may be mentioned that he drew up for each one of those who took part in the Harton Colliery experiment, instructions, telling them by what trains to travel, where to change, and so forth, with the

same minuteness that one might for a child who was taking his first journey alone; and he himself packed up soap and towels with the instruments lest his astronomers should find themselves in [County] Durham, out of reach of these necessaries of civilization.

A note delivered to the British astronomer William Lassell, which contained Adams' data, was accidentally destroyed by a maid before Lassell had a chance to make use of it. (When he received the note, he was in bed with a sprained ankle.) And James Challis, another British astronomer, who actually began the search for the new planet, remarked to a colleague at dinner that he had recently observed a curious disc-shaped star; the colleague wanted to take a look at once to see if this might be the missing planet. But before they could set off for the observatory, Mrs. Challis insisted on giving them tea, and by the time they got there the sky had clouded over.

By 1846, Leverrier had independently arrived at Adams' conclusions, and he, too, sent a manuscript to Airy. Airy at last seemed impressed, but he did not mention in his correspondence with Leverrier that Adams had already done practically the same thing. Now Airy became concerned lest the credit for discovering the new planet should escape the British astronomers, and he began writing letters urging them to intensify their search and suggesting methods, largely ineffective. (It turned out later that Challis had actually observed the planet twice in the first four days of his search but had confused it with a star.)

Leverrier had comparable difficulties in arousing the interest of French astronomers, and in September of 1846 he wrote in desperation to the German astronomer Johann Galle begging him to begin an immediate search. Galle managed to persuade the director of the Berlin Observatory to let him use the telescope, and that same night he and a young assistant found the new planet precisely where

Adams and Leverrier said it would be. So ended the story of the discovery of Neptune.

Dr. Grosser goes on to discuss the equally farcical outburst after the discovery of the planet. Airy's disinclination to inform Leverrier of Adams' work led to a period of intense bad feeling between English and Continental astronomers. (For a while, Leverrier wanted the planet named after him.) However, by 1847 emotions had cooled down, and Dr. Grosser concludes his fine book with a description of the first meeting of Adams and Leverrier. An eyewitness wrote, "One of the pleasantest things in my life to look back to is a walk I had with Adams and Leverrier, the two men evidently admiring one another and perfectly free from jealousy."

If there is a moral to Dr. Grosser's story, it may be that scientists are prone to the same sort of temperamental vagaries as the practitioners of any other creative activity. Scientists and artists are not as different emotionally as is often supposed.

4

Setting Back the Clock :
The Bomb and Beyond

To anyone who has seen an atomic explosion, one of
its most impressive aspects is the "transformation."
Before the explosion, one is in the presence of a complex, inert mechanical device, which, by the process of
the explosion, is suddenly transformed into an insane,
almost incomprehensible inferno. This is true of any
chemical explosion, of course, but the difference in
scale is so great that the experience is *qualitatively*
different. When the first atomic device was exploded
at Alamogordo, in the summer of 1945, one of the
physicists witnessing the growing fireball had a fleet-
ing nightmare that it was going to keep growing until
it had consumed the entire world, and Dr. Oppenheimer, who had for many years been a student of

Indian philosophy and religion, thought of a fragment from the *Bhagavad-Gita:*

> If the radiance of a thousand suns
> were to burst into the sky,
> that would be like
> the splendor of the Mighty One.

The scientists working on the bomb project who were in a position to know what they were working on were quite aware that the bomb would introduce a completely new force into world politics. From the very beginning, they understood that an enormous educational effort would be necessary to make people understand that the world had been wholly transformed, for better or worse. In the fall of 1945, a group of men involved in the Manhattan Project decided to put out a newsletter as a means of beginning this education. The first issue of this *Bulletin of the Atomic Scientists,* which was, and still is, edited by Professor Eugene Rabinowitch, a distinguished physical chemist, appeared in December of that year. It had an initial circulation of five or six thousand, but it has since become a full-fledged magazine, with a circulation of almost thirty thousand. Over the years, it has published a superb collection of articles about the era we have now entered, and some of the best have recently been reprinted by Basic Books in *The Atomic Age,* edited by the late Morton Grodzins, a political scientist at the University of Chicago, and by Professor Rabinowitch, who is at the University of Illinois. *The Atomic Age* is a striking and fascinating book. In their introduction, the editors tell us:

> The power of the fissioned atomic nucleus had been revealed at Alamogordo in June, 1945, to scientists working on the Manhattan Project, and revealed to the world at large at Hiroshima and Nagasaki in August of the same year. The *Bulletin* began as an emergency action, under-

taken by scientists who saw urgent need for an immediate educational program. One purpose was to make fellow scientists aware of the new relationships between their own world of science and the world of national and international politics. A second was to help the public understand what nuclear energy and its application to war meant for mankind. It was anticipated that the atomic bomb would be only the first of many dangerous presents from Pandora's box of modern science. Consequently, it was clear that the education of man to the realities of the scientific age would be a long, sustained effort.

From almost its very first issue, a clock—"the clock of doom"—has appeared with great frequency on the cover of the *Bulletin,* and its hands have always been close to midnight. After the explosion of the first Russian atomic device, in October of 1949, the hands were set closer to twelve, and they were set even farther forward after the explosion of the first Russian hydrogen bomb, in September of 1953. Following the signing of the test-ban treaty, they were moved back to seven minutes before midnight. The essays in this collection have been arranged to reflect these changes of mood and outlook. There are four sections: "Failure," "Peril," "Fear," and "Hope." Under "Failure," the editors have included the by now well-known Franck Report, written for Secretary of War Henry Stimson in June, 1945, before the successful test at Alamogordo, by a group of scientists at the "Metallurgical Laboratory" of the University of Chicago. "Metallurgical Laboratory" was the code name for the part of the bomb project that was being carried on in Chicago, and the report was the work of a committee headed by the Nobel Prize-winning physicist James Franck. One of several comments on the future of nuclear weapons that had been solicited from the atomic-bomb laboratories by Stimson, it urged that the bomb be used first in a supervised United Nations demonstration for the benefit of the Japanese, to be held "on the desert or a barren island," rather than on a target in Japan. The authors of the report felt that such an internationally supervised demonstration might prevent a vast nuclear-arms race. The suggestion was not adopted, and in 1947, in an article in *Harper's,* also reprinted in this book, Stimson offered the reasoning against it that finally prevailed in the Interim Committee, a group of prominent men, including some scientists, who had the responsibility of advising the President about the implications of atomic weapons:

> The Interim Committee carefully considered such alternatives as a detailed advance warning or a demonstration in some uninhabited area. Both of these suggestions were discarded as impractical. They were not regarded as likely to be effective in compelling a surrender of Japan, and both of them involved serious risks. Even the New Mexico tests would not give final proof that any given bomb was certain to explode when dropped from an airplane. Quite apart from the generally unfamiliar nature of atomic explosives, there was the whole problem of exploding a bomb at a predetermined height in the air by a complicated mechanism which could not be tested in the static tests of New Mexico. Nothing would have been more damaging to our effort to obtain surrender than a warning or a demonstration followed by a dud—and this was a real possibility. Furthermore, we had no bombs to waste. It was vital that a sufficient effect be quickly obtained with the few we had.

The bombings of Hiroshima and Nagasaki followed.

After the explosions, the Western powers made a sincere attempt to achieve some sort of international control of atomic energy through the United Nations. Several of the articles in the "Failure" section, including two especially eloquent ones by Robert Oppenheimer, summarize the total frustration that was experienced in the efforts to come to terms with the Russians. The reason is now obvious: the Russians were working furiously to develop their own atomic weapons, and a successful agreement to control weapons development would have frozen the situation. Although it had been clear to Western atomic scientists from the very beginning that no secrecy on our part could keep the Russians or anyone else from getting the bomb (the point was made in a rhyming alphabet put together during the war by Edward Teller: "S stands for Secret; you can keep it forever/Provided there's no one abroad who is clever"), great surprise was caused by the disclosure that the Russians had began work on their own bomb even before the successful test at Alamogordo, having apparently started about the same time we did—in 1940. And while we knew virtually nothing of their work, they had considerable knowledge of ours, through espionage. The Russians must have learned useful details about the engineering of the bomb from men like Klaus Fuchs, but probably the most important things they learned were the degree to which we were committed to the Manhattan Project and the prospects for its success. Anyone who knows how scientific projects operate would find it difficult to believe that a few engineering details learned through espionage could have been of much help in an operation as complex as building an atomic bomb. The most vital secret was that the bomb could be constructed at all, and this secret was, of course, revealed at Alamogordo.

However, the fact that espionage had penetrated an area as closely guarded as Los Alamos was disturbing to both the scientists and the public. It cast doubt on the security system, and—more important, since it was discovered at a time when Americans were just beginning to realize and react to the terrifying implications of the worldwide proliferation of atomic weapons—it helped to prompt a fanatical drive for security, which, in its excesses, came close to persuading scientists not to enter or remain in government service. No security system could have given complete protection from someone like Fuchs. In a thoughtful article in the *Bulletin* in 1951, the chemist T. Harrison Davies studies the effects of espionage at Los Alamos. He quotes from an interview with Gordon Dean, then chairman of the Atomic Energy Commission, just after the conviction of Fuchs. The questioner asked, "Have you any idea what is wrong with human beings or with our system in these democracies of ours that these people will do the things that Fuchs did? Does the scientist have less regard for loyalty to his country than other people? Is he a world citizen who wants to give everything away? What is the reason that Fuchs got into this thing?" Mr. Dean replied, "I don't think that you can say that scientists are an entirely different breed in that respect. . . . Fuchs is the type of man who, while he might have been caught had there been a real security check on him, might never be caught by any kind of investigation, because apparently he owes his allegiance to nothing that ordinary humans owe theirs to. He is going to make his own decisions regardless of any rules he purports to operate under. What do you do with a man like that? Usually he is a very intelligent man. He is an independent man. He is an idealist of some kind. He might be a Communist-idealist, but he is a man of ideals of some kind. You don't usually spot this kind in a check."

The early nineteen-fifties were a grim time for the scientific community, and many of the essays under "Fear" recall the unpleasantness of the period. There is a brilliant analysis of the legal aspects of the Oppenheimer case by Harry Kalven, Jr., a professor of law at the University of Chicago, who has also contributed an equally striking review of the legal framework of the congressional hearings on Linus Pauling in 1960. There are several articles on the problems that foreign scientists encountered in getting United States visas after they had been invited here to teach or to attend scientific meetings. Edward A. Shils, a sociologist at the University of Chicago, recounts the case of Professor Rudolf E. Peierls, a distinguished German-born British mathematical physicist who had worked here during the war on the Manhattan Project. After the war, Professor Peierls applied for a visa so that he could attend a physics conference in Chicago dealing with matters that were in no way classified. His visa was held up for many months, and, to quote the account, "during this period, while the consul and the Visa Division were pondering or disregarding Professor Peierls' application, he was in the United States on a British diplomatic passport participating in an official Anglo-American conference on the declassification of atomic-energy information, in which the information to which he had access was very highly classified." Such things are a sharp reminder of what can happen when fanaticism gets the upper hand over common sense.

In the section of *The Atomic Age* called "Peril," there is a wide range of views about a world in which we and the Russians live, as Oppenheimer has put it, "like two scorpions in a bottle." There are discussions of biological warfare, disarmament, nuclear deterrence, and fallout. One of the most interesting is a brief note by the physicist Freeman Dyson on the danger of bomb shelters:

> The basic question which ought to be considered first in any discussion of nuclear war is not "How many people die in the first attack?" but "How can one imagine the war coming to an end?" In the absence of bomb shelters, the two questions are perhaps equivalent. In that case, the war might reasonably end in a day or a week through the death of the combatant populations. But if shelters are built and effective, then I do not know how the war can end before one side or the other finally runs out of weapons. If past history is any guide, the military machines on both sides will continue to grind until there is nothing left for them to grind. . . . Our present policy of peace through deterrence,

so long as we have no bomb shelters, is a policy of finite risk. At the very worst, if deterrence fails, the populations of the nuclear powers may die, but the rest of the world will survive to carry on the aspirations of the human race. Only if we plunge into the vicious circle of building more and more massive bomb shelters do we risk the whole future of humanity itself.

The editors have ended on a note of cautious hope. Nothing can nullify the existence of the bomb. However, old attitudes are changing. The bomb has locked us all together willy-nilly in a reluctant but nonetheless very real international community. In the concluding essay in *The Atomic Age,* entitled "Pushing Back the Clock of Doom," Professor Rabinowitch says:

> Future generations may then come to see, in the years which now appear as an era of darkness, confusion, desperation, and deadly danger, the time when a break was first made with the age-long divisive tradition of mankind; when world community began to become a reality.
>
> Three broad changes in man's awareness of human relations are pushing us in this hopeful direction: a change in man's relation to war; a change in man's attitude toward the rule of force; and a growing feeling of personal and national responsibility for the security and prosperity of mankind as a whole, and not only of one's own country.
>
> A generation ago, the belief in the naturalness of war, in the glory of victorious battles, in the rationality of the use of military power as a tool of national policy was universal. In a Russian "student calendar" which I used to buy every year before the First World War, there was a table showing the number of battles each country had fought in its history with the comment, "France, the most civilized of all countries, has also engaged in the greatest number of battles." This attitude toward war is now dead. What was once the faith of a few exalted religious leaders and the reasoned conclusion of a few humanist philosophers—that war is evil

and that the establishment of permanent peace must be the considered aim of mankind—has now become a common, everyday belief of men and women all over the world.

Any optimism about the future of a world blanketed by opposing atomic weapons must be guarded, because it is based on the shaky assumption that reason will prevail over instinct and madness. Pondering this, I am often reminded of the fable of the centipede and the frog. The centipede comes to the banks of a stream that it cannot cross because it cannot swim. A friendly frog offers to carry the centipede across the stream, provided that the centipede promises not to sting him. "You see," explains the frog, "if you sting me while I am swimming across with you on my back, I will die, and then, because you can't swim, you will drown." "I see," says the centipede. "It sounds very reasonable." In the middle of the stream, the centipede stings the frog. As the frog is dying and the centipede is about to drown, the frog asks, "How could you have done such a foolish thing? Now we are both going to die." "I know," says the centipede. "I didn't *want* to sting you, but I couldn't help it, for it is my instinct."

5

Science and Politics in Russia

THE English translation of *Life in the Universe* (Twayne), written by the noted Russian biochemist A. Oparin in collaboration with a Russian astronomer, V. Fesenkov, is a peculiar and somewhat disappointing book. About twenty-five years ago, Oparin wrote a monograph, *The Origin of Life,* that has become a recognized scientific classic. In it he attempted to trace, step by step, the evolutionary process by which life developed from non-living matter. The writing is wonderfully lucid and can be followed even by a reader who does not have a great deal of scientific background. Much of the new book, though (which contains one chapter by Oparin, six chapters by Fesenkov, and one chapter and an introduction written jointly), is modern Russian scientific writing at its worst. There are heroic trumpetings of the glories of Russian technology ("It must be pointed out, however, that owing to the enormous achievements of Soviet radioelectronic engineering and the development of powerful guided rockets it was possible, for the first time in the history of man, also to obtain a picture of the back of our satellite [the moon]") that belong in *Pravda* and not in a scientific text. There is simple misinformation of all kinds; for example, on page 139, Fesenkov, in a wild and irrelevant blast at American journalism, is annoyed by something that he claims appeared in *The New Yorker* a hundred and twenty years ago. There are horribly long and involuted sentences that mix scientific exposition with Marxist dialectic: "This hypothesis, for the first time considering the process of development of the cosmic bodies, which were until then believed to have been immutable from the very moment of their supposed 'creation,' was of great progressive importance for its epoch and was highly appraised by F. Engels." How can anyone read prose like that?

Some fields, such as genetics, have already been ruined for Russian science by the intrusion of politics and ideology. In genetics, Lysenko derived directly from Marxist dialectic the principle that acquired characteristics are hereditary. Unfortunately for Russian genetics, the principle is scientifically false. One wonders, in general, how Russian scientists manage to get as much done as they do, in the face of the burden of claptrap that a book like this indicates they carry along. In Soviet physics, the effects of dialectic are much more subtle. Physics is vital to technology, and if Russian political philosophy interferes too much with Russian technology, then too bad for political philosophy. Nonetheless, in otherwise objective Soviet textbooks in physics the reader will sometimes come upon curious little dialectical messages. These seem halfhearted, and even absurd, like commercials from the sponsor. For example, at the end of an extremely technical presentation of one of the most difficult fields of modern physics, quantum electrodynamics, the two authors, A. I. Akhiezer and V. B. Berestetsky, find it necessary to remark that "these phenomena are a new confirmation of a well-known thesis of V. I. Lenin on the inexhaustibility of the properties of the electron and the infinity of nature." It would be interesting to know whether the authors really believe this. The New York *Times* of April 15, 1962, quotes a distinguished Russian physicist, Professor Pyotr Kapitsa, in what is described as "a withering attack against efforts to declare scientific theories true or false on the basis of Marxist dialectics." He is paraphrased as saying, "Dialectics alone cannot solve any scientific problem, and attempts to apply it as the unique clue to scientific correctness have hampered the progress of Soviet science." It is a remarkable statement for a Russian scientist to make in print.

Despite its drawbacks, the Oparin-Fesenkov book has a certain fascination—basically, because of its subject matter: Does life exist on other planets or in other solar systems? It is a question that has fascinated men for centuries, and Oparin and Fesenkov have no doubt about its answer:

> In our metagalactic system there are hundreds of millions of galaxies and each galaxy may be composed of hundreds of thousands of millions of stars. Even in our galaxy, which numbers approximately 150,000 million stars, there may be hundreds of thousands of planets on which life is likely to originate and develop. Our infinite Universe must also contain an infinite number of inhabited planets.

But how did life get there? The authors reject the notion that life is eternal, unchanging, and uniformly distributed throughout the universe, although they do it, again, on dialectical grounds.:

> Engels also levelled his crushing criticism on all the theories which spring from the principle of the eternity of

life, and showed the incompatibility of this principle with consistent materialism.

And they reject the notion that organisms spread from planet to planet by, say, riding on meteors. Many meteorites have been examined, and there is no solid evidence that they contained samples of what might have been living matter from outer space. Hence, Oparin and Fesenkov feel that life, if it exists elsewhere, must have evolved in a manner similar to the way it evolved on earth:

> Life is not transported, like "Vesta's inextinguishable torch," from one celestial body to another in the form of ready-made germs, but originates anew each time the requisite conditions are on hand in the process of the development of matter. Consequently, the origin of life is not a "fortunate," extremely improbable event, but quite a regular phenomenon subject to a deep scientific analysis and all-round study.

As they point out, the evolution of human life appears to depend heavily on the presence of water. According to most theories, life on earth began in the sea, and the mixture of hydrogen and the heavier elements that made up the primeval sea were essential to the early development of living organisms. There does not seem to be any significant amount of water vapor in the atmospheres of the planets in our solar system, and this makes it unlikely that life exists on them—or, at least, life that resembles the earthly varieties. It is known, because of irregularities in the motion of double stars (pairs of stars, very close to each other, that orbit around a common central point), that *some* distant stars have planets. These are much too faint to be seen, even with the most powerful telescopes, and so one has no idea whether they are suitable abodes for human beings. These remote outposts *might* support life, which may exist in forms that do not resemble us even faintly. There have been theories that on very hot planets creatures could have evolved whose chemistry is based on compounds of heat-resistant silicon rather than on carbon, like ours. Maybe yes and maybe no. In any case, these things are discussed to some extent in the book, and if Oparin and Fesenkov had been content to stick with scientific exposition the results might have been splendid. As it is, however, only a very dedicated reader will find it worthwhile to sort out the legitimate scientific speculations from the rest. A scientific text is a poor forum for political propaganda.

6

Bold New World : Is Science a Glorious Entertainment ?

DEAN (of Columbia University) JACQUES BARZUN's controversial book *Science: The Glorious Entertainment* (Harper & Row) has both the strengths and the weaknesses of a brilliant cartoon. There is wit, clarity of line, elegance, and irony, and there is also exaggeration for effect. Indeed, one is often led to wonder how Dean Barzun intends some of what he has written to be taken. Is he being funny, serious, mischievous, rhetorical, inflammatory, philosophical, metaphorical, or all of these at the same time, or all of these one after another? His introduction is not entirely illuminating. In describing how he is using examples, he notes, "That is why, in the present work, which is primarily descriptive, and which, like its predecessors, often uses for illustration not what is merely typical, but what is especially worthy of regard, I sometimes employ the rhetoric of argument—the form that most naturally incites the internal action called thought. To the reader it should not greatly matter whether or not he agrees with the conclusions I reach. The point of offering them is to reduce confusion and provide a spur to reasoning. For the aim of a critic, beyond that of saying what he thinks, is to make two thoughts grow where only one grew before." As the Italians say, *"Se non è vero, è ben trovato."*

Despite lapses into capriciousness, apparently for the sake of provoking the reader, and despite what I feel are some clear-cut misunderstandings about the quality of modern science, Barzun's book has a real fascination and serves a real purpose. Just because he is not a scientist, he can, without the restraint one might feel if one were actually engaged in one of the sciences, flail away at the numerous suppositions that underlie the modern scientific enterprise and its influence on society as a whole. And most scientists would accept and endorse most of his analyses. For one, there is his discussion of the contemporary attitude toward The Machine (or what he calls Techne). As he emphasizes, never before has there been a society so ready to surrender itself to The Machine. Science-fiction writers have long speculated about societies of machines that are plotting to take us over. But here, as elsewhere, they have underestimated the true phenomenon; man is apparently engaged in a pell-mell race to build machines, like the electronic computer, that will take over his functions one by one. I would be among the last to downgrade computers when they are used with discretion and tact as an aid to research, but their effects on many disciplines—both quantitative ones, like physics, and nonquantitative ones, like literary stylistic analysis—have often been simply disruptive. Some problems are posed merely because they can be programmed for a computer and not because they are in themselves interesting. (I have been asked, when I was working in a research establishment, whether I could think up a problem for the local computer, because it seemed a pity to keep it idle. In fact, inasmuch as machines are getting faster and more numerous, one wonders whether there can possibly continue to be enough sensible problems for them to go around.) Yet as striking as the impact of computers and automation has been on scientists and scholars, it is nothing to what it has been on society in general. For one thing, scientists have not been displaced by computers—at least, not yet. (As a graduate student, I once asked the late Professor John von Neumann whether he thought computers would replace the mathematician. His answer was "Sonny, don't worry about it.") But automation is changing the whole concept of labor. Manual labor, especially in large factories and assembly plants, is slowly disappearing. It has been pointed out that the muscular disorders that are concomitants of the more traditional forms of work are now being supplanted by the nervous breakdown. The human nervous system has not evolved to the point where it can stand the strain of a job whose primary requirement is pushing buttons every so often to keep a complex machine in line. Barzun puts this situation very well:

> The machine in any case forces us to unceasing self-defense. We use up life in response to signs, being artificially surrounded by matter in violent motion. Our sorry integument is never more than an inch away from things that burn and crush, cut and poison; we move among charged wires, adapt our speed to their commands, and remake our thoughts in the image of their broken idiom. We look for the light, heed the buzzer, turn the dial, distinguish color and symbols on lamps and cards, remem-

ber numbers and codes, decipher acronyms—no purpose is exempt: pleasure, travel, domesticity, the pursuit of art and learning. We perish, nullified, if we lose the serial number, the trade name, mislay the key or ticket or device or formula or token.

And he adds:

These are the requirements that overwork our nerves and make them an object of perpetual concern in common speech. Techne has relieved our muscles of strain at the expense of our nerve-ends. But our disorder is even greater than we admit, for in place of traditional work techne has made us pursue extraordinary forms of non-work. The primitive task of exerting force and mind upon some material object has disappeared in the abstraction of symbols on paper. In work other than farming and mining—and sometimes even there—men are busied with signs; they neither toil nor think but watch and tend. Across the nation they form a collective nervous system for the muscles of the machine. What they give is alertness to signals in order that other signals may be transmitted in turn; everything depends on the "flow of information" on "data processing." We may see in this something like a projection of the railroad signalman in his tower, abstracted into a collective, impersonal anxiety and agitation in the dark.

A return to the non-technological past is impossible short of a global cataclysm, and a moment's reflection will convince most people that it would hardly be desirable anyway. Most of us are much better off than we would have been in any past society except under very special circumstances. Barzun calls the idea that we can have at one and the same time the technological simplicity of the past and the numerous advantages of the present the Fallacy of Utopian Addition. If one accepts the benefits of technology, one must pay the price, but that is all the more reason to question whether a particular apparent technological advance makes us happier, richer people or just increases the appetite for further meaningless acquisition and futile leisure.

It might be imagined that a scientist looking about our Scientific Age would find no end of satisfaction in what he sees, for everywhere there are the manifestations of science and scientists at work. But the pleasure of this prospect is soon tempered by the realization that much of what he is looking at is not really science at all but a new kind of semiquantitative, jargonistic pseudo-scholarship that is merely masquerading in the costumes of science. As a rule, the scientist who comes upon this spectacle simply turns away from it and goes on about his own particular task. One reason is his attitude of live and let live toward people who appear to be well intentioned and who are figuratively (and sometimes literally) his colleagues. Barzun does not turn away, and watching him at work on pseudo-science with scalpel and crowbar is a delight. In example after example he shows how glibly and uncritically applied "scientific method" simply produces pompous distortions of common sense. An especially nice one is his account of a project "at a large and renowned institute which nestles close to a leading university in the midwest," a project that "brought together businessmen, academics, and civil servants to study Originality." The report of the conference read, in part, "Organizations, including business organizations, need creative talent. In April, 1958, businessmen and social scientists met together to examine research which had been done on creativity and conformity." This is what they found:

> People high on originality are usually high on intelligence as well. . . . Original people tend to prefer the complex. . . . Original people tend to have more energy and effectiveness. . . . Group pressures inhibit originality; groups discourage deviate (*sic*) opinions. . . . These pressures are at work in all organizations. . . . Original people

do conform to group pressures, but they conform less than unoriginal people. . . . There are different kinds of conformity behavior. The kind which occurs depends upon the personality of the individual and on the situation in which he finds himself. Support for a deviate opinion, however small, reduces the amount of conformity. . . . There are steps that management can take to increase originality.

We are surrounded by pseudo-science. The newspapers, television, books, and even the visual arts bombard us daily with impressions that have merely the shape of scientific truths and discoveries. The mind reels and rebels, and one is tempted to cry out, with Sir William Petty, a contemporary of Newton, "As for Pitty, let it bee applyed to ye Ignorance, Incapacity & small obstinancy of ye World."

The hallmark of a scientific truth is that it can be put into quantitative statements that are testable. Scientific truths never disappear; an experiment done honestly and reliably will, no matter how many times it is performed, produce essentially the same answer. With this in mind, Barzun observes that the belief that, say, the behavioral sciences have not borne fruit because they are "young" does not hold water. "There is," he says, "no such thing as a young science; there may be a small science or a short science, such as mathematics in Greek times or chemistry in the early nineteenth century. What was known was little, but every bit of it was genuine in form and most of it solid in contents." One may not agree with Barzun's blanket statement that the "social sciences today have yet to show one universal element or one controlling 'law,' one unit of measurement, one exactly plotted universal variable, or one invariant relation," but the opposite view —that human behavior can be summarized in simple mathematical laws—is hardly less of an exaggeration.

Because genuine scientific truths can never disappear, scientific theories are never entirely discarded. It is a misunderstanding to say that twentieth-century physics (i.e., the theory of relativity and the quantum theory) has "refuted" Newton's laws, if by "refuted" one means that these laws have been entirely displaced. Newton's laws were invented to deal with the relatively slow motions of massive objects (slow compared to the velocity of light and massive compared to the mass of an electron), and as long as they are applied to such objects they will yield predictions that are almost wholly valid—as valid, certainly, as is necessary for most of the applications of the laws by, for example, engineers. The new theories telescope into the old ones in their common domain of application. Niels Bohr called this fact about scientific theories the Correspondence Principle. When he devised the quantum theory of the orbits of electrons in atoms, one of the ingredients that went into his derivation was the principle that the new laws should agree with the old ones wherever the old ones were valid. Likewise, the formulas of the theory of relativity dovetail smoothly with the formulas of Newtonian mechanics when the velocities of particles are truly small compared to that of light. It appears to me that a lack of appreciation of the connection between the new theories and the old ones has led Barzun to suppose that the new theories are more abstract and arbitrary than they really are and that the old theories are simpler than they really are. He writes:

> If science had stood still on the apparently firm base of Newton's four laws, had only refined its measurements of conservation and atomic weights, had succeeded in subsuming electricity under mechanics and proving the existence of the ether, always increasing its power to predict until it filled out the grand system foreseen by the Galileos, Descartes, Newtons, Goethes, and Darwins, the peoples of Europe and America might shortly have mastered, if not the scientific habit of mind, at least the scientific vision, and the historian of ideas might have spoken with literal truth of a "scientific revolution."

He adds:

> But just when it had captured power and authority, nineteenth-century science had to face insurrection within, a radicalism sprung from the anti-mechanical facts of electricity. As these difficulties were tackled one by one and revealed the strange workings of both the subatomic and stellar worlds, the great vision broke up, the fragments became less and less graspable, specialities multiplied, the proofs by observation and common sense gave way to mathematical demonstration.

As if there were no mathematical demonstrations in, say, Newton's *Principia*. Barzun's attitude toward modern science as revealed by this and other passages in his book reminds me of a distortion of Pope's *Essay on Man* that was popular when I was a student:

> Nature and nature's laws lay hid in night
> When God created Newton and there was light.
> But came the Devil and He, with a mighty Ho,
> Created Einstein, who restored the status quo.

This is not to argue that modern scientific theories are simple. But the idea that the theories of the past are more intuitive and more solid is based on an optical illusion induced by the passage of time. Anyone, even a contemporary scientist, who studies Newton's *Principia*, with its fantastic array of geometric arguments and quasi-theological presuppositions, acquires a better notion of just how difficult and just how non-intuitive it was. Yet with time the ideas of "classical" science become distilled and popularized, and they ultimately seep into the common-sense attitudes of both philosophers and the man in the street. All of this is put succinctly in a wonderful essay, *Modern Physics and Common Sense,* that is incorporated in *Modern Science and Its Philosophy* (Collier Books), by Philipp Frank.

Professor Frank wrote:

A glance at the history of science also reveals that the wide gap between these two kinds of theory ["intuitive" and "abstract"] is not understood in the same manner at every period of the history of science. Thus, at the time of its discovery, Newton's theory of motion was regarded as an abstract, merely mathematical theory; in our own day, however, it is often cited as an example of an intuitive theory, especially when philosophers wish to establish the abstract character of the theory of relativity and of quantum mechanics by contrasting them with an intuitive theory. In truth, however, the alleged difference between Newtonian and relativistic mechanics depends only on the undeniable fact that the difficult and complicated calculations and deductions required for understanding Einstein's theory of relativity are not required for understanding the phenomena of everyday experience. For these phenomena can be formulated with the help of the more simple Newtonian theory of mechanics. Hence the statement that a theory like Einstein's is abstract and nonintuitive simply means that it is more complex than is necessary for a theory that need describe only the facts of daily experience.

And that is exactly the point. The new theories have come about because new experience has forced them upon us. The quantum theory was not the product of a physicist's whim; classical physics simply did not account for what happened inside the atom. Physicists, often with the greatest reluctance, were forced to rethink the foundations of their science. What resulted was not something less than Newtonian physics but something more—a new physics that included the old as well. It seems to me that it is just here that Barzun has failed to understand what modern science has accomplished. For he says, "True to the Faustian ideal in its elevated form, science seeks only to know; it is as pure as any human effort can be. It directs itself along any imaginative path, often one of negation, in order to make new—satisfying thus man's deep instinct of anarchy and perpetual revolution." The image created by this caricature is of scientists idly speculating here and playfully rearranging nature there. Indeed, in calling science a "Glorious Entertainment," this is apparently just what Barzun does mean. In fact, he says, "Out of man's mind in free play comes the creation Science. It renews itself, like the generations, thanks to an activity which is the best game of *homo ludens*: science is in the strictest and best sense a glorious entertainment."

The lesson of modern science is very nearly the opposite. Each new domain of nature uncovered has revealed new order among the phenomena. The new laws are in every way as solid and as satisfying as the old, and they strengthen one's confidence that the mind of man is not too weak an instrument to grasp the fixed regularities in the universe. With Einstein, one can say, "The eternal mystery of the world is its comprehensibility."

7

Keeping Up
with the Scientists :
Two Centuries

The New Scientist—Essays on the Methods and Values of Modern Science, edited by Paul C. Obler and Herman A. Estrin and published by Doubleday Anchor, is a collection of essays whose broad aim is to characterize modern science and its relation to society in general. Among the many authors who have contributed to it are P. W. Bridgman, Gerald Holton, Bertrand Russell, and C. P. Snow. Mr. Obler has written a short preface. Though some of the essays are damaged by the intrusion of a kind of mock-technical, pseudo-scientific jargon in places where simple English would do ("For methodological reasons science is perfectly right in restricting itself to the description and mathematical conceptualization of the mutual relationships among objects; but these objects are determined as being, and as being this and that, and presuppose therefore, logically, determining thought, that is, the subject which, by his thought, determines the being and the being-what of the objects"), others are so striking and the subject they treat is of such real concern that the book is well worth reading.

Today, in all the advanced technological societies, we are witnessing a remarkable phenomenon—the enormous support by governments of research in pure science, the results of which are really understandable to only a tiny fraction of the population. In the democratic societies, this means the support of basic research by taxation and ultimately by popular approval. Undoubtedly, much of this approval has been granted because of a confusion between science and technology, or because in many instances (especially under the stimuli of modern war) there has been a very small time lag between discoveries in pure science and their application in technology. Professor Holton, a physicist and historian of science at Harvard, in the first essay in the collection, says, "The bomb is taking the place of the microscope, Wernher Von Braun the place of Einstein, as symbols for modern science and scientists." In another age this confusion might not have had serious consequences, but as long as present-day science is dependent on government and popular support it is important that this support be given on a realistic basis and not under the illusion that there is an obvious connection between, say, building a large particle accelerator and our posture in national defense, or between research in genetics and cures for cancer. There are connections, but they are usually rather indirect, and if public support of scientific research is offered on the assumption that these connections are more immediate, then, as is always the case with illusion, there is bound to be the unhappy day of reckoning.

The root of the problem is a massive ignorance, in most of the broad intellectual community, of what science really is. Indeed, for many intellectuals it is almost "in" not to want to understand science. As Holton puts it:

> When the man in the street—or many an intellectual—hears that you are a physicist or mathematician he will usually remark with a frank smile, "Oh, I never could understand that subject"; while intending this as a curious compliment, he betrays his intellectual dissociation from scientific fields. It is not fashionable to confess to a lack of acquaintance with the latest ephemera in literature or the arts, but one may even exhibit a touch of pride in professing ignorance of the structure of the universe or one's own body, of the behavior of matter, or one's own mind.

Oddly, this attitude seems to be just about peculiar to the present day. The intellectual reaction against science is coinciding with one of the most important periods of scientific ferment and achievement. But scientific culture was once taken for granted as part of the furnishings of an educated man. Holton notes:

> Every great age has been shaped by intellectuals of the stamp of Hobbes, Locke, Berkeley, Leibnitz, Voltaire, Montesquieu, Rousseau, Kant, Jefferson, and Franklin—all of whom would have been horrified by the proposition that cultured men and women could dispense with a good grasp of the scientific aspect of the contemporary world picture.

Whatever the scientist may think of the anti-scientific attitude he finds around him, he cannot afford to dismiss it, if for no other reason than that public and government support has become essential for so much of what he wants to do in his research. And the inevitable concomitant of ignorance is fear, the fear of what one does not understand.

In his excellent contribution to this book, C. P. Snow begins by saying:

> Scientists are the most important occupational group in the world today. At this moment, what they do is of passionate concern to the whole of human society. At this moment, the scientists have little influence on the world effect of what they do. Yet potentially, they can have great influence. The rest of the world is frightened both of what they do—that is, of the intellectual discoveries of science—and of its effect. The rest of the world, transferring its fears, is frightened of the scientists themselves, and tends to think of them as radically different from other men.

And he adds:

> I believe that there is a spring of moral action in the scientific activity which is at least as strong as the search for truth. The name of the spring is *knowledge*. Scientists *know* certain things in a fashion more immediate and more certain than those who don't comprehend what science is. Unless we are abnormally weak or abnormally wicked men, this knowledge is bound to shape our actions. Most of us are timid; but to an extent, knowledge gives us guts.

However—and this is the heart of the matter—many of the results of modern science are difficult to understand. They are far removed from the domain of common sense and everyday experience, and no popularization, however well done, can completely bridge the gap. Even a serious student of physics must work for many years to understand at all deeply a conceptual structure like the quantum theory. But any intelligent layman can get *some* grasp of the basic ideas and, above all, can discover that these ideas are worth an attempt to understand them. Great scientific discoveries are often as beautiful as great creations in the fine arts. Snow puts it this strongly:

> Anyone who has ever done any science knows how much aesthetic joy he has obtained. That is, in the actual *activity*

of science, in the process of making a discovery, however humble it is, one can't help feeling an awareness of beauty. The subjective experience, the aesthetic satisfaction, seems exactly the same as the satisfaction one gets from writing a poem or a novel, or composing a piece of music. I don't think anyone has succeeded in distinguishing between them.

Scientists are aware that this is a magnificent age in science and they are eager to share and communicate the excitement and content of the new discoveries. But this requires an enlightened audience and a reintegration of scientific culture into the rest of the cultural fabric. As Oppenheimer has said, it is possible for us to create together "an immense network of intimacy, illumination, and understanding. Everything cannot be connected with everything in the world we live in. Everything can be connected with anything."

Part III

SCIENCE AND SCIENCE FICTION

1

The Future
Is Practically Here :
A Tribute to
Arthur C. Clarke

SCIENCE FICTION is not for everyone. Too often it involves a parade of metallic, humorless puppet characters that are put through a series of what have become routine situations involving time machines, spaceships, death rays, and eerie contacts with extraterrestrial beings. There is usually a full complement of essentially meaningless but exotic-sounding gadgets aboard, and these are operated at top speed by people whose names sound like a rare earth or a Himalayan mountain guide—"Captain Linax, I have the Worldlings on the gravitoscope" or "Trigon sensed that something was wrong the second that he stepped out of the magnetic air lock." As has been frequently observed, it is, on the whole, mediocre fiction and worse science. But every discipline manages to produce a few colossi, and science fiction has had its share. Jules Verne and H. G. Wells come to mind at once, along with more recent authors such as Čapek, Olaf Stapledon, A. E. Van Vogt, and the even more recent (and brilliant) English writer Arthur C. Clarke. Some of these men have used science fiction as a medium for social and political commentary. Wells' *The War of the Worlds* is, in addition to being a splendid story, a spoof of Victorian complacency and smugness:

> Even the daily papers woke up to the disturbance at last, and popular notes appeared here, there, and everywhere concerning the volcanoes upon Mars. The serio-comic periodical *Punch*, I remember, made a happy use of it in the political cartoon.

In any case, all of the exceptional science-fiction writers have in common vivid imaginations and a considerable amount of scientific understanding, which gives their work structure and plausibility. In that sense, scientific laws are to science fiction what metre is to verse. No matter how strange the writer's fantasy seems, it must give one the feeling that what is being described is logically and scientifically possible (at least, in principle, in the future), otherwise the description becomes unintelligible. Clarke has commented:

> Fantasy? Of course; the reality of our Universe *is* fantastic. We live in an age when we can keep up with tomorrow—or even today—only by letting our imaginations freewheel any-

where they care to travel, as long as they keep within the bounds of logic and the known laws of Nature.

As a science-fiction writer, Clarke has all of the essentials. In the first place, he has had a good deal of scientific training. Just after the war, he took a Bachelor of Science degree in physics and mathematics at King's College, in London, and for many years he has been a member of the British Interplanetary Society. Out of this experience have come a number of excellent popular scientific books, such as *The Challenge of the Spaceship,* that are not only fun to read but technically sound. In 1945, twelve years before the Sputnik and seventeen years before the Telstar, Clarke realized that satellites could be used for relaying electronic communications. He wrote a paper on this for *Wireless World,* but the whole idea seemed at the time too far-fetched to try to patent. Clarke notes, "Had I realised how quickly this idea would materialise, I would certainly have attempted to patent it—though it is some slight consolation to know that an application would probably have failed in 1945."

But Clarke's forte is an inexhaustible imagination and energy. His short stories run into the hundreds, and he has written a number of full-length novels. Of the latter, *Against the Fall of Night* and *Childhood's End* are top-ranking. (*Against the Fall of Night* was his first novel, written in 1937. In 1946 he rewrote it under a new title, *The City and the Stars.* Either version exhibits Clarke at his best.) Both are set in the far future and are concerned with the ultimate evolution of the human race, which Clarke seems to feel will be into a kind of state of pure mind. In *Childhood's End,* the Overlords, who are kindly and rather melancholy super-creatures, come to Earth from a planet forty light-years away to preside over the evolutionary transition. The Overlords are sad because the human race, despite its inferiority, has been chosen for the evolution. The Earth has now become expendable, and the book ends with Karellen, the Commander of the Overlords, watching its last moments from his spaceship:

> Karellen raised his hand and the picture changed once more. A single brilliant star glowed in the center of the screen; no one could have told, from this distance, that the Sun had ever possessed planets or that one of them had now been lost. For a long time Karellen stared back across that swiftly widening gulf, while many memories raced through his vast and labyrinthine mind. In silent farewell he saluted the men he had known, whether they had hindered or helped him in his purpose. No one dared disturb him or interrupt his thoughts: and presently he turned his back upon the dwindling Sun.

Pure fantasy it is, but there is a strange plausibility about the book, and one gets caught up and moved by it. Even Clarke's popular scientific writing is colored by his imagination, although it is always kept in check by the requirements of scientific accuracy. In *The Challenge of the Spaceship* there is a short essay, written in the style of a travel brochure—*So You're Going to Mars*—that describes how an interplanetary trip will look to a tourist. It is written with a perfectly straight face, and the journey unfolds with the calm inevitability of an ocean voyage:

> One of the big moments of the trip will come when you realize that Mars has begun to show a visible disk. The first feature you'll be able to see with the naked eye will be one of the polar caps, glittering like a tiny star on the edge of the planet. A few days later the dark areas—the so-called seas—will begin to appear, and presently you'll glimpse the prominent triangle of the Syrtis Major. In the week before landing, as the planet swims nearer and nearer, you'll get to know its geography pretty thoroughly.

Clarke's book *Tales of Ten Worlds* (Harcourt, Brace & World) is a collection of some of his most recent short stories. Several of these stories reflect his latest interest, undersea exploration. He now lives in Ceylon and spends a good deal of his time exploring the Pacific. He has written half a dozen books on the sea, and he feels that what he has learned in facing the challenges of undersea diving will prepare him for what will be encountered in interplanetary travel. But all of the new stories are the vivid blend of reality and irreality that is characteristic of Clarke's writing. I was especially struck by one of them—*Before Eden.* It is set in the not very distant future, when planetary exploration is already well under development. Two Americans are exploring Venus. Venus is a hot planet, and they are wearing special thermal suits that shield them from the heat. They are near the Venusian Pole, and it is wintertime, so the temperature has dropped to only two hundred degrees. They are looking for life. (Clarke does not expect that intelligent life will be found on the planets, but he thinks that unusual forms of plants and perhaps animals will certainly be turned up.) They come upon a weird plant that reacts to light by changing color, like a kaleidoscope, and is able to propel itself in search of food. In their excited wish to study the plant, they forget that they can contaminate it with earthly bacteria, which can kill it, unless they are tremendously careful. They handle the plant carefully, but they leave behind some debris, which the plant feeds on. There are bacteria in the debris, and the plant is contaminated. In turn, it contaminates the few forms of life, all of them fragile, on the planet. By coming to study life on Venus, man has destroyed it. As Clarke puts it, "Beneath the clouds of Venus, the story of Creation was ended."

In the hands of a master like Clarke, science fiction can be both exciting and instructive. It may also be a guide to us as we look toward the future.

2

How About
a Little Game ?
Stanley Kubrick

On pleasant afternoons, I often go into Washington Square Park to watch the Master at work. The Master is a professional chess player—a chess hustler, if you will. He plays for fifty cents a game; if you win, you get the fifty, and if he wins, he gets it. In case of a draw, no money changes hands. The Master plays for at least eight hours a day, usually seven days a week; in the winter he plays indoors in one or another of the Village coffeehouses. It is a hard way to make a living, even if you win all your games; the Master wins most of his, although I have seen him get beaten several games straight. It is impossible to cheat in chess, and the only hustle that the Master perpetrates is to make his opponents think they are better than they are. When I saw him one day recently, he was at work on what in the language of the park is called a "potzer"—a relatively weak player with an inflated ego. A glance at the board showed that the Master was a rook and a pawn up on his adversary—a situation that would cause a rational man to resign the game at once. A potzer is not rational (otherwise, he would have avoided the contest in the first place), and this one was determined to fight it out to the end. He was moving pawns wildly, and his hands were beginning to tremble. Since there is no one to blame but yourself, nothing is more ranking than a defeat in chess, especially if you are under the illusion that you are better than your opponent. The Master, smiling as seraphically as his hawk-like, angular features would allow, said, "You always were a good pawn player—especially when it comes to pushing them," which his deluded opponent took to be a compliment. At a rook and four pawns down, the potzer gave up, and a new game began.

My acquaintance with the Master goes back several years, but it was only recently that I learned of a connection between him and another man I know—the brilliant and original film-maker Stanley Kubrick, who has been responsible for such movies as *Paths of Glory, Lolita,* and *Dr. Strangelove.* The Master is not much of a moviegoer—his professional activities leave little time for it—and, as far as I know, he has never seen one of Kubrick's pictures. But his recollection of Kubrick is nonetheless quite distinct, reaching back to the early nineteen-fifties, when Kubrick, then in his early twenties (he was born in New York City on July 26, 1928), was also squeezing out a small living (he estimates about three dollars a day, "which goes a long way if all you are buying with it is food") by playing chess for cash in Washington

Square. Kubrick was then living on Sixteenth Street, off Sixth Avenue, and on nice days in the spring and summer he would wander into the park around noon and take up a position at one of the concrete chess tables near Macdougal and West Fourth streets. At nightfall, he would change tables to get one near the street light. "If you made the switch the right way," he recalls, "you could get a table in the shade during the day and one nearer the fountain, under the lights, at night." There was a hard core of perhaps ten regulars who came to play every day and, like Kubrick, put in about twelve hours at the boards, with interruptions only for food. Kubrick ranked himself as one of the stronger regulars. When no potzers or semi-potzers were around, the regulars played each other for money, offering various odds to make up for any disparities in ability. The best player, Arthur Feldman, gave Kubrick a pawn—a small advantage—and, as Kubrick remembers it, "he didn't make his living off me." The Master was regarded by the regulars as a semi-potzer—the possessor of a flashy but fundamentally unsound game that was full of pseudo traps designed to enmesh even lesser potzers and to insure the quickest possible win so that he could collect his bet and proceed to a new customer.

At that time, Kubrick's nominal non-chess-playing occupation (when he could work at it) was what it is now—making films. Indeed, by the time he was twenty-seven he had behind him a four-year career as a staff photographer for *Look,* followed by a five-year career as a film-maker, during which he had made two short features and two full-length films—*Fear and Desire* (1953) and *Killer's Kiss* (1955). By all sociological odds, Kubrick should never have got into the motion-picture business in the first place. He comes from an American Jewish family of Austro-Hungarian ancestry. His father is a doctor, still in active practice, and he grew up in comfortable middle-class surroundings in the Bronx. If all had gone according to form, Kubrick would have attended college and probably ended up as a doctor or a physicist—physics being the only subject he showed the slightest aptitude for in school. After four desultory years at Taft High School, in the Bronx, he graduated, with a 67 average, in 1945, the year in which colleges were flooded with returning servicemen. No college in the United States would even consider his application. Apart from everything else, Kubrick had failed English outright one year, and had had to make it up in the summer. In his recollection, high-school English courses consisted of sitting behind a book while the teacher would say, "Mr. Kubrick, when Silas Marner walked out of the door, what did he see?" followed by a prolonged silence caused by the fact that Kubrick hadn't read *Silas Marner,* or much of anything else.

When Kubrick was twelve, his father taught him to play chess, and when he was thirteen, his father, who is something of a camera bug, presented him with his first camera. At the time, Kubrick had hopes of becoming a jazz drummer and was seriously studying the technique, but he soon decided that he wanted to be a photographer, and instead of doing his schoolwork he set out to teach himself to become one. By the time he left high school, he had sold *Look* two picture stories—one of them, ironically, about an English teacher at Taft, Aaron Traister, who had succeeded in arousing Kubrick's interest in Shakespeare's plays by acting out all the parts in class. After high school, Kubrick registered for night courses at City College, hoping to obtain a B average so that he could transfer to regular undergraduate courses, but before he started going to classes, he was back at *Look* with some more pictures. The picture editor there, Helen O'Brian, upon hearing of his academic troubles, proposed that he come to *Look* as an apprentice photographer. "So I backed into a fantastically good job at the age of seventeen," Kubrick says. Released from the bondage of schoolwork, he also began to read everything that he could lay his hands on. In retrospect, he feels that not going to college and having had the four years to practice photography at *Look* and to read on his own was probably the most fortunate thing that ever happened to him.

It was while he was still at *Look* that Kubrick became a film-maker. An incessant moviegoer, he had seen the entire film collection of the Museum of Modern Art at least twice when he learned from a friend, Alex Singer (now also a movie director), that there was apparently a fortune to be made in producing short documentaries. Singer was working as an office boy at the March of Time and had learned —or thought he had learned—that his employers were spending forty thousand dollars to produce eight or nine minutes of film. Kubrick was extremely impressed by the number of dollars being spent per foot, and even more impressed when he learned, from phone calls to Eastman Kodak and various equipment-rental companies, that the cost of buying and developing film and renting camera equipment would allow him to make nine minutes of film, complete with an original musical score, for only about a thousand dollars. "We assumed," Kubrick recalls, "that the March of Time must have been selling their films at a profit, so if we could make a film for a thousand dollars, we couldn't lose our investment." Thus bolstered, he used his savings from the *Look* job to make a documentary about the middleweight boxer Walter Cartier, about whom he had previously done a picture story for *Look*. Called *Day of the Fight,* it was filmed with a rented spring-wound thirty-five-millimetre Eyemo camera and featured a musical score by Gerald Fried, a friend of Kubrick's who is now a well-known composer for the movies. Since Kubrick couldn't afford any professional help, he took care of the whole physical side of the production himself; essentially, this consisted of screwing a few ordinary photofloods into existing light fixtures. When the picture was done—for thirty-nine hundred dollars—Kubrick set out to sell it for forty thousand. Various distributing companies liked it, but, as Kubrick now says ruefully, "we were offered things like fifteen hundred dollars and twenty-five hundred dollars. We told one distributor that the March of Time was getting forty thousand dollars for *its* documentaries, and he said, 'You must be crazy.' The next thing we knew, the March of Time went out of business." Kubrick was finally able to sell his short to R.K.O. Pathé for about a hundred dollars more than it had cost him to make it.

Kubrick, of course, got great satisfaction out of seeing his documentary at the Paramount Theatre, where it played with a Robert Mitchum–Ava Gardner feature. He felt that it had turned out well, and he figured that he would now instantly get innumerable offers from the movie industry—"of which," he says, "I got none, to do anything." After a while, however, he made a second short for R.K.O. (which put up fifteen hundred dollars for it, barely covering expenses), this one about a flying priest who travelled through the Southwest from one Indian parish to another in a Piper Cub. To work on the film, Kubrick quit his job at *Look,* and when the film was finished, he went back to waiting for offers of employment, spending his time playing chess for quarters in the park. He soon reached the reasonable conclusion that there simply wasn't any money to be made in producing documentaries and that there were no film jobs to be had. After thinking about the millions of dollars that were being spent on making feature films, he decided to make one himself. "I felt that I certainly couldn't make one worse than the ones I was seeing every week," he says. On the assumption that there were actors around who would work for practically nothing, and that he could act as the whole crew, Kubrick estimated that he could make a feature film for something like ten thousand dollars, and he was able to raise this sum from his father and an uncle, Martin Perveler. The script was put together by an acquaintance of Kubrick's in the Village, and, as Kubrick now describes it, it was an exceedingly serious, undramatic, and pretentious allegory. "With the exception of Frank Silvera, the actors were not very experienced," he says, "and I didn't know anything about directing *any* actors. I totally failed to realize what I didn't know." The film, *Fear and Desire,* was about four soldiers lost behind enemy lines and struggling to regain their identities as well as their home base, and it was full of lines like "We spend our lives looking for our real names, our permanent addresses." "Despite everything, the film got an art-house distribution," Kubrick says. "It opened at the Guild Theatre, in New York, and it even got a couple of fairly good reviews, as well as a compliment from Mark Van Doren. There were a few good moments in it. It never returned a penny on its investment."

Not at all discouraged, Kubrick decided that the mere fact that a film of his was showing at a theatre at all might be used as the basis for raising money to make a second one. In any case, it was not otherwise apparent how he was going to earn a living. "There were still no offers from anybody to do anything," he says. "So in about two weeks a friend and I wrote another script. As a contrast to the first one, this one, called *Killer's Kiss,* was nothing but action sequences, strung together on a mechanically constructed gangster plot."

Killer's Kiss was co-produced by Morris Bousel, a relative of Kubrick's who owned a drugstore in the Bronx. Released in September, 1955, it, too, failed to bring in any revenue (in a retrospective of his films at the Museum of Modern Art two summers ago, Kubrick would not let either of his first two films be shown, and he would probably be just as happy if the prints were to disappear altogether), so, broke and in debt to Bousel and others, Kubrick returned to Washington Square to play chess for quarters.

The scene now shifts to Alex Singer. While serving in the Signal Corps during the Korean War, Singer met a man named James B. Harris, who was engaged in making Signal Corps training films. The son of the owner of an extremely successful television-film-distribution company, Flamingo Films (in which he had a financial interest), Harris wanted to become a film producer when he returned to civilian life. As Harris recalls it, Singer told him about "some guy in the Village who was going around all by himself making movies," and after they got out of the Army, introduced him to Kubrick, who had just finished *Killer's Kiss*. Harris and Kubrick were both twenty-six, and they got on at once, soon forming Harris-Kubrick Pictures Corporation. From the beginning, it was an extremely fruitful and very happy association. Together they made *The Killing, Paths of Glory,* and *Lolita.* They were going to do *Dr. Strangelove* jointly, but before work began on it, Harris came to the conclusion that being just a movie producer was not a job with enough artistic fulfillment for him, and he decided to both produce and direct. His first film was *The Bedford Incident,* which Kubrick considers very well directed. For his part, Harris regards Kubrick as a cinematic genius who can do anything.

The first act of the newly formed Harris-Kubrick Pictures Corporation was to purchase the screen rights to *Clean Break,* a paperback thriller by Lionel White. Kubrick and a writer friend named Jim Thompson turned it into a screenplay, and the resulting film, *The Killing,* which starred Sterling Hayden, was produced in association with United Artists, with Harris putting up about a third of the production cost. While *The Killing,* too, was something less than a financial success, it was sufficiently impressive to catch the eye of Dore Schary, then head of production for M-G-M. For the first time, Kubrick received an offer to work for a major studio, and he and Harris were invited to look over all the properties owned by M-G-M and pick out something to do. Kubrick remembers being astounded by the mountains of stories that M-G-M owned. It took the pair of them two weeks simply to go through the alphabetical synopsis cards. Finally, they selected *The Burning Secret,* by Stefan Zweig, and Kubrick and Calder Willingham turned it into a screenplay—only to find that Dore Schary had lost his job as a result of a major shuffle at M-G-M. Harris and Kubrick left soon afterward. Sometime during the turmoil, Kubrick suddenly recalled having read *Paths of Glory,* by Humphrey Cobb, while still a high-school student. "It was one of the few books I'd read for pleasure in high school," he says. "I think I found it lying around my father's office and started to read it while waiting for him to get finished with a patient." Harris agreed that it was well worth a try. However, none of the major studios took the slightest interest in it. Finally, Kubrick's and Harris's agent, Ronnie Lubin, managed to interest Kirk Douglas in doing it, and this was enough to persuade United Artists to back the film, provided it was done on a very low budget in Europe. Kubrick, Calder Willingham, and Jim Thompson wrote the screenplay, and in January of 1957 Kubrick went to Munich to make the film.

Seeing *Paths of Glory* is a haunting experience. The utter desolation, cynicism, and futility of war, as embodied in the arbitrary execution of three innocent French soldiers who have been tried and convicted of cowardice during a meaningless attack on a heavily fortified German position, comes through with simplicity and power. Some of the dialogue is imperfect, Kubrick agrees, but its imperfection almost adds to the strength and sincerity of the theme. The finale of the picture involves a young German girl who has been captured by the French and is being forced to sing a song for a group of drunken French soldiers about to be sent back into battle. The girl is frightened, and the soldiers are brutal. She begins to sing, and the humanity of the moment reduces the soldiers to silence, and then to tears. In the film, the girl was played by a young and pretty German actress, Suzanne Christiane Harlan (known in Germany by the stage name Suzanne Christian), and a year after the film was made, she and Kubrick were married. Christiane comes from a family of opera singers and stage personalities, and most of her life has been spent in the theatre; she was a ballet dancer before she became an actress, and currently she is a serious painter, in addition to managing the sprawling Kubrick household, which now includes three daughters.

Paths of Glory was released in November, 1957, and although it received excellent critical notices and broke about even financially, it did not lead to any real new opportunities for Kubrick and Harris. Kubrick returned to Hollywood and wrote two new scripts, which were never used, and worked for six months on a Western for Marlon Brando, which he left before it went into production. (Ultimately, Brando directed it himself, and it became *One-Eyed Jacks.*) It was not until 1960 that Kubrick actually began working on a picture again. In that year, Kirk Douglas asked him to take over the direction of *Spartacus,* which Douglas was producing and starring in. Shooting had been under way for a week, but Douglas and Anthony Mann, his director, had had a falling out. On *Spartacus,* in contrast to all his other films, Kubrick had no legal control over the script or the final form of the movie. Although Kubrick did the cutting on *Spartacus,* Kirk Douglas had the final say as to the results, and the consequent confusion of points of view produced a film that Kubrick thinks could have been better.

While *Spartacus* was being edited, Kubrick and Harris bought the rights to Vladimir Nabokov's novel *Lolita.* There was immense pressure from all sorts of public groups not to make *Lolita* into a film, and for a while it looked as if Kubrick and Harris would not be able to raise the money to do it. In the end, though, the money was raised, and the film was made, in London. Kubrick feels that the weakness of the film was its lack of eroticism, which was inevitable. "The important thing in the novel is to think at the outset that Humbert is enslaved by his 'perversion,'" Kubrick says. "Not until the end, when Lolita is married and pregnant and no longer a nymphet, do you realize—along with Humbert—that he loves her. In the film, the fact that his sexual obsession could not be portrayed tended to imply from the start that he was in love with her."

It was the building of the Berlin Wall that sharpened Kubrick's interest in nuclear weapons and nuclear strategy, and he began to read everything he could get hold of about the bomb. Eventually, he decided that he had about covered the spectrum, and that he was not learning anything new. "When you start reading the analyses of nuclear strategy, they seem so thoughtful that you're lulled into a temporary sense of reassurance," Kubrick has explained. "But as you go deeper into it, and become more involved, you begin to realize that every one of these lines of thought leads to a paradox." It is this constant element of paradox in all the nuclear strategies and in the conventional attitudes toward them that Kubrick transformed into the principal theme of *Dr. Strangelove.* The picture was a new departure for Kubrick. His other films had involved putting novels on the screen, but *Dr. Strangelove,* though it did have its historical origins in *Red Alert,* a serious nuclear suspense story by Peter George, soon turned into an attempt to use a purely intellectual notion as the basis of a film. In this case, the intellectual notion was the inevitable paradox posed by following any of the nuclear strategies to their extreme limits. "By now, the bomb has almost no reality and has become a complete abstraction, represented by a few newsreel shots of mushroom clouds," Kubrick has said.

"People react primarily to direct experience and not to abstractions; it is very rare to find anyone who can become emotionally involved with an abstraction. The longer the bomb is around without anything happening, the better the job that people do in psychologically denying its existence. It has become as abstract as the fact that we are all going to die someday, which we usually do an excellent job of denying. For this reason, most people have very little interest in nuclear war. It has become even less interesting as a problem than, say, city government, and the longer a nuclear event is postponed, the greater becomes the illusion that we are constantly building up security, like interest at the bank. As time goes on, the danger increases, I believe, because the thing becomes more and more remote in people's minds. No one can predict the panic that suddenly arises when all the lights go out—that indefinable something that can make a leader abandon his carefully laid plans. A lot of effort has gone into trying to imagine possible nuclear accidents and to protect against them. But whether the human imagination is really capable of encompassing all the subtle permutations and psychological variants of these possibilities, I doubt. The nuclear strategists who make up all those war scenarios are never as inventive as reality, and political and military leaders are never as sophisticated as they think they are."

Such limited optimism as Kubrick has about the long-range prospects of the human race is based in large measure on his hope that the rapid development of space exploration will change our views of ourselves and our world. Most people who have thought much about space travel have arrived at the somewhat ironic conclusion that there is a very close correlation between the ability of a civilization to make significant space voyages and its ability to learn to live with nuclear energy. Unless there are sources of energy that are totally beyond the ken of modern physics, it is quite clear that the only source at hand for really elaborate space travel is the nucleus. The chemical methods of combustion used in our present rockets are absurdly inefficient compared to nuclear power. A detailed study has been made of the possibilities of using nuclear explosions to propel large spaceships, and, from a technical point of view, there is no reason that this cannot be done; indeed, if we are to transport really large loads to, say, the planets, it is essential that it be done. Thus, any civilization that operates on the same laws of nature as our own will inevitably reach the point where it learns to explore space and to use nuclear energy about simultaneously. The question is whether there can exist any society with enough maturity to peacefully use the latter to perform the former. In fact, some of the more melancholy thinkers on this subject have come to the conclusion that the earth has never been visited by beings from outer space because no civilization has been able to survive its own technology. That there *are* extraterrestrial civilizations in some state of development is firmly believed by many astronomers, biologists, philosophers, physicists, and other rational people—a conclusion based partly on the vastness of the cosmos, with its billions of stars. It is presumptuous to suppose that we are its only living occupants. From a chemical and biological point of view, the processes of forming life do not appear so extraordinary that they should not have occurred countless times throughout the universe. One may try to imagine what sort of transformation would take place in human attitudes if intelligent life should be discovered elsewhere in our universe. In fact, this is what Kubrick has been trying to do in his latest project, *2001: A Space Odyssey*, which, in the words of Arthur Clarke, the co-author of its screenplay, "will be about the first contact"—the first human contact with extraterrestrial life.

It was Arthur Clarke who introduced me to Kubrick. We met in New York a few years back, when he was working on a book about the future of scientific ideas and wanted to discuss some of the latest developments in physics. I always look forward to his occasional visits from Ceylon, and when he called me up one evening some time ago, I was very happy to hear from him. He lost no time in explaining what he was up to. "I'm working with Stanley Kubrick on the successor to *Dr. Strangelove*," he said. "Stanley is an amazing man, and I want you to meet him." It was an invitation not to be resisted, and Clarke arranged a visit to Kubrick soon afterward.

Kubrick was at that time living, on the upper East Side, in a large apartment whose décor was a mixture of Christiane's lovely paintings, the effects of three rambunctious young children, and Kubrick's inevitable collection of cameras, tape recorders, and hi-fi sets. (There was also a short-wave radio, which he was using to monitor broadcasts from Moscow, in order to learn the Russian attitude toward Vietnam. Christiane once said that "Stanley would be happy with eight tape recorders and one pair of pants.") Kubrick himself did not conform at all to my expectations of what a movie mogul would look like. He is of medium height and has the bohemian look of a riverboat gambler or a Rumanian poet. (He has now grown a considerable beard, which gives his broad features a somewhat Oriental quality.) He had the vaguely distracted look of a man who is simultaneously thinking about a hard problem and trying to make everyday conversation. During our meeting, the phone rang incessantly, a messenger arrived at the door with a telegram or an envelope every few minutes, and children of various ages and sexes ran in and out of the living room. After a few attempts at getting the situation under control, Kubrick abandoned the place to the children, taking me into a small breakfast room near the kitchen. I was immediately impressed by Kubrick's immense intellectual curiosity. When he is working on a subject, he becomes completely immersed in it and appears to absorb information from all sides, like a sponge. In addition to writing a novel with Clarke, which was to be the basis of the script for *2001*, he was reading every popular and semi-popular book on science that he could get hold of.

During our conversation, I happened to mention that I had just been in Washington Square Park playing chess. He asked me whom I had been playing with, and I described the Master. Kubrick recognized him immediately. I had been playing a good deal with the Master, and my game had improved to the point where I was almost breaking even with him, so I was a little stunned to learn that Kubrick had played the Master on occasion, and that in his view the Master was a potzer. Kubrick went on to say that he loved playing chess, and added, "How about a little game right now?" By pleading another appointment, I managed to stave off the challenge.

I next saw Kubrick in London, where I had gone to a physicists' meeting and where he was in the process of organizing the actual filming of *2001*. I dropped in at his office in the M-G-M studio in Boreham Wood, outside London, one afternoon, and again was confronted by an incredible disarray—papers, swatches of materials to be used for costumes, photographs of actors who might be used to play astronauts, models of spaceships, drawings by his daughters, and the usual battery of cameras, radios, and tape recorders. Kubrick likes to keep track of things in small notebooks, and he had just ordered a sample sheet of every type of notebook paper made by a prominent paper firm—about a hundred varieties—which were spread out on a large table. We talked for a while amid the usual interruptions of messengers and telephone calls, and then he got back to the subject of chess: "How about a little game right now?" He managed to find a set of chessmen—it was missing some pieces, but we filled in for them with various English coins—and when he couldn't find a board he drew one up on a large sheet of paper. Sensing the outcome, I remarked that I had never been beaten five times in a row—a number that I chose more or less at random, figuring that it was unlikely that we would ever get to play five games.

I succeeded in losing two rapid games before Kubrick had to go back to London, where he and his family were living in a large apartment in the Dorchester Hotel. He asked me to come along and finish out the five games—the figure appeared to fascinate him—and as soon as he could get the girls off to bed and order dinner for Christiane, himself, and me sent up to the apartment, he produced a second chess set, with all the pieces and a genuine wooden board.

Part of the art of the professional chess player is to unsettle one's opponent as much as possible by small but legitimate annoying incidental activities, such as yawning, looking at one's watch, and snapping one's fingers softly—at all of which Kubrick is highly skilled. One of the girls came into the room and asked, "What's the matter with your friend?"

"He's about to lose another game," said Kubrick.

I tried to counter these pressures by singing "Moon River" over and over, but I lost the next two games. Then came the crucial fifth game, and by some miracle I actually won it. Aware that this was an important psychological moment, I announced that I had been hustling Kubrick and had dropped the first four games deliberately. Kubrick responded by saying that the poor quality of those games had lulled him into a temporary mental lapse. (In the course of making *Dr. Strangelove,* Kubrick had all but hypnotized George C. Scott by continually beating him at chess while simultaneously attending to the direction of the movie.) We would have played five more games on the spot, except that it was now two in the morning, and Kubrick's working day on the *2001* set began very early.

The Sentinel, a short story by Arthur Clarke in which *2001* finds its genesis, begins innocently enough: "The next time you see the full moon high in the south, look carefully at its right-hand edge and let your eye travel upward along the curve of the disk. Around about two o'clock you will notice a small dark oval; anyone with normal eyesight can find it quite easily. It is the great walled plain, one of the finest on the moon, known as the Mare Crisium—the Sea of Crises." Then Clarke adds, unobtrusively, "Three hundred miles in diameter, and almost completely surrounded by a ring of magnificent mountains, it had never been explored until we entered it in the late summer of 1996." The story and the style are typical of Clarke's blend of science and fantasy. In this case, an expedition exploring the moon uncovers, on the top of a mountain, a little pyramid set on a carefully hewed-out terrace. At first, the explorers suppose it to be a trace left behind by a primitive civilization in the moon's past. But the terrain around it, unlike the rest of the moon's surface, is free of all debris and craters created by falling meteorites—the pyramid, they discover, contains a mechanism that sends out a powerful force that shields it from external disturbances and perhaps signals to some distant observer. When the explorers finally succeed in breaking through the shield and studying the pyramid, they become convinced that its origins are as alien to the moon as they are themselves. The astronaut telling the story says, "The mystery haunts us all the more now that the other planets have been reached and we know that only Earth has ever been the home of intelligent life in our universe. Nor could any lost civilization of our own world have built that machine. . . . It was set there upon its mountain before life had emerged from the seas of Earth."

But suddenly the narrator realizes the pyramid's meaning. It was left by some far-off civilization as a sentinel to signal that living beings had finally reached it:

Nearly a hundred thousand million stars are turning in the circle of the Milky Way, and long ago other races on the worlds of other suns must have scaled and passed the heights that we have reached. Think of such civilizations, far back in time against the fading afterglow of Creation, masters of a universe so young that life as yet had come only to a handful of worlds. Theirs would have been a loneliness we cannot imagine, the loneliness of gods looking out across infinity and finding none to share their thoughts.

They must have searched the star-clusters as we have searched the planets. Everywhere there would be worlds, but they would be empty or peopled with crawling, mindless things. Such was our own Earth, the smoke of the great volcanoes still staining the skies, when that first ship of the peoples of the dawn came sliding in from the abyss beyond Pluto. It passed the frozen outer worlds, knowing that life could play no part in their destinies. It came to rest among the inner planets, warming themselves around the fire of the sun and waiting for their stories to begin.

These wanderers must have looked on Earth, circling safely in the narrow zone between fire and ice, and must have guessed that it was the favorite of the sun's children. Here, in the distant future, would be intelligence; but there were countless stars before them still, and they might never come this way again.

So they left a sentinel, one of millions they have scattered throughout the universe, watching over all worlds with the promise of life. It was a beacon that down the ages has been patiently signalling the fact that no one had discovered it.

The astronaut concludes:

I can never look now at the Milky Way without wondering from which of those banked clouds of stars the emissaries are coming. If you will pardon so commonplace a simile, we have set off the fire alarm and have nothing to do but to wait.

I do not think we will have to wait for long.

Clarke and Kubrick spent two years transforming this short story into a novel and then into a script for *2001,* which is concerned with the discovery of the sentinel and a search for traces of the civilization that put it there—a quest that takes the searchers out into the far reaches of the solar system. Extraterrestrial life may seem an odd subject for a motion picture, but at this stage in his career Kubrick is convinced that any idea he is really interested in, however unlikely it may sound, can be transferred to film. "One of the English science-fiction writers once said, 'Sometimes I think we're alone, and sometimes I think we're not. In either case, the idea is quite staggering,'" Kubrick once told me. "I must say I agree with him."

By the time the film appears, according to Kubrick's estimate, he and Clarke will have put in an average of four hours a day, six days a week, on the writing of the script. (This works out to about twenty-four hundred hours of writing for two hours and forty minutes of film.) Even during the actual shooting of the film, Kubrick spends every free moment reworking the scenario. He has an extra office set up in a blue trailer that was once Deborah Kerr's dressing room, and when shooting is going on, he has it wheeled onto the set to give him a certain amount of privacy for writing. He frequently gets ideas for dialogue from his actors, and when he likes an idea he puts it in. (Peter Sellers, he says, contributed some wonderful bits of humor for *Dr. Strangelove.*)

In addition to writing and directing, Kubrick supervises every aspect of his films, from selecting costumes to choosing the incidental music. In making *2001,* he is, in a sense, trying to second-guess the future. Scientists planning long-range space projects can ignore such questions as what sort of hats rocket-ship hostesses will wear when space travel becomes common (in *2001* the hats have padding in them to cushion any collisions with the ceiling that weightlessness might cause), and what sort of voices computers will have if, as many experts feel is certain, they learn to talk and to respond to voice commands (there is a talking computer in *2001* that arranges for the astronauts' meals, gives them medical treatments, and even plays chess with them during a long space mission to Jupiter—"Maybe it ought to sound like Jackie Mason," Kubrick once said), and what kind of time will be kept aboard a spaceship (Kubrick chose Eastern Standard, for the convenience of communicating with Washington). In the sort of planning that NASA does, such matters can be dealt with as they come up, but in a movie everything is immediately visible and explicit, and questions like this must be answered in detail. To help him find the answers, Kubrick has assembled around him a group of thirty-five artists and designers, more than twenty special-effects people, and a staff of scientific advisers. By the time the picture is done, Kubrick figures, he will have consulted with people from a generous sampling of the leading aeronautical companies in the United States and Europe, not to mention innumerable scientific and industrial firms. One consultant, for instance, was Professor Marvin Minsky, of M.I.T., who is a leading authority on artificial intelligence and the construction of automata. (He is now building a robot at M.I.T. that can catch a ball.) Kubrick wanted to learn from him whether any of the things that he was planning to have his computers do were likely to be realized by the year 2001; he was pleased to find out that they were.

Kubrick told me he had seen practically every science-fiction film ever made, and any number of more conventional films that had interesting special effects. One Saturday afternoon, after lunch and two rapid chess games, he and Christiane and I set out to see a Russian science-fiction movie called *Astronauts on Venus,* which he had discovered playing somewhere in North London. Saturday afternoon at a neighborhood movie house in London is like Saturday afternoon at the movies anywhere; the theatre was full of children talking, running up and down the aisles, chewing gum, and eating popcorn. The movie was in Russian, with English subtitles, and since most of the children couldn't read very well, let alone speak Russian, the dialogue was all but drowned out by the general babble. This was probably all to the good, since the film turned out to be a terrible hodgepodge of pseudo science and Soviet propaganda. It featured a talking robot named John and a talking girl named Masha who had been left in a small spaceship orbiting Venus while a party of explorers—who thought, probably correctly, that she would have been a nuisance below—went off to explore. Although Kubrick reported that the effects used were crude, he insisted that we stick it out to the end, just in case.

Before I left London, I was able to spend a whole day with Kubrick, starting at about eight-fifteen, when an M-G-M driver picked us up in one of the studio cars. (Kubrick suffers automobiles tolerably well, but he will under almost no circumstances travel by plane, even though he holds a pilot's license and has put in about a hundred and fifty hours in the air, principally around Teterboro Airport; after practicing landings and takeoffs, flying solo cross-country to Albany, and taking his friends up for rides, he lost interest in flying.) Boreham Wood is a little like the area outside Boston that is served by Route 128, for it specializes in electronics companies and precision industry, and the M-G-M studio is hardly distinguishable from the rather antiseptic-looking factories nearby. It consists of ten enormous sound stages concealed in industrial-looking buildings and surrounded by a cluster of carpenter shops, paint shops, office units, and so on. Behind the buildings is a huge lot covered with bits and pieces of

other productions—the façade of a French provincial village, the hulk of a Second World War bomber, and other
debris. Kubrick's offices are near the front of the complex
in a long bungalow structure that houses, in addition to
his production staff, a group of youthful model-makers
working on large, very detailed models of spacecraft to be
used in special-effects photography; Kubrick calls their
realm "Santa's Workshop." When we walked into his
private office, it seemed to me that the general disorder
had grown even more chaotic since my last visit. Tacked to
a bulletin board were some costume drawings showing
men dressed in odd-looking, almost Edwardian business
suits. Kubrick said that the drawings were supposed to be
of the business suit of the future and had been submitted
by one of the innumerable designers who had been asked
to furnish ideas on what men's clothes would look like in
thirty-five years. "The problem is to find something that
looks different and that might reflect new developments in
fabrics but that isn't so far out as to be distracting,"
Kubrick said. "Certainly buttons will be gone. Even now,
there are fabrics that stick shut by themselves."

Just then, Victor Lyndon, Kubrick's associate producer
(he was also the associate producer of *Dr. Strangelove*
and most recently of *Darling*), came in. A trim, ath-
letic-looking man of forty-six, he leans toward the latest
"mod" styling in clothes, and he was wearing an elegant
green buttonless, self-shutting shirt. He was followed by a
young man wearing hair down to his neck, a notably non-
shutting shirt, and boots, who was introduced as a brand-
new costume designer. (He was set up at a drawing table
in Santa's Workshop, but that afternoon he announced
that the atmosphere was too distracting for serious work,
and left; the well-known British designer Hardy Amies was
finally chosen to design the costumes.) Lyndon fished from
a manila envelope a number of shoulder patches designed
to be worn as identification by the astronauts. (The two

principal astronauts in the film were to be played by Keir Dullea, who has starred in *David and Lisa* and *Bunny Lake Is Missing,* and Gary Lockwood, a former college-football star and now a television and movie actor.) Kubrick said that the lettering didn't look right, and suggested that the art department make up new patches using actual NASA lettering. He then consulted one of the small notebooks in which he lists all the current production problems, along with the status of their solutions, and announced that he was going to the art department to see how the drawings of the moons of Jupiter were coming along.

The art department, which occupies a nearby building, is presided over by Tony Masters, a tall, Lincolnesque man who was busy working on the Jupiter drawings when we appeared. Kubrick told me that the department, which designs and dresses all sets, was constructing a scale model of the moon, including the back side, which had been photographed and mapped by rocket. Looking over the Jupiter drawings, Kubrick said that the light in them looked a little odd to him, and suggested that Masters have Arthur Clarke check on it that afternoon when he came out from London.

Our next stop was to pick up some papers in the separate office where Kubrick does his writing—a made-over dressing room in a quiet part of the lot. On our way to it, we passed an outbuilding containing a number of big generators; a sign reading "DANGER!—11,500 VOLTS!" was nailed to its door. "Why eleven thousand five *hundred?*" Kubrick said. "Why not twelve thousand? If you put a sign like that in a movie, people would think it was a fake." When we reached the trailer, I could see that it was used as much for listening as for writing, for in addition to the usual battery of tape recorders (Kubrick writes rough first drafts of his dialogue by dictating into a recorder, since he finds that this gives it a more natural flow) there was a phonograph and an enormous collection of records, practically all of them of contemporary music. Kubrick told me that he thought he had listened to almost every modern composition available on records in an effort to decide what style of music would fit the film. Here, again, the problem was to find something that sounded unusual and distinctive but not so unusual as to be distracting. In the office collection were records by the practitioners of *musique concrète* and electronic music in general, and records of works by the contemporary German composer Carl Orff. In most cases, Kubrick said, film music tends to lack originality, and a film about the future might be the ideal place for a really striking score by a major composer.

We returned to the main office, and lunch was brought in from the commissary. During lunch, Kubrick signed a stack of letters, sent off several cables, and took a long-distance call from California. "At this stage of the game, I feel like the counterman at Katz's delicatessen on Houston Street at lunch hour," he said. "You've hardly finished saying 'Half a pound of corned beef' when he says 'What else?' and before you can say 'A sliced rye' he's saying 'What else?' again."

I asked whether he ever got things mixed up, and he said rarely, adding that he thought chess playing had sharpened his naturally retentive memory and gift for organization. "With such a big staff, the problem is for people to figure out what they should come to see you about and what they should *not* come to see you about," he went on. "You invariably find your time taken up with questions that aren't important and could have easily been disposed of without your opinion. To offset this, decisions are sometimes taken without your approval that can wind up in frustrating dead ends."

As we were finishing lunch, Victor Lyndon came in with an almanac that listed the average temperature and rainfall all over the globe at every season of the year. "We're

looking for a cool desert where we can shoot some sequences during the late spring," Kubrick said. "We've got
our eye on a location in Spain, but it might be pretty hot
to work in comfortably, and we might have trouble controlling the lighting. If we don't go to Spain, we'll have to
build an entirely new set right here. More work for Tony
Masters and his artists." (Later, I learned that Kubrick did
decide to shoot on location.)

After lunch, Kubrick and Lyndon returned to a long-
standing study of the space-suit question. In the film, the
astronauts will wear space suits when they are working
outside their ships, and Kubrick was very anxious that they
should look like the space suits of thirty-five years from
now. After numerous consultations with Ordway and
other NASA experts, he and Lyndon had finally settled on a
design, and now they were studying a vast array of samples
of cloth to find one that would look right and photograph
well. While this was going on, people were constantly
dropping into the office with drawings, models, letters,
cables, and various props, such as a model of a lens for one
of the telescopes in a spaceship. (Kubrick rejected it because it looked too crude.) At the end of the day, when my
head was beginning to spin, someone came by with a
wristwatch that the astronauts were going to use on their
Jupiter voyage (which Kubrick rejected) and a plastic
drinking glass for the moon hotel (which Kubrick thought
looked fine). About seven o'clock, Kubrick called for his
car, and by eight-thirty he had returned home, put the
children to bed, discussed the day's events with his wife,
watched a news broadcast on television, telephoned Clarke
for a brief discussion of whether nuclear-powered spacecraft would pollute the atmosphere with their exhausts
(Clarke said that they certainly would today but that by
the time they actually come into use somebody will have
figured out what to do about poisonous exhausts), and

taken out his chess set. "How about a little game?" he said in a seductive tone that the Master would have envied.

On December 29, 1965, shooting of the film began, and in early March the company reached the most intricate part of the camerawork, which was to be done in the interior of a giant centrifuge. One of the problems in space travel will be weightlessness. While weightlessness has, because of its novelty, a certain glamour and amusement, it would be an extreme nuisance on a long trip, and probably a health hazard as well. Our physical systems have evolved to work against the pull of gravity, and it is highly probable that all sorts of unfortunate things, such as softening of the bones, would result from exposure to weightlessness for months at a time. In addition, of course, nothing stays in place without gravity, and no normal activity is possible unless great care is exercised; the slightest jar can send you hurtling across the cabin. Therefore, many spacecraft designers figure that some sort of artificial gravity will have to be supplied for space travellers. In principle, this is very easy to do. An object on the rim of a wheel rotating at a uniform speed is subjected to a constant force pushing it away from the center, and if the size of the wheel and the speed of its rotation are adjusted, this centrifugal force can be made to resemble the force of gravity. Having accepted this notion, Kubrick went one step further and commissioned the Vickers Engineering Group to make an actual centrifuge, large enough for the astronauts to live in full time. It took six months to build and cost about three hundred thousand dollars. The finished product looks from the outside like a Ferris wheel thirty-eight feet in diameter and can be rotated at a maximum speed of about three miles an hour. This is not enough to parallel the force of gravity—the equipment inside the centrifuge has to be bolted to the floor—but it has enabled Kubrick to achieve some remarkable photographic effects. The interior, eight feet wide, is fitted out with an enormous computer console, an electronically operated medical dispensary, a shower, a device for taking an artificial sunbath, a recreation area, with a Ping-pong table and an electronic piano, and five beds with movable plastic domes—hibernacula, where astronauts who are not on duty can, literally, hibernate for months at a time. (The trip to Jupiter will take two hundred and fifty-seven days.)

I had seen the centrifuge in the early stages of its construction and very much wanted to observe it in action, so I was delighted when chance sent me back to England in the early spring. When I walked through the door of the *2001* set one morning in March, I must say that the scene that presented itself to me was overwhelming. In the middle of the hangarlike stage stood the centrifuge, with cables and lights hanging from every available inch of its steel-girdered superstructure. On the floor to one side of its frame was an immense electronic console (not a prop), and, in various places, six microphones and three television receivers. I learned later that Kubrick had arranged a closed-circuit-television system so that he could watch what was going on inside the centrifuge during scenes being filmed when he could not be inside himself. Next to the microphone was an empty canvas chair with "Stanley Kubrick" painted on its back in fading black letters. Kubrick himself was nowhere to be seen, but everywhere I looked there were people, some hammering and sawing, some carrying scripts, some carrying lights. In one corner I saw a woman applying makeup to what appeared to be an astronaut wearing blue coveralls and leather boots. Over a loudspeaker, a pleasantly authoritative English voice—belonging, I learned shortly, to Derek Cracknell, Kubrick's first assistant director—was saying, "Will someone bring the Governor's Polaroid on the double?" A man came up to me and asked how I would like my tea and whom I was looking for, and almost before I could reply "One lump with lemon" and "Stanley Kubrick," led me, in a semi-daze, to an opening at the bottom of the centrifuge. Peering up into the dazzlingly illuminated interior, I spotted Kubrick lying flat on his back on the floor of the machine and staring up through the viewfinder of an enormous camera, in complete concentration. Keir Dullea, dressed in shorts and a white T-shirt, and covered by a blue blanket, was lying in an open hibernaculum on the rising curve of the floor. He was apparently comfortably asleep, and Kubrick was telling him to wake up as simply as possible." "Just open your eyes," he said. "Let's not have any stirring, yawning, and rubbing."

One of the lights burned out, and while it was being fixed, Kubrick unwound himself from the camera, spotted me staring openmouthed at the top of the centrifuge, where the furniture of the crew's dining quarters was fastened to the ceiling, and said, "Don't worry—that stuff is bolted down." Then he motioned to me to come up and join him.

No sooner had I climbed into the centrifuge than Cracknell, who turned out to be a cheerful and all but imperturbable youthful-looking man in tennis shoes (all the crew working in the centrifuge were wearing tennis shoes, not only to keep from slipping but to help them climb the steeply curving sides; indeed, some of them were working while clinging to the bolted-down furniture halfway up the wall) , said, "Here's your Polaroid, Guv," and handed Kubrick the camera. I asked Kubrick what he needed the Polaroid for, and he explained that he used it for checking subtle lighting effects for color film. He and the director of photography, Geoffrey Unsworth, had worked out a correlation between how the lighting appeared on the instantly developed Polaroid film and the settings on the movie camera. I asked Kubrick if it was customary for movie directors to participate so actively in the photographing of a movie, and he said succinctly that he had never watched any other movie director work.

The light was fixed, and Kubrick went back to work behind the camera. Keir Dullea was reinstalled in his hibernaculum and the cover rolled shut. "You better take your hands from under the blanket," Kubrick said. Kelvin Pike, the camera operator, took Kubrick's place behind the camera, and Cracknell called for quiet. The camera began to turn, and Kubrick said, "Open the hatch." The top of the hibernaculum slid back with a whirring sound, and Keir Dullea woke up, without any stirring, yawning, or rubbing. Kubrick, playing the part of the solicitous computer, started feeding him lines.

"Good morning," said Kubrick. "What do you want for breakfast?"

"Some bacon and eggs would be fine," Dullea answered simply.

Later, Kubrick told me that he had engaged an English actor to read the computer's lines in the serious dramatic scenes, in order to give Dullea and Lockwood something more professional to play against, and that in the finished film he would dub in an American-accented voice. He and Dullea went through the sequence four or five times, and finally Kubrick was satisfied with what he had. Dullea bounced out of his hibernaculum, and I asked him whether he was having a good time. He said he was getting a great kick out of all the tricks and gadgets, and added, "This is a happy set, and that's something."

When Kubrick emerged from the centrifuge, he was immediately surrounded by people. "Stanley, there's a black pig outside for you to look at," Victor Lyndon was saying. He led the way outside, and, sure enough, in a large truck belonging to an animal trainer was an enormous jet-black pig. Kubrick poked it, and it gave a suspicious grunt.

"The pig looks good," Kubrick said to the trainer.

"I can knock it out with a tranquillizer for the scenes when it's supposed to be dead," the trainer said.

"Can you get any tapirs or anteaters?" Kubrick asked.

The trainer said that this would not be an insuperable problem, and Kubrick explained to me, "We're going to use them in some scenes about prehistoric man."

At this point, a man carrying a stuffed lion's head approached and asked Kubrick whether it would be all right to use.

"The tongue looks phony, and the eyes are only marginal," Kubrick said, heading for the set. "Can somebody fix the tongue?"

Back on the set, he climbed into his blue trailer. "Maybe the company can get back some of its investment selling guided tours of the centrifuge," he said. "They might even feature a ride on it." He added that the work in the machine was incredibly slow, because it took hours to rearrange all the lights and cameras for each new sequence. Originally, he said, he had planned on a hundred and thirty days of shooting for the main scenes, but the centrifuge sequences had slowed them down by perhaps a week. "I take advantage of every delay and breakdown to go off by myself and think," he said. "Something like playing chess when your opponent takes a long time over his next move."

At one o'clock, just before lunch, many of the crew went with Kubrick to a small projection room near the set to see the results of the previous day's shooting. The most prominent scene was a brief one that showed Gary Lockwood exercising in the centrifuge, jogging around its interior and shadowboxing to the accompaniment of a Chopin waltz—picked by Kubrick because he felt that an intelligent man in *2001* might choose Chopin for doing exercise to music. As the film appeared on the screen, Lockwood was shown jogging around the complete interior circumference of the centrifuge, which appeared to me to defy logic as well as physics, since when he was at the top he would have needed suction cups on his feet to stay glued to the floor. I asked Kubrick how he had achieved this effect, and he said he was definitely, absolutely not going to tell me. As the scene went on, Kubrick's voice could be heard on the sound track, rising over the Chopin: "Gain a little on the camera, Gary! . . . Now a flurry of lefts and rights! . . . A little more vicious!" After the film had run its course, Kubrick appeared quite pleased with the results, remarking, "It's nice to get two minutes of usable film after two days of shooting."

Later that afternoon, I had a chance to see a publicity short made up of some of the most striking material so far filmed for *2001*. There were shots of the space station, with people looking out of the windows at the earth wheeling in the distance; there was an incredible sequence, done in red, showing a hostess on a moon rocket appearing to walk on the ceiling of the spaceship; there was a solemn procession of astronauts trudging along on the surface of the moon. The colors and the effects were extremely impressive.

When I got back to the set, I found Kubrick getting ready to leave for the day. "Come around to the house tomorrow," he said. "I'll be working at home, and maybe we can get in a little game. I still think you're a complete potzer. But I can't understand what happens every fifth game."

He had been keeping track of our games in a notebook, and the odd pattern of five had indeed kept reappearing. The crucial tenth game had been a draw, and although I had lost the fifteenth, even Kubrick admitted that he had had an amazingly close call. As for the games that had not been multiples of five, they had been outright losses for me. We had now completed nineteen games, and I could sense Kubrick's determination to break the pattern.

The next morning, I presented myself at the Kubricks'

house, in Hertfordshire, just outside London, which they have rented until *2001* is finished. It is a marvellous house and an enormous one, with two suits of armor in one of the lower halls, and rooms all over the place, including a panelled billiard room with a big snooker table. Christiane has fixed up one room as a painting studio, and Kubrick has turned another into an office, filled with the inevitable tape recorders and cameras. They moved their belongings from New York in ninety numbered dark-green summer-camp trunks bought from Boy Scout headquarters—the only sensible way of moving, Kubrick feels. The house is set in a lovely bit of English countryside, near a rest home for horses, where worthy old animals are sent to live out their declining years in tranquillity. Heating the house poses a major problem. It has huge picture windows, and Arthur Clarke's brother Fred, who is a heating engineer, has pointed out to Kubrick that glass conducts heat so effectively that he would not be much worse off (except for the wind) if the glass in the windows were removed entirely. The season had produced a tremendous cold spell, and in addition to using electric heaters in every corner of the rooms, Kubrick had acquired some enormous thick blue bathrobes, one of which he lent me. Thus bundled up, we sat down at the inevitable chessboard at ten in the morning for our twentieth game, which I proceeded to win on schedule. "I can't understand it," Kubrick said. "I know you are a potzer, so why are you winning these fifth games?"

A tray of sandwiches was brought in for lunch, and we sat there in our blue bathrobes like two figures from Bergman's *The Seventh Seal,* playing on and taking time out only to munch a sandwich or light an occasional cigar. The children, who had been at a birthday party, dropped in later in the day in their party dresses to say hello, as did Christiane, but the games went on. I lost four in a row, and by late afternoon it was time for the twenty-fifth game, which, Kubrick announced, would settle the matter once and for all. We seesawed back and forth until I thought I saw a marvellous chance for a coup. I made as if to take off one of Kubrick's knights, and Kubrick clutched his brow dramatically, as though in sharp pain. I then made the move ferociously, picking off the knight, and Kubrick jumped up from the table.

"I knew you were a potzer! It was a trap!" he announced triumphantly, grabbing my queen from the board.

"I made a careless mistake," I moaned.

"No, you didn't," he said. "You were hustled. You didn't realize that I'm an actor, too."

It was the last chess game we have had a chance to play, but I did succeed in beating him once at snooker.

3

Life in the Universe

ᴀɴʏ coherent discussion of the existence, or non-existence, of extraterrestrial life must begin with a statement of the rules and limitations of the game. If one is willing to assume that the laws of nature elsewhere in the universe are quite different from what they are in regions accessible to our measuring instruments, one can come to any conclusion one likes about life in such regions, and, from a scientific point of view, the discussion loses any real interest. The scientifically interesting question is (assuming that the laws of nature in the part of the universe that we can observe and study are similar to or identical with the laws that apply to Earth and the solar system) : Is it likely, or unlikely, in terms of our present knowledge, that life—living matter—is confined uniquely to Earth? My guess is that in a poll of contemporary scientists the great majority would say that, though there is absolutely no direct evidence of the existence of extraterrestrial life (such as the discovery, say, of a meteorite from outer space containing the remains of non-Earthly organisms), the indirect evidence makes it extremely likely that life is a widespread phenomenon in the universe.

The chain of reasoning for this has grown quite long, and it involves several scientific disciplines. It has also, because of the current "space fad," been the subject of so many books and articles that one hardly knows where to begin reading. Two of the best summaries, I think, are contained in a generally excellent and highly readable book, *We Are Not Alone,* by Walter Sullivan, the science editor of the *Times* (McGraw-Hill), and, on a more technically sophisticated level, in *The Origin of the Solar System* (Macmillan), a collection of semi-popular articles that first appeared in the astronomy journal *Sky & Telescope.* Mr. Sullivan's book was first published in 1964, but in view of the knowledge gained from the Mariner IV photographic mission to Mars, in July of 1965, he has revised it. Mr. Sullivan is a believer. In his mind, there is no doubt that extraterrestrial intelligent life exists and that we should attempt to come in contact with it. How to do this occupies a good deal of the book. *The Origin of the Solar System,* published in 1966, is a more staid and an excellently annotated (by the astronomer Thorton Page, of Wesleyan University, and his wife) assortment of articles by some of our most distinguished astronomers and physicists. An especially nice feature of it is that many of the articles are arranged in chronological order, and this enables one to see at a glance how rapidly ideas in the field have been changing. The subject of the collection is nominally the solar system, but most of the writers regard the solar system as a model of how planetary systems could have evolved anywhere in the universe, and several of them end up by stating the arguments for extraterrestrial life almost as enthusiastically as Mr. Sullivan.

All such arguments begin with some observations about the magnitude of the visible universe. A typical galaxy—such as our own Milky Way—contains at least a hundred billion stars. Within the part of the universe visible to us—say, several billion light-years of it—there are at least a hundred billion galaxies. As the great American astronomer Edwin Hubble asked, "It seems reasonable to assume —doesn't it?—that among the myriads of stars that we now know to be in the grand universe there are innumerable ones that have planets associated with them. Many of these planets must be suitable for supporting life. On the whole, one is inclined to think that there may be countless other worlds with life, even life such as we do not know or cannot conceive on the basis of our earthly experience." The key word is "reasonable"; Hubble's conclusion is "reasonable" only if it can be demonstrated that there is nothing unique about our own star—the sun—which, after all, is the only star that we know for certain supports planets of which one, at any rate, supports life. The burden of the argument, and most of the discussion in *The Origin of the Solar System,* rests on showing that the sun is a typical, comparatively cool, middle-aged star.

Before we proceed to this matter, a slight historical detour may be enlightening. We have become so conditioned by the marvels and sophistication of the space age that it is easy to forget—a point emphasized by Mr. Sullivan—that three and a half centuries ago Giordano Bruno was burned at the stake in Rome for proclaiming a point of view much like Hubble's. Prior to the Renaissance, science was dominated by the Aristotelian cosmology, according to which extraterrestrial matter obeyed physical laws entirely different from ours. (The moon was, however, considered a possible haven for life as early as the writings of Plutarch and Lucian.) It is a legacy of the Renaissance, primarily because of the telescopic discoveries of Galileo, that the laws of nature as discovered on Earth have been assumed to apply to the rest of the universe. We have come so far in three hundred and fifty years that, to our contemporary eye, Hubble's statement appears almost obvious. Lest we overcongratulate ourselves, it is also worth pointing out that the second step of the argument for extraterrestrial life—that, given a suitable environment, life can evolve anywhere—is based on evolutionary biology, which is still considered immoral and unteachable in parts of the United States (Scopes lost a decision in the Monkey Trial in Tennessee, and it is still against the law to teach evolution in that state), and which, until the latest change of regime in the Soviet Union, could condemn a biologist to enforced obscurity and perhaps prison.

Back to the sun. The only parts of it that can be directly observed are the surface—the photosphere—and the gaseous regions above the surface, the chromosphere and the corona. Electromagnetic radiation that has its origins in the interior is trapped there. The only particles coming from the interior of the sun that might be detected are the neutrinos manufactured in the nuclear reactions that are responsible for the sun's energy production. These reactions take place deep in the interior of the sun. So far, no experiments have been sufficiently sensitive to detect solar neutrinos. The surface temperature of the sun is eleven thousand degrees Fahrenheit, and it is believed that the interior, where the nuclear cooking is going on, must have a temperature of twenty or thirty million degrees. (One of the persistent puzzles of solar physics is that the outermost region of the sun—the corona, which is made wonderfully visible during total eclipses—has a temperature of at least a million degrees and is thus much hotter than the photosphere, which lies below it. This is thought to be the result of shock waves in the gas that are caused by disturbances in the photosphere; the turbulence created by these waves heats up the chromosphere and the corona.) As stars go, twenty or thirty million degrees is fairly cool, but the sun is constantly getting hotter. (It has been estimated that, because of this, Earth is heating up at a rate of one degree every hundred million years.) As the sun gets hotter, new kinds of nuclear reactions become possible, and so the solar fuel is used up at a faster rate. The sun should continue to supply Earth with a comfortable heat bath for ten billion years more. Since the age of Earth in its present, solidified form is about four billion years, the processes in the sun must have been operating in their present form for at least that long. The quantitative theory of the sun's radiation is only thirty years old. It is due in large part to Hans Bethe, and it is beautifully summarized by him in *The Origin of the Solar System*. It is based on the fact that in many nuclear reactions the masses of the particles that emerge are less than the masses of the particles that enter the reactions, and, according to Einstein's formula $E = mc^2$, this difference in mass is converted into energy. Because c, the velocity of light, is such an enormous number, the amount of energy produced in these reactions is substantial even though the loss of mass is comparatively small. (The conversion of just a one-gram mass into energy would keep a hundred-watt bulb burning for thirty thousand years.) That is why the sun has managed to shine for such a long time. The fact that Einstein's formula had something to do with solar energy was realized early in this century; however, Bethe was the first scientist who made a systematic study of the nuclear reactions that were possible in the sun, and he narrowed them down to a couple, whose rates he could estimate rather accurately. Prior to Einstein's discovery, the mechanism of solar radiation was a complete mystery. Chemical burning (that is, plain, everyday combustion) is much too feeble a process to account for the tremendous energy given off by the sun—a situation that has been summarized in the aphorism that the sun is too hot to burn. All the other pre-Einstein estimates about the generation of solar energy gave lifetimes for the sun of less than a hundred million years—estimates that were sharply contradicted when the age of Earth was established accurately in this century by radioactive-dating methods. It is now known that a large number of the stars in the Milky Way—that is, billions of stars—are at a stage in their evolution comparable to the sun's, so, in Hubble's terms, "myriads" of stars are capable (in theory) of supporting planetary life. Otto Struve, a Russian-born astrophysicist who fled Russia after the Revolution and worked until his death, in 1963, in the United States, and who is generally regarded as the greatest astronomer of his generation, sums up the status of the sun in *The Origin of the Solar System:* "If we imagine as astronomer about three hundred light-years from where we are now, and let him observe the sun from that distance, it would appear to him as an inconspicuous, single star of apparent magnitude 7, having a pronounced reddish color, and a surface temperature of about eleven thousand degrees. He should be totally unaware of the existence of any of the planets, not to speak of the comets, asteroids, zodiacal light, or corona." This is not a flattering view of the uniqueness of our faithful star, but if life is a widespread phenomenon, then uniqueness is the last thing one would expect of the sun.

As with many astronomers, extraterrestrial life became Struve's *violon d'Ingres.* Perhaps his interest was kindled by one of the astronomical discoveries that he made important contributions to—the discovery that stars of the sun's type and cooler than it rotate very slowly. It is known that the sun rotates at a rate of two kilometres a second, taking twenty-five days to complete a rotation. These figures are fairly typical of the cool stars. The hot stars, presumably in rapid evolution, rotate much faster. In the solar system, the planets, which contain less than one per cent of the total mass of the system (the rest is the mass of the sun), have, strikingly, ninety-eight per cent of the system's angular momentum. Angular momentum is the quantity physicists use to measure the amount of rotational momentum, and it is a remarkable fact about the solar system that the light, whirling planets carry most of the system's angular momentum. To Struve, this fact had to do with the explanation of how the planets were formed. One can imagine that in the early stages of its evolution the sun was a rapidly whirling object surrounded by an enormous gaseous cloud. In time, the sun threw off parts of this gaseous envelope. There are still intermittent solar explosions in which glowing pieces of the sun's surface are hurled hundreds of thousands of miles away, and these occurrences may resemble, on a reduced scale, the processes that took place earlier in the sun's history. (These explosions eject charged particles that reach Earth, where they disrupt radio transmission and cause visual phenomena like the northern lights.) Many astrophysicists believe that, as a result of complicated electromagnetic interactions, the young sun transferred its angular momentum to the surrounding gas. The magnetic fields set up around the sun acted as a frictional brake, and so the gas took up most of the sun's spin. The planets, in the course of eons, condensed out of this spinning gas, which would explain why they carry so much angular momentum. (Historically, this explanation of the formation of planets can be traced back to the speculations of Descartes and Kant. For a while, it was abandoned in favor of a theory that the sun had lost its angular momentum by colliding with another star. Since stellar collisions are extremely improbable, this theory made planetary formation a very unlikely phenomenon. But the collision hypothesis has fallen out of favor in the last thirty years, for it has been demonstrated that in such a collision the matter torn out of the sun would simply explode rather than condense into planets.) If this explanation is correct, it is quite natural to suppose that there are planetary systems associated with stars of low angular momentum. Such stars are the ones that are in the most stable phase of their evolution, which makes them the best candidates for supporting life. Struve summarizes, "Since all those properties of the sun which we can observe in other stars are normal for a large group of reddish dwarfs [small stars], it is at least plausible that those other properties that we cannot now test outside the solar system are also common to all or most of them. In other words, it is far more reasonable to start with the working hypothesis that planets are normally present in the vicinity of cool dwarfs than it is to suppose that our planetary system is unique, or very rare."

This evidence for the existence of planets near stars other than the sun is, of course, rather indirect. However, there is much direct evidence, and this leaves little doubt that planetary systems exist elsewhere in the universe. This evidence involves the irregularities in the motions of stars. Almost two-thirds of the known stars are multiple; what appears to be a single star is often composed of two or more stars in motion around each other. The simplest such configuration is the binary one—two stars revolving around their common center of mass. Many of these binary configurations exhibit irregular wobbles in their motions. The natural explanation of these motions is that the two stars are being affected by a third body travelling near them; viz., a planet. Sometimes a star that seems single, even through a telescope, will wiggle in its motion. In some cases, the "invisible" companion that is affecting its motion has finally shown up in photographs and turned out to be a faintly glowing object that is between the sun and Jupiter in mass (Jupiter is the largest of the planets, with a mass three hundred and eighteen times the mass of Earth). One tremendously interesting star, known to astronomers as Barnard's star, almost without doubt has a satellite planet about the size of Jupiter. It is described in *The Origin of the Solar System* by the astronomer Peter van de Kamp, the director of the Sproul Observatory, at Swarthmore, which was responsible for much of the recent study of it. Dr. van de Kamp reports:

In 1916, E. E. Barnard discovered that an inconspicuous star in Ophiuchus has the exceptionally large proper motion [proper motion refers to the extremely small motion of the stars with respect to each other, as seen from the Earth. The "constellations" are really not fixed, but the relative motions of the stars that compose them during, say, a year are so small that it takes very exact measurements to observe them at all. Conventionally, relative astronomical distances are measured in terms of angles rather than, for example, miles, the angles of separation between the astronomical objects. Three hundred and sixty degrees is the amount of angle in an entire circle. Each degree of angle is divided into sixty minutes and each minute into sixty seconds. The proper motions usually amount to changes in the angular separations of stars, in a year, of fractions of seconds of angle] of 10.3 seconds of arc [i.e., angle] per year, which is still the record [among all known stars]. This 9.5 magnitude star is drifting northward by a moon's diameter in about a hundred and eighty years. It has the further distinction of being closer to the sun than any other known star except the triple system of Alpha Centauri. Physically, Barnard's star is a red dwarf, having only about one sixth the diameter of our sun. Very recently, an intensive astrometric study at Sproul Observatory has revealed that this fast-moving obect has an invisible companion which is in some ways even more remarkable.

Dr. van de Kamp goes on to point out that because it is so close to Earth, and because of its enormous proper motion, Barnard's star is an especially favorable object for the study of irregularities in a star's motion. And, indeed, instead of moving across the sky in a sedate line, Barnard's star moves with a well-defined wavelike serpentine motion. The pattern repeats itself every twenty-four years—a fact that can be explained if Barnard's star has an invisible companion that moves around the parent star once every twenty-four years; in Dr. van de Kamp's words, "Barnard's star is shifted by the gravitational attraction of an unseen companion." The computation of planetary orbits is an extremely exact science, and by using the mass of the star and the characteristics of its motion, it can be shown "that the mass of the unseen companion is only about 0.0015 [the mass of the] sun—a mere one and a half times as massive as Jupiter! Such an object must be regarded as a planet rather than a star. . . . It can hardly appear brighter than about thirtieth magnitude [that it would shine at all would be due to the fact that it would reflect the light from Barnard's star, just as Jupiter reflects the light of the sun]—far too dim for us to detect it by any current techniques [that is, to see it directly]. No wonder its image is not found on our 1937–1946 plates, when the apparent separation of Barnard's star and its companion was more than two seconds of arc!"

Since there are hundreds of billions of stars, it is all but impossible not to conclude that there are hundreds of billions of planets. This is to say that there must be billions of empty stages on which it is possible for the drama of life to be enacted, and the question is how many of these stages are now being used. The most naïve answer to this question is approximately one-ninth of them—using the fact that there are nine planets in the solar system and on one, at least, there is life. Before we return to this somewhat oversimplified reasoning, a few comments about life, or its absence, in the rest of the solar system are in order. Proceeding outward from the sun, the first of the so-called terrestrial planets—Mercury, Venus, Earth, and Mars—is Mercury. Mercury is only slightly larger than the moon. (An all but total lack of atmosphere on the moon, which is responsible for violent temperature extremes on the dark and light halves of the moon, and which allows it to be bathed in a continuous stream of sterilizing ultraviolet radiation from the sun, precludes life in any conceivable form on our nearest neighbor, although one is always tempted to hedge absolute statements of this kind with the Shakespeare-like note that there may be more things in heaven and earth than in our currently accepted natural philosophy). On its bright side (the side that at any given time faces the sun), it has a temperature of at least seven hundred and fifty degrees; on its dark side, the temperature is estimated to be exceedingly low. The atmosphere of Mercury is still a matter of conjecture, but it is quite likely that the bright side has little or none. It was thought until recently that any gases on the dark side were frozen solid. But now Mercury is known to rotate on its axis with a period of fifty-nine days, which means that the sun heats up the entire surface of the planet. Venus has a mass of about four-fifths that of Earth. It has a high surface temperature—six hundred degrees or more—and a thick atmosphere composed in part of a heavy layer of carbon dioxide and clouds. A few lonely visionaries maintain that beneath the clouds there may be Venusian seas teeming with life, but, as the physicist Edward M. Purcell said, in another context, this idea probably "belongs back where it came from, on the cereal box." Next is Earth, which, despite the dangers posed by our all but uncontrollable technological rapacity, remains a relatively sound abode for life. Mars is such a complicated case that I will come back to it later. After Mars, the next planet is Jupiter, the largest planet. In the words of one of my favorite astronomy books, *Pictorial Guide to the Planets*, by Joseph H. Jackson, its "atmosphere would hardly be exhilarating to breathe. Ammonia, methane, and hydrogen have been identified in it." It has a surface temperature of about minus two hundred degrees. Perhaps some use can be made of it when the gradual heating of the sun makes life on Earth intolerable, but it is a good bet that there is nothing living there now. The same gloomy report holds for Saturn, Uranus, Neptune, and Pluto, all of which appear to have murderous atmospheres, and are even colder than Jupiter.

To return to Mars. No object in the heavens, with the possible exception of the sun and moon, has been studied so extensively or has been so much written about as the Red Planet. Mars is 141,637,000 miles from the sun; Earth is 92,956,000 miles from it. The Martian year—the time it takes for Mars to make a single revolution around the sun—is 686.98 Earth days (the Martian day is about as long as our day). Mars has one-tenth the mass of Earth. It is the relatively small mass of Mars that accounts for the fact that its atmosphere is so tenuous. Earth's atmosphere is held to Earth by the pull of gravity, though the light gases at the top of the atmosphere are continually being lost into outer space. Traces of water vapor and oxygen have been detected in the Martian atmosphere, but the density of the atmosphere is probably less than one per cent of Earth's. The surface temperatures on Mars apparently vary between about minus eighty degrees at the poles to plus eighty degrees at high noon on the equator. All in all, it is not a very attractive environment for life.

The great interest in Mars, which has amounted at times to near-hysteria, is due to the peculiarities observed on its surface. (One noted astrophysicist recently bemoaned the fact that "so much nonsense has been written about the planet in various branches of literary endeavor that it is easy to forget that Mars is still an object of serious scientific investigation.") Because of its thin atmosphere, the surface of Mars is highly visible, and it could be intimately studied if our own atmosphere did not interfere so drastically with telescopic observations. The history of the study of the Martian surface, nicely summarized in one of the chapters of Sullivan's book, begins in the seventeenth century, when Christiaan Huygens noted that there were white caps on the Martian poles. These caps increase in the Martian fall and winter and shrink in the spring and summer, and sometimes, in the words of Jackson, "they develop gouges and ridges and sometimes leave islands of white beyond their line of retreat." The caps are presumably frost, which melts or sublimates—that is, passes directly from the solid to the gaseous state without first liquefying—when the planet heats up. Most of the surface appears to consist of "deserts," which give off a reddish or "a buff orange hue." However, there are dark regions, first noted by the eighteenth-century astronomer Sir William Herschel, and certain of these regions, which some observers say are basically gray, with touches of blues and greens, grow and shrink, often rather quickly, with the seasons. The dark regions have caused some of the most dramatic speculations about Mars by scientists, beginning with Herschel, who thought they might indicate the existence of vegetation. Jackson says, "Often the dark markings return again within a few weeks after they have been covered by dust in one of the Martian storms; could this be rejuvenation, explained by vegetation growing up through the dust?" Most astronomers now agree that whatever the dark areas may be, they are not composed of objects containing chlorophyll. Chlorophyll is the key to the metabolic system of plants. In the process of photosynthesis, the energy of sunlight is used to convert—with the aid of chlorophyll—carbon dioxide and water into glucose sugar and phosphates. During this process, oxygen is released into the atmosphere; the present oxygen in the atmosphere of Earth is probably the accumulation from photosynthesis. The sugars and phosphates can be stored in the plant for later use as sources of energy. The development of chlorophyll-using plants freed plants, and therefore, ultimately, the primitive animals, from their dependence on much more inefficient energy sources, such as ultraviolet light. The release of oxygen into the atmosphere increased its efficiency as a blanket against ultraviolet light, which in large amounts is detrimetal to life. Chlorophyll is so essential in the ecology of life on Earth that the first thing one would want to know about the Martian dark spots is whether they contain it. Chlorophyll strongly reflects yellow and yellow-green light, and it has been found by telescopic observation that the Martian dark spots do not reflect these colors any more strongly than do the neighboring deserts. This does not mean that there is no plant life on Mars; it means, rather, that such life, if it exists, will be difficult or impossible to verify by telescope.

The feature of the Martian surface that has excited the greatest speculation is the "canals." The canals, or *canali,* were first reported in 1877 by Giovanni Virginio Schiaparelli, an Italian astronomer. According to him, their architecture appeared to be perfect, "being drawn with absolute geometrical precision, as if they were the work of rule or compass." Schiaparelli was cautious about concluding that the canals were the work of intelligent beings, but his contemporaries had a field day. Among them was Percival Lowell, the brother of Amy Lowell and Abbott Lawrence Lowell, the Harvard president. He was so interested in the canals and the information that Schiaparelli's eyes were failing that in his thirties he gave up a career as an Orientalist to become an astronomer. He created an observatory in Flagstaff, Arizona, which became a center for planetary observation. He came to the conclusion that what Schiaparelli had seen were bands of land irrigated by canals, rather than the canals themselves. This meant to him that intelligent life was guiding the destiny of Mars, and he decided (his view is rather uncritically shared by many modern writers) that if intelligent life exists, it must be superior to and more benign than the forms we are familiar with. "Irrigation, unscientifically conducted, would not give us such truly wonderful mathematical fitness in the several parts of the whole as we there behold. A mind of no mean order would seem to have presided over the system we see." He adds, perhaps because of his knowledge of Boston politicians, "A mind certainly of considerably more comprehensiveness than that which presides over the various departments of our own public works. Party politics, at all events, have had no part in them; for the system is planet-wide. . . . Certainly what we see hints at the existence of beings who are in advance of, not behind, us in the journey of life." Much as one might like to have Martian neighbors, current observations indicate that it is most unlikely that the canals are the work of humanoids. They appear to be irregularly shaped streaks, perhaps made up of the materials that form the other dark Martian regions. The pictures sent back by Mariner IV show the Martian surface to be as awesomely inhospitable as the surface of the moon—a surface gouged by craters, perhaps caused by the impact of meteorites. It has been said that a rocket fired at Earth from Mars, carrying the same equipment and following a similar trajectory, would probably not reveal life on Earth, and the question of whether there is life on Mars and what forms it has taken is still open.

This brings us to the crucial question: What is the origin of life? If life on Earth is a unique phenomenon, of perhaps divine origin, the fact that it has occurred on at least one of nine solar planets does not necessarily tell us anything about its distribution in the universe. On the other hand, if living organisms can generate themselves from inanimate chemicals, there may be reason to suppose that life is distributed in the universe almost as widely as the stars. The history of this question is a fascinating one. Early thinkers, such as the pre-Socratic evolutionary speculators of Greece, took it almost for granted that life could be generated spontaneously from matter. In the

Middle Ages, the Renaissance, and the beginning of the nineteenth century, both scientists, such as Newton and Harvey, and most laymen felt that while Man might have a divine origin, parasites—rodents and insects—could be generated directly from decaying matter. As Sullivan points out, early-nineteenth-century experiments with electricity seemed, at any rate to the experimenters, to show that living creatures could be produced by passing an electric current through a chemically prepared stone. Many textbooks treat these experiments, and to a considerable extent justifiably, with slightly comic overtones, and go on to speak of Pasteur's refutation of them, in the eighteen-sixties, as a triumph of the scientific method. Pasteur prepared a broth, containing yeast, that was subject to fermentation—a chemical transformation caused by the activity of the yeast. He put the broth in sealed flasks and boiled the contents. As long as the flasks remained sealed and there was no bacterial contamination, there was no fermentation, despite the claims of some of his contemporaries that bacteria could generate spontaneously in the broth and cause it to ferment. (It has been pointed out that Pasteur was "lucky" in his choice of yeast, since many bacteria, such as the hay bacillus, are heat-resistant and cannot be killed by boiling. This sort of luck occurs often in the careers of great scientists, and Pasteur himself once remarked, "In the field of experimentation, chance favors only the prepared mind.") Pasteur was convinced that his experiments proved that living matter cannot arise spontaneously out of non-living matter—which he felt was a triumph for science.

In fact, it was very nearly the opposite. If life has been generated only from life, in an infinite regress, any hope for a scientific explanation of its origin is vain—a fact that appears to have been recognized, soon after, by Darwin. Darwin traced the origin of species back farther and farther, to simpler and simpler forms, and he was inevitably confronted with the question of whether the "continuity" of evolution could be traced back beyond the first living species. He wrote, just before his death, that the "principle of continuity renders it probable that the principle of life will hereafter be shown to be a part, or a consequence, of some general law." He also recognized that the conditions that exist on Earth, while they are favorable for the continuity of life, may not be the optimum conditions for its origination, and, indeed, that conditions in the distant past, when life began, were entirely different from what they are now. "It is often said that all the conditions for the first production of a living organism are now present, which could ever have been present. But if (and oh! what a big if!) we could conceive in some warm little pond, with all sorts of ammonia and phosphoric-acid salts, light, heat, electricity, etc., present, that a protein compound was chemically formed ready to undergo still more complex changes, at the present day such matter would be instantly devoured or absorbed, which would not have been the case before living creatures were formed." In this brief and remarkable paragraph, Darwin anticipated the substance and flavor of the contemporary scientific discussion of the origins of life.

What is alive? It is easy to answer this question if one considers the extremes in the spectrum between living and non-living things. A man is alive, but an electron is not alive. One may begin to narrow the spectrum. A bacterium (the biggest is about a five-thousandth of an inch in diameter and the smallest about a twenty-five-thousandth of an inch in diameter) is alive, and a protein molecule is not alive. Is a virus alive? A virus is an object of perhaps a thousandth of the diameter of the smallest bacterium. It cannot even be seen through an ordinary microscope. A concentrated sample of viruses—say, the virus that causes the disease in tobacco plants that mottles their leaves (the tobacco-mosaic virus) —has the crystalline structure of a substance like sugar, and yet these apparently inanimate crystals can infect tobacco plants. A virus is now known to consist of a string of DNA—the molecule that contains the "genetic code"—surrounded by a protein coat. Viruses "reproduce" themselves by attaching themselves to bacteria and injecting their DNA into them. The virus DNA makes use of the materials of the host cell to construct replicas of itself—a process that eventually kills the bacteria, which break open, letting the newly made viruses out to repeat the process with new bacteria. But proteins can be synthesized in the laboratory, and so can DNA. In 1957, Arthur Kornberg and his associates at Washington University, in St. Louis, produced a simplified artificial DNA from the separated materials known to be in the DNA molecule. This DNA duplicated itself just as the DNA does in the living cell. Is the DNA alive?

In a superb new book on genetics by George and Muriel Beadle (he is a Nobel Prize-winning geneticist and president of the University of Chicago), *The Language of Life* (Doubleday), this question is answered as follows:

Life, according to Webster's Third New International Dictionary, is:

1a: Animate being: the quality that distinguishes a vital and functional being from a dead body or purely chemical matter. . . .

b: The principle or force by which animals and plants are maintained in the performance of their functions and which distinguishes by its presence animate from inanimate matter;

c: The state of a material complex or individual characterized by the capacity to perform certain functional activities including metabolism, growth, reproduction, and some form of responsiveness or adaptability. . . .

By any of the definitions above, men are alive. So are trout. And spiders. And earthworms. And bacteria. But what about viruses? They can reproduce and evolve, given the cells of one of those other organisms to grow in. They can't "perform certain functional activities including metabolism," but they certainly *can* direct metabolic processes for their own benefit. Given a choice between calling them animate or inanimate matter, wouldn't one be tempted to call them "animate"?

Viruses are essentially DNA with a protein coat, and that coat is primarily protective. So, if viruses are alive, couldn't one say that DNA molecules are alive too—even artificial ones? Kornberg's artificial DNA's can reproduce, and presumably can evolve.

But Kornberg's artificial DNA's were made from "purely chemical matter," compounds that were inert until he put them together. Perhaps there is something hidden in them, a vital force unique to these particular compounds? If so, couldn't one say that adenine, thymine, guanine, and cytosine nucleotides are alive?

But they are composed of varying arrangements of elemental atoms—the same kind of atoms that compose the water you drink and the sugar you eat. As we said earlier, physicsts have done experiments that have "created" the elements, step by step, from hydrogen. Are hydrogen atoms alive?

As you can see, there is no logical place to break the chain: hydrogen → the elements → chemical compounds → nucleic acids → proteins → viruses → bacteria → higher organisms. And since there is no logical place to break the chain, any definition of life must necessarily be arbitrary—given the present state of man's knowledge.

Perhaps a more exact way to phrase it would be: "In the continuum of being, is there a boundary between life and non-life?"

The question remains unanswered. But one is tempted to believe that science has made the question meaningless.

This point of view certainly offends traditional beliefs and distinctions. (The Beadles quote a freshman at Chicago who, after completing the required course in biology, said, "It's fascinating stuff. But I've decided that I don't believe it.") Yet most scientists would probably accept it. However, even granted that life and non-life merge into each other, this is a far cry from accounting for the steps that lead to the evolution of life on Earth. One can state with certainty that the atmosphere of prehistoric Earth was entirely different from its atmosphere today. It is probable that there was no free oxygen, or very little. Oxygen was later produced by the photosynthesis taking place in the green plants. It has been suggested that the primitive atmosphere might have had as its major ingredients oxygen (in water), carbon (in methane), nitrogen (in ammonia), and hydrogen (in hydrogen gas). But there remains the question of how these primitive compounds came to be joined together into the complex molecules characteristic of living things.

In the early nineteen-fifties, Harold Urey, then of the University of Chicago, suggested that ultraviolet light, or electrical discharges, might have broken up these four molecules, allowing them to recombine into more complex organic compounds of the type that ultimately enter the DNA molecule. In 1952, a graduate student, Stanley Miller, working in Urey's laboratory in Chicago, performed a series of experiments in which a vapor mixture of these substances was subjected for a week to a sixty-thousand-volt high-frequency spark. At the end of the week, it was discovered that amino acids, sometimes strung together as small proteins, were produced by this discharge. This is an important step in the construction of organic substances, but it is still a long way from a simple protein to the enormously complicated DNA molecule, and it leaves unanswered the question of how the building blocks were first strung together into DNA, and the almost impossibly complicated one of how the first recognizably living forms arose out of these chemicals.

However, the other planets in our solar system have in their atmospheres most of the chemicals listed above, and more, which naturally suggests that the synthesis of complicated organic molecules is going on all the time in some planetary atmospheres in our own solar system and elsewhere in the universe. But even if one grants that the phenomenon of life is widespread, this life would not necessarily resemble human life in any way. It need not even be intelligent. Scientists' opinions about this range from a strong negative (as expressed in a brilliant essay, *The Nonprevalence of Humanoids,* by the Harvard paleontologist George Gaylord Simpson, who wrote, "The assumption, so freely made by astronomers, physicists, and some biochemists, that once life gets started anywhere, humanoids will eventually and inevitably appear is plainly false. The chance of duplicating man on any other planet is the same as the chance that the planet and its organisms have had a history identical in all essentials with that of the earth through some billions of years. Let us grant the unsubstantiated claim of millions or billions of possible planetary abodes of life; the chances of such historical duplication are still vanishingly small") to a statement by the distinguished biologist Melvin Calvin, who wrote, "We can assert with some degree of scientific confidence that cellular life as we know it on the surface of the earth does exist in some millions of other sites in the universe. This does not deny the possiblity of the existence of still other forms of matter which might be called living which are foreign to our present experience. . . . We have now removed life from the limited place it occupied a moment ago, as a rather special and unique event . . . to a state of matter widely distributed throughout the universe."

No scientist would claim that the existence of intelligent extraterrestrial life has been proved. But it is nonetheless interesting to speculate on what it might mean if there were humanoids elsewhere in the universe. It has been argued that if there were many humanoid civilizations, some would have been likely to develop technologies, and some of these technologies could be much more advanced than ours. Technology is presumably linked to scientific curiosity and scientific achievement, so a civilization that has an advanced technology would presumably have the same curiosity about the universe that we do, or so the conventional argument goes. Thus, such a civilization would begin to wonder if it was alone in the universe, just as we are wondering if we are alone. Might that civilization not try to signal us, or someone else? In 1959, the thought occurred, more or less simultaneously, to two groups of scientists that the existing radio telescopes—enormous antenna arrangements that pick up radio signals from outer space—could be used to "listen" for signals from intelligent life on distant planets. This idea has been a favorite of science-fiction writers for decades, but the advances in radio telescopes suggested that it might be a practical possibility. The principle, proposed independently by the physicists Giuseppe Cocconi and Philip Morrison, both then at Cornell, and by the astronomer Frank D. Drake, now at Cornell, was based on the speculation of the Dutch astronomer Hendrick Christoffel van de Hulst that interstellar hydrogen would emit a characteristic radio signal, with a wavelength of exactly twenty-one centimetres. It is known that there are interstellar hydrogen clouds and that the atoms making up these clouds collide. The twenty-one-centimetre radiation occurs after some of the collisions have excited the atomic hydrogen in the clouds. The twenty-one-centimetre radiation has the ability to penetrate Earth's upper atmosphere, which blocks out most of the other radiation from outer space, and radio telescopes can be built to detect it. In fact, in 1951, a Dutch group—and independently, a little before, an American group, at Harvard (Edward M. Purcell and Harold I. Ewen)—built such detectors, and with them observed the twenty-one-centimetre radiation from interstellar gas clouds. Now, the argument ran, if a civilization was really sophisticated, it might try to signal on the twenty-one-centimetre line, and the signals could be picked up by the radio telescopes. Cocconi and Morrison did not have such a telescope, but they wrote to Sir Bernard Lovell, director of the huge English radio telescope at Jodrell Bank. Lovell said that the Jodrell Bank telescope had more pressing business. Meanwhile, Drake, who was involved with our huge radio telescope at Green Bank, West Virginia, had had the same idea, and he had a telescope. Drake initiated Project Ozma, the search for intelligent extraterrestrial life (named for the Princess of the Land of Oz), and on April 8, 1960, the telescope was pointed at Epsilon Eridani, a sunlike star eleven light-years away. Sullivan writes, "Shortly after the antenna had been aimed at Epsilon Eridani, and before the loudspeaker had been switched on, the needle inscribing [the recording paper], as Drake put it, 'went bang off scale.' Some very strong signal was coming in! The volume was turned down, and the needle wrote a series of high-speed pulses, at a rate of roughly eight per second, so uniformly spaced that they could only be the product of intelligent beings. When the loudspeaker was turned on, the pulses could be heard, coming in with machinelike precision." A few weeks later, Drake discovered that he had been picking up airborne transmissions from a secret military radar project. During the rest of the project, no further intelligent signals were heard.

It is generally assumed that communication with extraterrestrial civilizations would be a good thing. It would certainly be a bizarre form of communication. Signals from distant stars can take tens or hundreds of years to reach Earth. A communication from a distant source could come from a civilization long ago vanished. However, the usual idea is that advanced extraterrestrial civilizations are benign, and that if we ever established contact with them it might change our Earthly attitudes for the better. In

April of 1964, the physicist Freeman J. Dyson, of the Institute for Advanced Study, who has been interested in space travel and astrophysics for many years, wrote a chilling letter, questioning this assumption, to the *Scientific American*. Just before, the late James R. Newman had written a long review in that magazine of a book on interstellar communication edited by A. G. W. Cameron, a well-known astrophysicist, and Dyson, who had contributed to it, said:

> James R. Newman's review of *Interstellar Communication* in your February issue is written with his usual mixture of wit and wisdom. As one of the authors I am grateful for the general blessing he has given to our enterprise, and I only wish to rebut two of his offhand pronouncements I consider untrue.

The first part of Dyson's letter deals with the question of interstellar-space travel, which some people feel is impossible because of the fantastic distances involved. Dyson remarks that it is really a problem in biology, since it is conceivable that forms of hibernation will be found that will enable people to travel for years and maybe centuries without aging. "Many of us, no doubt including Newman, would find thousand-year trips unappealing, but we have no right to impose our tastes on others."

Then comes the main part of the letter:

> Newman's second objectionable statement is his gibe at "a few of the contributors to this book" who "are silly enough to impute to the societies of other planets the same murderous impulses, military ambitions, obsessions and follies that shape our own civilization." I do not know if he includes me in this category, but I hope he does. I am glad to speak for all scientists interested in interstellar communication who do not share Newman's peculiarly optimistic preconceptions. Our business as scientists is to search the universe and find out what is there. What is there may conform to our moral sense or it may not. Our business is to

try to imagine and find means to detect the possible manifestations of intelligence in the universe. It is just as un-
scientific to impute to remote intelligences wisdom and
serenity as it is to impute to them irrational and murderous
impulses. We must be prepared for either possibility and
conduct our searches accordingly. I personally cannot accept
Newman's view that interstellar communication will necessarily be "the perfect, deliberate, philosophical discourse."
Intelligence may indeed be a benign influence, creating
isolated groups of philosopher-kings far apart in the heavens
and enabling them to share at leisure their accumulated
wisdom. Or intelligence may be a cancer of purposeless
technological exploitation, sweeping across a galaxy as irre-
sistibly as it has swept across our own planet. In this connection it is of importance that, even at the slow rate of interstellar travel that is unquestionably feasible, the technological cancer could spread over a whole galaxy in a few million
years, a time very short compared with the life of a planet.

All of us who think seriously about the detection of extraterrestrial intelligence know that we suffer from one basic
limitation. Our imagined detectors detect technology rather
than intelligence. And we have no idea whether or not a
truly intelligent society would retain over millions of years
an interest in or a need for advanced technology. Under
these circumstances it is best to admit frankly that we are
searching for evidence of technology rather than of intelligence. And we must be aware that we have perhaps a
greater chance of discovering first a technology run wild,
insane or cancerously spreading than a technology firmly
under control and supporting the rational needs of a superior intelligence.

It may be, then, that when we search for life elsewhere
in the universe, the footprints that we find will be too
much like our own.

About the Author

JEREMY BERNSTEIN is the only physicist on the staff of *The New Yorker,* and, in addition, the author of two books: *The Analytical Engine,* an introduction to computers, and *Ascent,* an account of mountaineering in the Alps—his hobby. More than thirty of Dr. Bernstein's papers have appeared in the scientific journals, and, since 1962, he has been associate professor of physics at New York University.

Dr. Bernstein was born in Rochester, New York, on December 21, 1929, attended Columbia Grammar School in New York City, and studied for eight years at Harvard University, from which he received his A.B., a Master's in Mathematics and a Doctorate in Physics. He then worked for two years as a Research Associate at the Harvard Cyclotron Laboratory, and two subsequent years at the Institute for Advanced Study at Princeton. He has been a physicist at Los Alamos and at Brookhaven National Laboratories, and he traveled to Europe on a National Science Foundation Post-Doctoral Fellowship in Paris, Vienna, and Geneva. Dr. Bernstein is now a frequent visiting physicist at CERN (Centre Européen pour la Recherche Nucléaire) in Geneva, and serves as a consultant to the General Atomics Corporation.